OCTOBER FURY

PETER A. HUCHTHAUSEN

John Wiley & Sons, Inc.

Copyright © 2002 by Peter Huchthausen. All rights reserved

Published by John Wiley & Sons, Inc., Hoboken, New Jersey
Published simultaneously in Canada

For general information about our products and services, please contact our Customer Care Department within the United States at (800) 762-2974, outside the United States at (317) 572-3993 or fax (317) 572-4002.

Wiley also publishes its books in a variety of electronic formats. Some content that appears in print may not be available in electronic books.

Library of Congress Cataloging-in-Publication Data:

Huchthausen, Peter A., date.
    October fury / Peter Huchthausen.
        p. cm.
    Includes bibliographical references and index.
    ISBN 0-471-41534-0 (acid-free paper)
    1. Cuban Missile Crisis, 1962. 2. United States. Navy—History—20th century.
3. Soviet Union. Voenne-Morskoæ Flot—History. 4. Destroyers (Warships)—
Cuba—History—20th century. 5. Submarines (Ships)—Cuba—History—
20th century. I. Title.

E841.H83 2002
973.922—dc21

                                                                2002071333

Printed in the United States of America

10 9 8 7 6 5 4 3

CONTENTS

PREFACE

The actions and maneuvers made by the Soviet and U.S. ships and submarines, related on the following pages, were reconstructed from interviews and conversations with members of the crews on both sides. The author corrected the dates, sequence, and locations of the actions given by the sources, based on their memories, using the antisubmarine warfare records of October and November 1962. The dialogue was formed directly from the accounts given by the men who were there. On the U.S. side indeed a larger number of ships and aircraft participated in each encounter than are mentioned. The three destroyers whose actions are described in detail, however, were the ships primarily responsible for forcing their Soviet prey to surface.

I am deeply grateful to Captain First Rank Lev Vtorygin, Russian Navy Retired, a close friend now for more than fourteen years, for his tenacity and zeal in finding the participants on the Soviet side, and recording their accounts. His many contributions were instrumental to my completing this narrative with accurate accounts from both sides. I am thankful to the Russian officers who gave their excellent accounts from memory, and am also indebted to the men of the three destroyers: Gary Slaughter of the USS *Cony*; Charles Rozier, John Hunter, Jim Jordan, and others from the USS *Charles P. Cecil*; and my many shipmates and friends of the USS *Blandy* for their invaluable input. I am especially indebted to Mrs. Grace Kelley, who helped so many former *Blandy* sailors rekindle the spirit and leadership of our beloved skipper, the late Edward G. Kelley.

PROLOGUE

If I take the wings of the morning
    And dwell in the uttermost parts of the sea,
Even there your hand will lead me
    And your right hand hold me fast.

Psalm 139:9–10

In the fall of 1962, the United States and the Soviet Union came as close as they ever would to global nuclear war. The confrontation came after Soviet premier Nikita S. Khrushchev was caught in the act of secretly deploying nuclear-tipped ballistic missiles to Fidel Castro's Cuba. What is not widely known is that the showdown with the Soviet Union nearly led to an exchange of tactical nuclear weapons at sea between ships and submarines of the opposing navies. We now know from participants on both sides that a naval shoot-out very nearly occurred. This account is based on the recollections of men who had their fingers on the triggers.

The gravity of the encounter was first revealed in 1992, when parts of the long-guarded files of the Central Committee of the Communist Party of the Soviet Union were opened. Although many KGB and Ministry of Defense files were released to researchers shortly after the dissolution of the Soviet Union in December 1991, the Central Committee files were stored separately and guarded as politically sensitive. Items from these files have been selectively released by the government of the Russian Federation.

Central Committee files released in January 1992 state that the Soviet Politburo had given their military commander in Cuba in 1962,

General Issa Pliyev, the authority to use tactical nuclear weapons against U.S. ships and landing forces without prior approval from Moscow. The following quote from a dispatch from Soviet defense minister Rodion Malinovsky to General Pliyev in Havana in early October 1962 was made public in 1992:

> Only in the event of a landing of the opponent's forces on the island of Cuba and if there is a concentration of enemy ships with landing forces near the coast of Cuba, in its territorial waters . . . and there is no possibility of receiving orders from the USSR Ministry of Defense, you are personally allowed as an exception to take the decision to apply the tactical LUNA missiles as a means of local destruction of the opponent on land and on the coast with the aim of a full crushing defeat of troops on the territory of Cuba and the defense of the Cuban Revolution.[1]

General Anatoly Gribkov, who was chief of operational planning on the Soviet General Staff in 1962, stated during a Cuban crisis reunion hosted by Fidel Castro in Havana in January 1992 that in addition to medium-range SS-4 missiles in Cuba, *Luna* (also known as *Frog* by NATO) missiles with nuclear warheads had already been provided to Soviet forces. These had one-hundred-kiloton warheads and a twenty-five-mile range. It has since been learned from Soviet records that the four submarines sent as the advance brigade to make its home port in Cuba as part of Operation *Kama* (the naval phase of Operation *Anadyr*, the code name for the overall plot to introduce strategic weapons in Cuba) had been equipped with tactical nuclear-tipped torpedoes and given the same authority to use them if an attack by U.S. Navy ships appeared imminent.

The Cuban missile crisis and its outcome provide a classic study of the successful use of diplomacy backed by superior sea power. The Soviet Navy was operating in unfamiliar waters with inferior naval forces and without air support. The advantageous naval position enjoyed by the United States forced a choice on Khrushchev between hostilities and certain defeat, or withdrawal and a major diplomatic setback. The major reversal for the Soviet leader eventually resulted in his political defeat and forced retirement.

The confrontation was a pivotal moment for the Soviet fleet, leading to resumption of an aggressive naval construction program, which continued until the implosion of the Soviet Union in 1991. By that time the USSR had achieved status as the world's largest and second most powerful navy.

Historians and command and control experts have pondered the Cuban missile crisis in great depth and continue to offer new analysis. During the thirty-year anniversary observations of the Cuban episode in 1992, a number of surviving senior decision makers from the three sides met in Havana and Moscow for reunions and roundtable critiques. New information revealed at those gatherings confirmed that the situation came even closer to a nuclear exchange than either the United States or the Soviet Union leadership realized. Escalation to a nuclear exchange might have resulted in grave injury to the United States, but it certainly would have led to a disastrous Soviet defeat. The results of the crisis had a profound impact on subsequent overall Soviet military policy as well as the naval construction program.

The Soviet Navy before the Cuban confrontation consisted of twenty-five conventional cruisers, fewer than one hundred destroyers, and large numbers of small combatants. It also included more than three hundred diesel-powered submarines, more than half of which were long-range attack boats. The Soviet Union already possessed more than the total number of diesel attack submarines Nazi Germany had operated at the peak of its strength in World War II.

Until 1962, however, Soviet naval forces were seldom deployed far from home waters. Despite our suspicions of the quality of the fleet at the time, we learned only in 1995 that Soviet submarine forces deployed during the crisis—all long-range diesel subs of the Project 641 type, called Foxtrot class in the West—had been equipped with nuclear-tipped torpedoes in Sayda Bay.

The Cuban confrontation served as a dramatic arena where the U.S. Navy, for the first time since World War II, looked seriously into the eyes of a genuine naval opponent, which, although still a light-weight, was capable of inflicting serious damage. Until this point the Soviet Navy had confined its operations to supporting the massive Soviet ground army in Europe and Asia. However, for many years the Soviets had dreamed of becoming a naval power.

One of the dreamers was Sergei Georgevich Gorshkov. As Peter the Great was known as the father of the Russian Navy, surely Admiral of the Fleet and twice Hero of the Soviet Union Gorshkov was father of the modern Soviet Navy. Gorshkov, who joined the navy at age seventeen, became an admiral at age thirty-one and served for twenty-seven years as its commander in chief, presiding longer and through more significant changes than any other single Soviet naval leader. His rapid rise to the rank of admiral was due largely to his brilliance as a naval commander during what the Russians call the Great Patriotic War (World War II). He emerged from the war as one of the few senior Soviet naval heroes, mostly due to his actions during the campaign in Odessa on the Black Sea and as commander of the Danube River Flotilla. The navy emerged from the war as a nearly intact but small force commanded by the popular Admiral Nikolai G. Kuznetsov.

In October 1955, two years after Nikita Khrushchev became Communist Party first secretary, the Soviet Black Sea Fleet 24,000-ton flagship battleship *Novorossysk* exploded and sank in Sevastopol Harbor with the loss of 608 navy men. (*Novorossysk* was the former Italian battleship *Giulio Caesar*, transferred to the USSR in 1949 as war reparations.) In the aftermath of the official investigation into the causes for the sinking—to this day still a major controversy in Russia—Khrushchev summarily removed and demoted navy commander in chief Kuznetsov, elevated war hero Admiral Gorshkov to commander in chief, and abruptly reversed Stalin's postwar naval expansion. Khrushchev directed the disposal of many large surface warships and a halt to their further construction. According to Khrushchev, a nonsailor:

> Navy surface ships are good only for carrying heads of state on official visits; they have outlived their time. They're good only as missile platforms. This year to date we have destined practically all cruisers to the scrap heap.

Khrushchev stopped the aggressive heavy cruiser construction projects in midcourse. He redirected naval thinking to a defensive strategy anchored on a strong submarine force and a surface fleet restricted to coastal defense on the flanks of a massive ground army. Khrushchev, with the support of his first defense chief, Marshal Georgii Zhukov, the celebrated World War II ground army commander, sought to cut costs of new military construction while still retaining a gigantic land force. Expenditures for new naval building were drastically reduced. As a result, by 1957 the Soviet Navy was reduced to a force of fewer than 500,000 men; more than 350 ships had been mothballed. The navy cuts had been accompanied by a controversial debate on the value of a conventional surface navy dominated by cruisers. The large diesel attack submarine construction program also was reduced and deferred in favor of building nuclear and missile submarines with more sophisticated capabilities.

The new navy chief, Gorshkov, then presided over the transformation of the defensive Soviet fleet into a powerful navy of the nuclear era. He proceeded with the disposal of obsolete battleships and older cruisers following Khrushchev's dictum, and stopped the new all-gun cruiser building plans, scrapping many unfinished hulls still on the building ways.

Gorshkov carried out the policies trumpeted in the droning jargon of the Communist Party Central Committee that called for a revolution in military affairs, and began transforming the conventional navy into an offensive, long-range missile and nuclear force. But the transformation was slow starting and fraught with difficulty. During the ensuing quarter century of extraordinary Soviet Navy expansion, the pattern of the enormous loss of life aboard *Novorossysk* would haunt the Soviet Navy as they launched unprecedented numbers of submarines and modern, lighter, and missile-equipped surface ships in the race to become the world's largest navy. The stampede into the nuclear power arena resulted in scores of serious accidents aboard their prototype classes of submarines. The first nuclear submarine, *K-3*, burned, killing thirty-nine, and their first nuclear-powered ballistic missile sub, *K-19*, suffered so many fatal accidents she was nicknamed "Hiroshima."

Then astonishingly in 1962 in Leningrad, during the height of the Cuban crisis, the mercurial Khrushchev reproached Admiral Gorshkov while the navy searched frantically for appropriate escorts for their merchant ships being challenged en route to Cuba. "We need ships with autonomy and long range as escorts to Cuba," roared the angry Khrushchev. "How could you be without any?"

"But sir," replied Gorshkov, "you ordered them destroyed."

"I ordered no such thing," countered the first secretary.

Khrushchev denied not only that he had given the order to destroy all large surface combatants but that he ever knew about the sinking of battleship *Novorossysk*, or that he knew of the sacking of Admiral Kuznetsov.

This was the situation in 1962 when the Soviet Union launched its secret Operation *Anadyr*.

PART I

Cuba Libre

Operation *Anadyr*

In early 1962, first secretary of the Communist Party and premier of the Soviet Union Nikita S. Khrushchev set into quiet motion an operation to deploy ballistic missiles, medium-range bombers, and a regiment of mechanized infantry troops to Cuba in a daring plan named *Anadyr*. The naval part of the plan called for the secret deployment of seven ballistic missile submarines to Mariel, a deepwater port twenty-five miles west of Havana, which would become their permanent base of operations. The naval plan, code-named Operation *Kama*, began on October 1, 1962, with a sortie of four long-range diesel attack submarines assigned to proceed undetected from the Soviet Northern Fleet port of Sayda Bay to Mariel as an advance reconnaissance and a preparatory move for the seven ballistic missile submarines and support ships, which would follow later.

This is a true story based on firsthand accounts of the Soviet submariners who were part of the first sortie and of the U.S. destroyermen who challenged their transit.

JULY 1962
MOSCOW

On July 7 a secret session convened in the Kremlin for all senior military officers involved in the planning and execution of Operation *Anadyr*. The attendance was limited to key figures of the operation. From the navy only Fleet Admiral Sergei Gorshkov, the commander in chief, attended. At the highly polished table in the ornate Hall of St. George,

7

a flushed Nikita Khrushchev personally appealed to his military leaders and Cuban experts from the Ministries of Foreign Affairs and State Security to protect the secrecy of the operation and urged the attendees to get started as soon as possible.

On July 10 the Soviet commander for the forces in Cuba, General Issa Pliyev, and his staff left Moscow for Havana in a flight of three VIP-configured TU-114 transports. The senior officers were in civilian clothes, all disguised as engineers, agricultural experts, or irrigation and drainage technicians en route to assist Cubans in a massive humanitarian aid program.

In mid-July the dry cargo ship *Maria Ulyanova* slipped her moorings quietly and sailed from Murmansk for the port of Cabañas, scheduled to arrive on July 26. She was the first of what would surge to a total of eighty-five cargo ships and transports to depart from ports all around the Soviet Union carrying military equipment to Cuba. Operation *Anadyr* had begun.

As predicted by the general staff, the first ships had made the transit with little attention shown by the Americans. The massive sealift was under way in the guise of an all-out humanitarian and economic assistance program for Cuba.

AUGUST 1962
MOSCOW

Early one morning a black Volga sedan traveled at high speed toward the blinding morning sun on the still-empty Kutuzovsky Prospekt in Moscow. The car sped past the ugly scar of the still unfinished memorial to the Soviet victory over fascism, for which the ground had been broken in 1950. The car's sole passenger was as oblivious to the symbol as he was to the circumstances about to overtake him with a speed that matched his race toward the center of Moscow, just emerging from a shroud of early morning steam rising from the late summer coolness.

Kontr Admiral Leonid Filippovich Rybalko sat in the front passenger seat, the custom of senior officers expected to display socialist equality. The practice, which had remained even during the recent relaxation under Khrushchev, usually vanished as soon as the official graduated to the larger and more luxurious Chaika or ZIL limousine. The day might come later, he thought, when he would sit snugly in the rear of a ZIL.

Rear Admiral Leonid F.
Rybalko in 1962 (courtesy
the Rybalko family)

The admiral, commander of the Fourth Red Banner, Order of Ushakov Submarine Squadron, watched the distant silhouette of the red
Kremlin walls grow closer as the car propelled without slowing past the
first signs of life on the foot of the Arbat, as early morning vendors
unpacked their pitiful wares. Soon the area would be jammed with
buyers swarming like ants looking for something of value. Lining up
was a part of every Russian life, born from the habit of waiting for the
nonexistent luxuries promised by communism but that never came.

The Volga turned right sharply on Yanesheva ulitsa, past the military guards in front of the Ministry of Defense building, then came to
a stop in the annex parking lot. Rybalko slipped out of the car, and
without looking back barked, "Wait here," before the driver shut off the
engine. The cool wind forced Rybalko to fasten the lower buttons on
his heavy overcoat, girding himself for the journey across the street to
the large white building. He strode through the arched tunnel, which
framed the defense ministry building like the view through the wrong
end of a telescope. Military police with high leather boots and white
guard belts stood by the main entrance like pink-cheeked infants, too
early grown and tucked into uniforms. The admiral used the formal
entrance of the ministry, instead of the side door reserved for the senior
members of the operations and intelligence staff who manned the busy

command center. He had used that door for the past two years but today he was a VIP reporting to the minister to officially receive his new assignment.

Rybalko returned the salutes of the main hall sentries and strode up the steps two at a time, showing that at age fifty-three he still had the energy of his youth. He walked briskly down the ornate hallway under the overpowering murals in socialist realism, which screamed from the walls in defiance to remind all who passed of the Soviet victory over the Nazis, the sole positive accomplishment of more than four decades of communism, Rybalko thought grimly. The visitor was subjected to the full barrage of the garish forms of the heroes of the Great Patriotic War—Zhukov, Rokossovskii, Bogdanov, Gorshkov, and others—who peered down like cherubs from the walls as he walked down the hall toward the imposing door that led into the minister's cavernous office.

Rybalko paused, gathered his breath, and pushed open the heavy door without knocking. As was the custom the minister stood waiting, not two steps inside the door. A clock on a mantel was chiming exactly the appointed time.

"*Zdorovye zhelayu* [To your health], Comrade Marshal," the admiral pronounced, smiling broadly. This was a military greeting used by juniors to seniors.

"Lyova." The minister used the familiar diminutive of the admiral's first name as he reached for the extended hand. The handshake of both men was strong and friendly.

"Good to see you, Rodion Yakovlevich," the admiral addressed the minister respectfully, using his first name and patronymic. Marshal Rodion Yakovlevich Malinovsky, twice-decorated Hero of the Soviet Union who once commanded the famous Soviet Sixth Corps on the southern front in the Great Patriotic War, had shared many crises with Rybalko. The marshal placed his arm on the admiral's shoulder, shook it slightly, and guided him firmly to a chair. He began to recall some of their adventures during the years of Stalin's postwar purges, and how their clever political maneuvers had kept them just one step ahead of the informers and alive. Their mutual efforts in behind-the-scene politics cemented the admiral's position with Malinovsky.

Rybalko waited for the marshal to sit first. He recalled that the marshal was from the backwaters of Tatarstan near Kazan: although a Russian, his squat build and large facial features dominated by flintlike eyes and high cheeks gave him a slightly wild and oriental look.

"Leonid, we're sending you on another adventure, this time in an area you know well." The marshal looked beyond Rybalko and thundered "Bring tea!" to a white-frocked orderly standing paralyzed by the door.

"Colonel, leave us alone," the marshal motioned to his executive assistant and aide, a wide-girthed giant wearing the black tabs and gold insignia of a tanker on his green army tunic. The aide nodded politely and withdrew quietly, moving his bulk with astonishing agility.

The marshal looked at Rybalko and considered the handsome officer with a gift for languages, fluent in Spanish from his training at the Moscow Military Political Institute. Rybalko was always a few steps ahead of everyone else, with his brilliant analytical brain, smooth demeanor, and high charm, which catapulted his tall, wide-shouldered presence into complete mastery of every situation.

"How's Galina? She getting used to the idea you'll be gone for a while on this new, open-ended assignment?" The marshal studied Rybalko's features for the telltale signs of aging. He noticed a few, but the admiral still retained his alert and boyish look. From experience the marshal knew this officer had an uncanny ability to make the smallest operational assignment blossom into a major achievement. There had been that time when Rybalko's submarine had torpedoed two Nazi troop ships attempting to land reinforcements during the siege of Leningrad in 1943, thus relieving pressure on the beleaguered Soviet forces attempting to slash their way in to relieve the blockade. Rybalko was always there when needed; his units never seemed to suffer the usual mechanical failures that plagued most of the pitiful wartime Soviet Baltic Fleet, which failed in most attempts to inflict some damage to the German Fleet. Rybalko had always succeeded where others failed. He was perfect for this new assignment, of utmost importance in the growing crisis.

Party First Secretary Nikita Khrushchev's meddling in the navy's postwar ship construction program had resulted in a serious lack of major surface combatants in the Soviet Fleet. Now, with the possibility of a grave confrontation looming in the Caribbean over Castro's Cuba, the fleet was incapable of mustering two cruisers at the ready to escort the brigade of long-range, diesel attack submarines now preparing to sortie from Polyarny in the Northern Fleet. The long-awaited nuclear-powered submarines promised by Fleet Admiral Sergei Gorshkov to be operational by the beginning of the 1960s had failed every engineering readiness test and were languishing in the Severodvinsk repair yards, in the process of being modified after repeated reactor problems. There were simply not enough nuclear-trained officers to take the new submarines safely to sea, nor to keep up with the overly optimistic building program thrust upon the navy and shipbuilding ministry by the Party Central Committee. The shipyards had been hard pressed to gather enough materials in advance for the accelerated Five-Year Plan of construction to try to keep pace with the burgeoning U.S. nuclear submarine threat; and they desperately needed trained crewmen.

It had been a bad year for Northern Fleet's Polyarny-based submarines. On January 27, 1961, a Project 613 (Whiskey class) diesel attack submarine, S-80 had gone missing, with all sixty-eight of her crew. (S-80 was eventually found on the bottom of the Barents Sea, having suffered a snorkel failure. She was raised and salvaged in July 1969. All the food on board had been consumed, and there was still emergency oxygen aboard. The entire crew had succumbed to carbon dioxide poisoning.)

Then the first nuclear-powered strategic missile submarine, Project 658 (Hotel class) K-19, also based in Polyarny, had suffered a reactor casualty on her first missile firing exercise, in July. The submarine had been heralded publicly as the Soviet Union's answer to the United States' new Polaris boats, and shown on Soviet television supposedly launching her ballistic missiles while submerged to make it appear she had the same capability as the USS *George Washington*. But the footage had been carefully faked. Rybalko had been astounded when he saw it. The K-19 he knew could fire only while surfaced. The navy propaganda office of the Political Directorate had managed to fabricate the effect that the submarine had different capabilities. In fact, the launching of her new missile had gone badly. After several false countdowns it finally lifted off but veered off course and self-destructed without reaching even half the maximum range. This, too, was carefully suppressed, and the political wizards dubbed into the TV film a flight of a totally unrelated Strategic Rocket Force missile launched from a stand on the Novaya Zemlya test range. Even the Moscow leadership had not known the submarine missile launch had failed.

Then, to make matters still worse, as K-19 was crossing the North Atlantic on her way back to her home port, one of her VM-A, 70-megawatt pressurized water reactors suffered a loss of primary cooling, a failure with no remedy since there had been no backup system installed. And there she was, wallowing helplessly in midocean with the reactor's uranium fuel elements overheating, certain disaster to the 128 crewmen aboard. In desperation the crew's engineers fabricated an auxiliary cooling system using stainless steel tubing cannibalized from several torpedoes and rigged a Rube Goldberg–like device linking one of the submarine's freshwater tanks to circulate water through the reactor for cooling. The foolishly brave engineers then climbed into the hot shielded reactor compartment, two at a time, and welded the jury-rigged cooling system in by hand. The eight men who worked inside the shielded reactor space wore only light chemical protection suits and oxygen breathing apparatuses. Then, to better see during the welding process through fogging lenses, they removed the masks. All eight were exposed to lethal doses of gamma and neutron radiation, and absorbed lethal quantities of alpha and beta contamination. Within minutes they suffered severe nausea, their faces swelled, and their tongues turned black. Within hours they broke out in beads of bloody perspiration and suffered painfully slow deaths, some pleading to be shot to allay the severe pain. Many of the other engineers working in the submarine's adjacent engineering spaces were severely poisoned by radiation, and the cesium and strontium poisons, by-products of the fission, spilled on the deck and tracked throughout the boat, spreading enough pollutants to contaminate all aboard. When the submarine met the rescue forces, most of the crew had suffered some degree of radiation exposure; all were evacuated from the submarine.

Thus, in mid-1962, when a real need arose for long-range nuclear submarines, there was none available. They were all in shipyards undergoing engineering backfitting to install redundant cooling systems for their reactor primary loops. Although Admiral Rybalko was not a nuclear engineer, he understood enough thermodynamics to know that you didn't send complex weapons platforms to sea with prototype, untested engineering equipment without backup systems. The accident aboard *K-19* was particularly difficult for the navy to squelch because there had been a near-mutiny aboard when some officers, instigated by the political officer, called the *zampolit,* felt the *K-19*'s commanding officer, Captain Nikolai Zateyev, was unduly risking their lives by taking the boat to a rendezvous for help from other fleet units of the exercise. These officers tried to compel him to beach the boat on nearby Jan Mayen Island, a NATO ocean surveillance facility, and to abandon her to save the lives of the remaining crew. The group of officers led by the *zampolit* approached the captain to force him to follow their plan. After a tense encounter Zateyev successfully rebuffed the group. The number of seriously radiated crewmen was so great that there were angry repercussions later as some threatened to expose the true story of what had transpired. In the end, the whole mess had been contained by security officers who forced all involved to swear oaths of secrecy to not reveal that the accident occurred, on threat of imprisonment. The submarine had made it home after evacuating the remaining crew to a rescue ship. The entire propulsion system was then pulled out in the yard and another of the same type installed. It was the first Soviet submarine ever to undergo a complete "hysterectomy," said Rybalko.

The whole scandalous K-19 episode had been successfully covered up by the Main Navy Staff; few civilians outside of the Northern Fleet area ever knew exactly what had happened. Those sailors who had received lethal doses of radiation were spirited away into various hospitals, where they were listed as "suffering severe trauma caused by stress." The eight who died were buried in secret graves, their families told only that they had perished in the line of duty. Thirteen others died later, and their bodies were sequestered in similar fashion.

In January 1962 another Polyarny submarine, the Project 641 (Tango class) B-37, suffered a torpedo explosion while moored to a pier in Polyarny. The explosion was so devastating that it killed the entire 122-man crew, sank the submarine moored to the other side of the same pier, the Project 613 (Whiskey class) S-350, and spewed torn and twisted deck plates and piping aloft, which rained down hundreds of yards away, smashing the homes of terrified Polyarny navy families.

For those reasons the Main Navy Staff had searched high and wide for a competent submariner for this top-security operation called *Anadyr*. They selected Leonid Rybalko and the time-tested long-range diesel boats of his Fourth Squadron, and at this point, the kontr admiral had not the faintest idea of where exactly that would take them. General Matvei Zakharov, chief of the Soviet General Staff from 1960 to 1963, had christened the Cuban deployment "Operation *Anadyr*," which had been the name of Stalin's plan in the 1950s to stage a million-man army in Chukhotka for use in attacking Alaska had the period of worsening postwar relations with the United States led to war.

Defense Minister Malinovsky was now in urgent need of a reliable and effective submarine commander who could be trusted to take the advance brigade of long-range, Project 641 (Foxtrot class) diesel attack submarines to sea and to proceed undetected to Mariel, Cuba, as the opening phase of the naval portion of Operation *Anadyr*. In the eyes of hard-core Reds like Malinovsky, this missile gamble in a Caribbean island under a tin-hat dictator who wasn't at this point even a confirmed communist was foolishness. The naval portion of Operation *Anadyr* (the name of a port in northeastern Siberia), which called for the covert movement of eleven submarines to Cuba, was called *Kama* after the river that runs from Siberia west into the Volga River. The naval plan called for the deployment of a contingent that would eventually include two ancient gun cruisers of the Project 68 *Chapayev* class, two missile destroyers, two squadrons of mine warfare craft, seven strategic missile Project 629 (Golf class) submarines forming the Eighteenth Division, and four long-range diesel attack Project 641 submarines forming the Sixty-ninth Brigade—all to be permanently stationed in Mariel, Cuba.

Premier Khrushchev had made the fateful decision on May 12, 1962, to deploy strategic weapons to Cuba under the cover of a massive aid program. The first Soviet delegation, made up of senior defense experts headed by General Sharav Rashidov, flew to Havana on May 28 for consultations with the Cuban leaders. The Cubans accepted the grandiose plan immediately. On June 13 Soviet General Staff Directive 79604 arrived at the Main Navy Staff headquarters at Griboyedova Street to lay out the plan for Operations *Anadyr* and *Kama*.

From the beginning some senior naval officers felt a tinge of doubt about the operation, which they believed to carry the seeds of its eventual failure. The total reliance on secrecy cloaking the movement of the strategic arms to Cuba based its ultimate success on the perceived assumption that the Americans would not unmask the plan and squelch it before it was a fait accompli. If the Soviets did not achieve the covert installation of the missiles and have the bombers operational quickly, the whole operation could become a high-order diplomatic crisis, leaving the USSR with a viable threat only partially in place—somewhat like a duelist being caught with his pistol only partially out of his holster at the start of a duel.

The deception that covered the operation was so far-reaching that to further reinforce the validity of the code name *Anadyr*, the General Staff ordered the inclusion of arctic equipment—skis, fleece-lined parkas, and the famed World War II *valenki*, winter boots made of felt—in the gear of the troops of the four motorized rifle regiments earmarked for duty in Cuba. This was to deceive unwitting junior commanders who would note the presence of winter gear in the paperwork and on loading piers, and convince them that the operation area was indeed to take place somewhere far colder than the Caribbean.

The eventual collapse of secrecy forced the Soviet leaders to lie outright in the United Nations and to the world in general about their intentions. There were other departures from normal Soviet behavior connected with this operation. For example, the chief of staff, General Zakharov, insisted that all participants in the Cuban operation draw special pay three months prior to their deployment, an unusual order, which, although popular, set curious minds spinning and loose tongues wagging. How to accomplish this broad plan and still keep the operation completely secret must have been a challenge even in a system noted for its lack of free-flowing information and its propensity for intrigue and suppression of truth. With little knowledge of these preparations, Admiral Rybalko was forming his own impressions about the operation.

❖

The door to the minister's office suddenly burst open, and in spurted the stumpy figure of Fleet Admiral of the Soviet Union Sergei Gorshkov, puffing after his short walk from the VIP elevator, red-faced and openly upset. Behind him walked the tall Admiral Vitali Fokin, first deputy commander in chief, who was overall coordinator of Operation *Kama*.

"Greetings, Comrade Minister. What brings one of *my* admirals to your office, Marshal?" Gorshkov was notoriously jealous of his officers' relations with the senior officers of other services, especially the minister of defense. He was painfully aware of Admiral Rybalko's close personal relationship with Malinovsky, but that hardly excused the marshal's summoning the junior admiral without waiting for the navy commander in chief to arrive in the minister's office. Malinovsky had been correct in the protocol of advising Gorshkov's office that Rybalko had been summoned, but it was a clever act by both Rybalko and the marshal that the two had met fifteen minutes prior to the senior admiral's arrival, an obvious yet seemingly innocent snub to Gorshkov.

"Comrade Fleet Admiral, I've known your best submariner as long as if not longer than you, and I already know you approve of his assignment."

"Leonid, this is the most independent navy assignment you'll ever see," the marshal said with sudden seriousness. The marshal envied

Rybalko slightly. He was still young and full of promise. Following his recent promotion to kontr admiral he had enjoyed a wonderful series of assignments, the prestigious position as commandant of the Frunze Higher Naval School in Leningrad, then command of the Fourth Submarine Squadron in Polyarny.

Rybalko feigned surprise, although he had already heard rumors of an assignment to take a squadron of long-range diesels into the United States' backyard. He often humored the marshal in this manner; it was a way of keeping close to him. The marshal was slowing down. The incredibly good luck of surviving the sweeping postwar party purges had been crowned when Malinovsky became Stalin's man and then was picked by the new premier Khrushchev as defense minister in 1957 over a whole series of more senior officers, including Admiral Gorshkov.

The marshal paused while the orderly brought in the tray of tea, clear glasses on silver metal holders, accompanied by a plate of lemons and a sugar bowl. "See, Leonid, we're living high here, we've even got lemon for our tea." He smiled broadly, eyes twinkling. "But the sugar's vile, Cuban stuff." He shook his head in mock despair. "My Masha can't even find lightbulbs for our quarters, and we live in Marshal Zhukov's old apartment! How's that for workers' paradise?" He grinned and offered tea to the three navy men.

"It's a good job for you," the marshal continued. "You already know that part of the Atlantic well. This time there will be an added element, not yet used in operations at sea."

"I understand, sir." Rybalko looked at the marshal without emotion. Quietly Rybalko felt sorry for the man. Malinovsky had once been known for his sharp focus on the issues, always operationally oriented and never a politician. Rybalko had no idea what the marshal was referring to as a new operational element.

Gorshkov interrupted to remind the marshal that he was really the operational commander of this mission, and began to spell out Rybalko's orders. "Kontr Admiral Rybalko," he began with exaggerated volume, "you are in no way to allow American antisubmarine forces to discover your submarines during the transit. Your assignment is to get to Mariel undetected by October 20 and to prepare for the subsequent deployment of seven ballistic missile submarines, which will follow with their support ships. You are to reconnoiter the waters surrounding Mariel and ensure they are free of American antisubmarine forces, fixed acoustic arrays, and to survey and report the hydroacoustic conditions of the area. The communications code words are all set, and will be broadcast in parallel on low-frequency schedules and on high-frequency single sideband, so you'll have to keep one boat near the surface at periscope depth to monitor HF. That will be particularly challenging if the Americans deploy their hunter-killer ASW forces."

"I'm familiar with Caribbean sonar conditions, sir—"

Gorshkov cut him off. "I'm aware of that, Comrade Admiral; that's why you were selected to command this force. Remember that you will command the only Soviet naval forces in the area, thanks to our new leadership." Gorshkov emphasized the words in an unveiled reference to Khrushchev's orders to halt the massive heavy cruiser building program in its tracks. The navy commander in chief fumed when he thought of the messy situation. He was now forced to deploy a puny brigade of diesels without escorts, instead of a flotilla of cruisers and destroyers. (Soviet attack submarines were organized into brigades, while strategic missile subs were formed into divisions. Squadrons could consist of a mix of attack brigades and missile divisions.) He was totally unprepared for what was developing in the Caribbean, but he would not let the navy be made a laughingstock, and he would get the submarines into the Caribbean if he had to break scores of officers to do it. That was precisely why he had selected Rybalko to head the force, which would be given the new designation of Twentieth Special Squadron. Although Gorshkov loathed the man, he would grant him the assignment especially because of his cozy relationship with the minister, that Mongolian-faced tank marshal.

"What you don't know, Admiral Rybalko, is that the new elements mentioned by the marshal are the special torpedo warheads your submarines will carry. You will load one such torpedo on each of your boats at Sayda Bay before getting under way. Your brigade commander and submarine commanding officers will have advance authorization to engage with the special weapons without the permission from fleet headquarters or the ministry in Moscow if attacked by American ships or aircraft."

Rybalko paled and looked at the admiral, then turned to the marshal, who was studying his face, watching for the reaction. "Sir, you're aware that few of our submarines have ever test-fired atomic weapons at sea?"

"Of course we're aware of that, Leonid Filippovich, but the warheads have been tested by MINATOM, the ministry that develops such weapons. Also one of the commanding officers in your Sixty-ninth Brigade—Captain . . . what's his name?" He looked around.

Admiral Fokin, standing to the side, offered, "That's Captain First Rank Nikolai Shumkov, commanding officer of *B-130.*" Vitali Fokin was the first deputy commander in chief under Gorshkov and had been given the task of preparing all naval forces participating in Operation *Kama.*

"Yes," Admiral Gorshkov continued. "Your Shumkov has fired two live nuclear torpedoes off Novaya Zemlya, one subsurface burst and one surface burst. For that he was awarded the Order of Lenin. That's enough."

Rybalko looked alarmed. "Sir, we still don't know the effects on the launch platforms of such weapons, or at what range the blast will be lethal to the firing unit. We might destroy our own subs if we fire one of these at an American target."

Gorshkov was visibly agitated; he did not enjoy discussing naval operational matters in the office of the minister. The marshal was an army ground force officer who knew little about naval weapons and warfare. Gorshkov wanted to cover these naval operational details away from this obviously ignorant tank officer.

Gorshkov came directly to the point, the real reason the junior admiral had been summoned to the defense ministry, which was normally unheard of for giving ordinary naval orders. "Your rules of engagement are quite clear. You will use these weapons if American forces attack you submerged or force your units to surface and then attack, or upon receipt of orders from Moscow."

Now Rybalko looked shocked. He glanced at the minister, who nodded slowly.

Admiral Gorshkov caught the look and the minister's nod, and grew more furious that this naval officer, his junior, was obviously doubting that these orders could be correct. Gorshkov added loudly, "Those rules have been approved by the Politburo, and the first secretary, and that is enough for us. We will follow orders. Admiral Fokin will give you detailed orders at the Main Navy Staff. When you finish the briefings at Griboyedova ulitsa you will fly immediately to Northern Fleet headquarters in Severomorsk. I'm aware of your command difficulties with the Sixty-ninth Brigade. Your new brigade commander will be the former chief of staff, Captain Vitali Agafonov."

Rybalko looked stunned. He knew that Agafonov had been the brigade chief of staff and that the brigade commander, Kontr Admiral Yevseyev, had been suddenly hospitalized. How in the world had Commander in Chief Gorshkov learned of this? It had taken place only hours before. Rybalko assumed the political officer network was doing its duty well, or had it been the third separate channel of the Security Office network, which often looked closely into these matters and reported via their channels directly to the main Naval Security in the *Kommitet Gosudarstvenny Bezopastnosty*, the KGB? It was rumored belowdecks that Yevseyev wasn't really ill. He was a known heavy drinker, and when word had come in advance that this mission was to be a highly sensitive, dangerous, and long deployment, Yevseyev had come down mysteriously with an extended bout of high blood pressure. Some believed that he had just chickened out. He was a veteran submariner of World War II and had seen a lot of action and suffered frequently from a nervous condition. In any case, Agafonov had been brigade chief of staff for some time and could easily take over command of the brigade. Rybalko became suddenly aware of the high-level scrutiny this operation would have focused on it, and the awareness brought mixed emotions.

Captain Vitali Agafonov had a superb record as a submarine commanding officer. Once, during a fire in the forward torpedo room of another ill-fated Polyarny-based diesel submarine, *B-139*, earlier that year, Agafonov had personally taken command and piloted the burning submarine out of the crowded nest and into more isolated waters in case her remaining torpedoes exploded. He succeeded, and became known as a brave officer and a real stalwart.

Rybalko stood silent and rigid, thinking rapidly. He understood that the rules of engagement virtually gave his submarine commanders personal authority to begin a nuclear war with the United States. This was incredible! He could hardly believe his ears. He was yanked back to reality by Gorshkov.

"Dismissed, Admiral." Gorshkov, in an obvious breach of military etiquette, dismissed the junior admiral from the minister's office without so much as a glance at the minister.

The marshal squinted, face reddening, at the feisty fleet admiral who stood feet widely planted, appearing as if ready to trade punches with the minister. Malinovsky took a deep breath, holding his temper. He was not prepared for a face-off with the stubborn fleet admiral; he had to get ready for his noon meeting with the Politburo and needed some time to prepare his proposed rules of engagement for General

Pliyev, the commander of Soviet ground and missile troops already in Havana in the early stages of *Anadyr*. Pressure was mounting, and he needed time. For all he knew they could be in a shooting war with the United States soon, and he knew his forces were woefully unprepared. Who else knew it would depend on his ability to dazzle the Politburo and the Ukrainian farmer, First Secretary Khrushchev, with fancy footwork.

The minister suddenly straightened his tunic and spat out "Z'*bogm*," the old Russian farewell, "Go with God." Then he added his dismissal to the junior admirals with a forced smile on his face.

As the office door closed behind the departing admirals the marshal turned, walked to the window, and looked out. The sudden silence pressed in on him as he reached in his inside tunic pocket and took out a cigarette. Looking out over the rooftops to the distant Arbat, he could see the daily growing crowds. He sighed as he pictured his Masha there in the masses looking for lemons. He tapped the cigarette on the lighter, then lit the cigarette. He noticed his reflection in the glare of the glass and saw the flame of the lighter in the window. His aide, the thick tanker, quietly emerged and walked over to the marshal. The colonel looked out the window and joined the silence. Brushing the marshal with his shoulder, he said, "I don't like that fleet admiral either, sir." As if reading the minister's mind, he added, "I don't trust his submarines."

The marshal registered no reaction and continued staring through the window at the lines of Russians huddled in front of shop doors and stands selling everything under the sun—long line after long line everywhere he looked, framed by his own reflection. He wondered how it would be to stand in line with Masha, or to be hungry. What would it be like if he couldn't find what he needed? He drew on his cigarette, then suddenly crushed it out angrily in the plate of cookies that sat untouched on the tea tray. Not one had been eaten because everyone knew they were stale. There were no fresh cookies anywhere in Moscow.

❖

In the small bedroom of their Moscow apartment Admiral Rybalko watched his wife, Galina, finish packing his old leather suitcase. She always repacked even after he had already put in everything he needed. Galina rearranged the case, brilliantly rolling things so there was double the space than when he packed. He wondered how she kept her spirits up during the current economic mess in Moscow. There were seldom staples that could be counted on to be in the desolate and barren shops. Still Galina continued in high spirits, as though it were all part of a game.

"Ready?" Galina smiled and slid the suitcase out to the hall. She took her husband's heavy blue overcoat off the hanger in the hall and began to brush it free of imaginary lint.

"Galina, that's not necessary." Leonid took her by the shoulders and embraced her and the overcoat. "It won't be a long separation." He suppressed his doubts about the mission.

She looked up at him and smiled, showing no sign of sadness. "I'll have this huge flat all to myself," she teased. "It's sinful, imagine all this space. Maybe Natasha will come and stay for some weeks! It would be a good change from her crowded flat." The admiral's mother, Natasha, lived with her two daughters and their families in the village of Klin north of Moscow, on the road to Leningrad. Galina scolded, "Lev, it's really unnecessary for her to live there, but then it's out of the Moscow pollution and better for her asthma and gives her the excuse to be independent from her high-ranking and dominating son." She grinned and turned away from her husband, who stood watching from the window.

"The car's here." The admiral helped Galina with her heavy coat, and then, while she secured her scarf in the intricate way she always did, he put on his heavy boots. Together they walked out of the apartment, carrying the heavy bag between them toward the elevator.

"This hall always smells of cooking oil and fish," Rybalko muttered.

"At least that's not as bad as the cigarette smoke on the first floor," Galina added. They entered the elevator together and, as they descended, Galina thought of their lovely dacha in Klin. Galina's dream was to live in their own home, one like the movies showed of private homes in the United States or England.

They stepped out into the windy late summer day and walked to the car. "Good morning, *Gospodzha* Admiral," the army driver said with a smile as he held the door for Galina. She slid into the left rear seat, while Rybalko broke the tradition and sat in the rear, next to her on the right.

"Need to be at Vnukovo Airport by noon." The admiral's tone was casual, not the normal tone when a senior addressed a driver. Rybalko was known for his outwardly soft manner with subordinates, but all who knew him were aware of his fierce reactions when he observed the slightest infractions of discipline or departure from excellence. He was a highly feared yet revered flag officer.

"Yes, sir, we'll take the Krylatskoi Shosse. It's faster and has fewer trucks." The Volga pulled out into the Moscow traffic and swirling black diesel exhaust.

They drove along silently through the wide Moscow streets. "Look," Galina exclaimed, "they have chicken for sale at the *Tsentralni Rynok!* I'll stop on the way back."

"Are things that bad, dear, that you have to rush out to buy when you don't even need it? I saw you had some in the kitchen already."

"My dear, you have to buy when you see things. I can trade it for marinated herring with Tatyana next door. She has a big supply her Sasha brought back from Murmansk. Plus on the other side of town they have lamb for sale by Kiev Station. Marina called and told me this morning. I can trade chicken for lamb."

The admiral shook his head. Galina had become an expert in hoarding and trading, an attribute necessary to survive in Moscow. The broader the network of friends, the richer the table she could lay for Leonid and his friends. The situation made him feel sick at heart. At least in the old days, if you had the rubles you could find things. Everything was available in Stalin's day except the guarantee of your privacy and security. As the saying went, "One died then with a full stomach."

❖

Admiral Rybalko walked with Galina toward the aircraft waiting at Vnukovo. He immediately noticed the lieutenant colonel in the uniform of the naval infantry standing by the ladder leading to the blue-and-white VIP-configured TU-42 aircraft. Standing in the small clutch at the bottom of the stairs were two senior officers from the Ministry of Defense Liaison Office—his former deputy, Rear Admiral Khuzhakov; and Colonel Gennady Tikhomirov, the gnarled oracle who had served nearly twenty years consecutively in the Intelligence Directorate. Galina walked close to her husband, clutching his arm silently, looking bright and fresh despite the impending farewell. She was used to seeing him off on duty trips, but she had been fortunate in accompanying him on most assignments, thereby playing a major role in the busy social life of three consecutive shore duty tours. This departure was somehow different.

Life had its ups and downs, but Galina was thankful for the opportunity to have been with him rather than remaining at home for the long deployments of the navy officers. She was proud of her husband's fast-moving career. Galina was more than a good navy wife. She was his partner, and he appreciated and loved her a great deal more than he showed.

Rybalko shook hands all around with the officers. He greeted his former aide. "It was kind of you to see me off, Valodiya. How's Irina?

"Fine, sir, sends her best. I'm not seeing you off, I'm escorting you to Severomorsk. I disembark there while you drive over to Polyarny after the briefings. The fleet admiral himself asked me to brief you on the way. I have lots to update you about." He pointed to a bulging briefcase standing at his feet.

The admiral kissed Galina, saluted the send-off group, and jogged up the ladder. His aide, Captain Second Rank Vladimir Popov, followed with his briefcase. Rybalko stopped briefly to wave, mimicking the popular VIP routine in Russia. He winked at Galina, gave the thumbs-up sign, and disappeared inside the aircraft. As he peered from the window by the senior seat, he saw Galina return the thumbs-up sign discreetly while standing to the rear of the others. She deserved better, he thought, determined to give her a better life someday, somehow.

Rybalko leaned over as the aircraft climbed and looked out at Moscow beneath the yellow shroud disappearing below. He recognized the beautiful domes of the old Church of Fili in the northwestern suburbs. The gold of the church's domes shimmered in the afternoon sunlight. As he squinted slightly in the glare, he watched the domes disappear into the haze.

"Moscow always looks better from a distance, doesn't it, sir?" his aide asked, breaking the silence.

Rybalko turned to the young submariner Popov seated next to him and wearing the submarine commander's badge on the right breast of his blue uniform. "Sure does. Look at that haze. Is Severomorsk that polluted?"

SEPTEMBER 1962
AT SEA

By the first of September the Soviet Navy had already shipped a full reserve supply of spare parts, ammunition, and missiles into Mariel. Then the ships began to bring in the missile-equipped small patrol boats of the Komar class for short-range coastal defense. These were intended to defend against amphibious forces and deemed urgent to be in place to help thwart a U.S. invasion, which at the time Soviet leaders considered to be inevitable.

In early September it was time for the three medium-range missile regiments to embark in their ships for the trip to Cuba. The overall missile division commander, Major General Igor Statsenko, was deeply concerned about his ability to load and transport his three regiments in complete secrecy, when the missiles themselves could fit only into holds with larger-than-normal-size hatches. The navy had suggested they load these ships in the closed port of Sevastopol, home port of the Black Sea Fleet in the Crimea, which was closed not only to foreigners but also to nonmilitary Soviet citizens, who required special passes to enter. Upon arrival in Sevastopol, the three regiments of missile troops were bivouacked in isolated warehouse areas and loaded quietly aboard large-hatch cargo ships. The first shipment of the sixty-seven-foot-long medium-range missiles was loaded aboard the merchant ship *Poltava*, in an isolated transport loading slip off the main harbor in Sevastopol, away from scrutiny by local residents of the predominantly navy town. Once the missiles were carefully loaded by crane into the holds, large concrete slabs, more than five tons each, were hoisted inside. These were the launch pads to accompany the missiles, ensuring that they could be erected quickly on arrival and be made operational without waiting for the transport and pouring of concrete on site in Cuba. The thousands of troops accompanying the missiles were crammed belowdecks in poorly ventilated compartments, and for more than three weeks endured terrible conditions, and were seasick and overcome by the oppressive heat. They were allowed topside only at night in small groups to breathe fresh air and to exercise. Frequently, U.S. reconnaissance aircraft flew over the ships, but were generally unable to identify the cargoes belowdecks. The shipping phase of the operation was colossal and initially successful at avoiding undue attention.

Over time, however, the United States increased its surveillance flights and began looking with peaked interest at the Soviet merchant traffic heading to the Caribbean. In early September two Soviet ships, *Indigirki* and *Aleksandrovsk*, sailed from the northern port of Severomorsk, and after an eighteen-day transit entered the port of Mariel with the first precious cargo of nuclear warheads, stowed in their main deck superstructure. *Indigirki* carried eighty cruise missile warheads for the

Komar class missile patrol boats, six nuclear warheads for the naval Il-28 bombers, and a dozen atomic warheads for the short-range, twenty-five-mile *Luna* coastal defense missiles. *Aleksandrovsk* carried twenty-four warheads for the R-14 intermediate-range missile, which remained in the ship's hold in the port of La Isabela, awaiting the missiles. (The R-14 missile had a range of just over two thousand miles and carried one nuclear warhead.) These two ships proceeded normally and, although detected and photographed by U.S. surveillance aircraft, did not cause any particular alarm. In 1962 the United States did not yet have the capability to detect nuclear weapons with gamma, neutron detectors, as in later years. The orders to the masters of *Indigirki* and *Aleksandrovsk* concerning self-defense had read: "Regarding the self-defense of your vessels *Indigirki* and *Aleksandrovsk*—during the transport of special cargo for the voyage—against pirate ships and aircraft you have been equipped with two 37mm automatic antiaircraft guns with 1,200 rounds for each. Open fire only in the event of an attempt to seize or to sink your ship, and report the same attempt simultaneously to Moscow."[1]

By mid-September the nuclear warheads for Soviet R-12 medium-range *Sopka* missiles and Il-28 medium-range bombers were in place in Cuba. (The R-12 missile had a range of 1,050 miles and carried a single nuclear warhead. The Il-28 medium bomber had a combat radius of 600 miles and was equipped in Cuba to carry six 8–12-kiloton atomic bombs.) The Soviet merchantmen unloaded the first six medium bombers from crates at the Cuban air base in San Julián. These were used naval aviation-subordinated aircraft and could deliver depth charges as well as conventional and nuclear bombs. There were only six nuclear bombs available for these aircraft at that field. The remainder of the atomic warheads were deployed with coastal defense *Luna* missiles. These twenty-five-mile missiles were to be used against amphibious landing forces and were authorized for release without prior authority from Moscow. The nuclear warheads for those were stockpiled at Santa Cruz del Norte. By the third week in September, 129 shipments had departed for Cuba, 94 had arrived at their destinations, and 35 were still en route. The loading in Soviet ports for the remaining shipments was due to be completed by October 20, and the final arrivals in Cuba were scheduled prior to November 5, before the U.S. congressional elections.[2]

The first serious alarm came on September 18, when a U.S. Navy frigate in the Mediterranean off the coast of Tunis queried a Soviet merchantman about the nature of his cargo. "Agricultural machinery," replied the Soviet master. However, his deck cargo consisted of large, irregularly sized crates containing disassembled fuselage parts of three Ilyushin-28 medium bombers. The Americans were suspicious and reported that the deck cargo appeared to consist of disguised aircraft. The Soviet merchantmen had been ordered to declare their cargoes as auto exports or agriculture machinery if challenged, stating that they were taking them to Havana. Initially, the merchant ship masters had departed the Soviet ports not knowing their ultimate destinations, with orders to sail toward the Azores, and at a particular checkpoint to open sealed envelopes, which would direct them to sail farther, to designated ports in Cuba. In that fashion there would be no chance to accidentally reveal the destinations before reaching the Azores, in the mid-Atlantic. The masters, their crews, and the Soviet soldiers embarked in the transports supposedly had no knowledge that they were heading to Cuba. It is difficult to believe that even in the Soviet Union, for an effort the size of the *Anadyr* operation, which involved the vast military complex of the huge nation and more than forty thousand men who were preparing to be stationed in the island nation, that some foreknowledge as to their destination had not leaked out. Nevertheless, the charade of secrecy continued. Ships carrying men of the four motorized rifle regiments to Cuba were limited to allowing only groups of twenty-five to thirty men on the weather decks at one time, the rest remaining below in the extreme heat and humidity inside the freighters, which would become extremely uncomfortable steaming in the Sargasso Sea and the Caribbean. After their first round-trip and while loading for the repeat voyages, most masters knew perfectly well that their shuttle runs were all to Cuban ports.

In the meantime, U.S. warships and reconnaissance flights were becoming curious at the massive sealift under way and began taking more strenuous efforts to identify their cargoes. In the cases where the size and configuration of the cargo—such as aircraft, helicopters, trucks, and armored personnel carriers—dictated parking the vehicles on deck, the equipment was covered and the aircraft disassembled, crated, and covered. However, it was impossible to hide all cargo loads completely, and soon U.S. surveillance ships and aircraft had identified the beginnings of the massive sealift of military cargo. The troops aboard ships wore civilian attire but could be recognized as Russian primarily by their striped jerseys, which often showed beneath their tropical shirts.

When in Cuba they were authorized to don Cuban military uniforms, but for the most part remained in civilian clothing. It was difficult if not impossible for the fair-haired, large-bodied Russian soldier or Asian conscript to pass as Cuban. All communications between the Ministry of Defense and the ships involved in the sealift were hand-carried by couriers, rather than being sent via radio or telephone.

On September 19 Soviet navy commander in chief and Admiral of the Fleet Sergei G. Gorshkov briefed the Ministry of Defense on the details of the NATO exercise called Fallex 62, which was under way throughout Europe, the Mediterranean, and the northern Atlantic. Gorshkov claimed the exercise was part of recurring maneuvers during which NATO forces exercised the transition to a full-blown nuclear war.

The Soviet naval staff watched with some apprehension as the U.S. Navy increased its activity in the Atlantic. Then, to the alarm of the Soviets and their Cuban allies, in early fall the U.S. Navy and Marines staged a large-scale amphibious landing exercise code-named Operation Ortsac (Castro spelled backward) on the island of Vieques off Puerto Rico. The Soviet naval leadership found it difficult to stand by and observe the continuing flow of men and matériel into these distant waters in unarmed carriers without responding with at least some visible escort presence. On September 19, 1962, in view of the increased surveillance and with the lurking fear of having his secret cargoes exposed, Premier Khrushchev authorized the Soviet General Staff to send the following message of instructions to all Soviet merchant ships:

> Soviet ships are part of the Soviet Union and any overt attack against them carried out by foreign ships or aircraft constitutes an act of aggression against the USSR. Upon receiving fire from foreign aircraft or warships the merchant ship commander is authorized to open fire. On being attacked the master will take all necessary measures to maintain order. When reporting attacks by the enemy you will encode your reports of attack.[3]

On September 25 the Soviet Defense Council acquiesced to pressure from Fleet Admiral Gorshkov to authorize the deployment of a squadron of navy surface combatants and auxiliaries simultaneously from the Northern, Baltic, and Black Sea Fleets into the Atlantic as a show of force to respond to the increase of U.S. naval forces, which were reacting to the massive influx of merchant ships carrying cargoes of all types, some obviously military, to ports in Cuba. At the last minute, before these units left home waters, both Khrushchev and Defense

Minister Malinovsky overruled the Defense Council and forced the aggressive Admiral Gorshkov to cancel the deployment of surface warships, since it would certainly have caused the Americans to react with even further vigor in the Caribbean. Marshal Malinovsky insisted that Operation *Kama* proceed as planned and that it was sufficient to have four long-range diesel attack submarines in the area with nuclear warheads aboard as a deterrent factor, and without surface escorts, which would certainly tip the Soviets' hand even further.

The extraordinary deception methods contributed to the success of the transit portion of the operation, but when the ships were offloaded and men and equipment moved to the launch sites, they became increasingly difficult to camouflage. Because of the frequent U.S. aerial surveillance, Soviet troops in Cuba moved overland to barracks only by night; as a result the Cubans began calling them "night crawlers."

For the fortunate Soviet troops who were airlifted to Cuba, the deception techniques were equally elaborate. Initial air transport manifests of staff and advisers for the Cuban Army were gathered together in Moscow and issued with passports stamped with entry visas for Conakry, Guinea, to keep them, and U.S. intelligence, in the dark concerning their final destination.

The following signal was transmitted to all ships in the Soviet Maritime Ministry by the Soviet General staff on September 27, 1962, as a result of reports of increased U.S. surveillance of their merchant ships that were part of Operation *Anadyr:*

> In the case it is impossible to defend against armed attack of your ship by foreign personnel boarding your ship by force, the head of the embarked military unit will destroy all documents aboard that contain military or state secrets. Upon threat of seizure of our ships by foreign ships the master and head of the embarked military unit will resist the attack and boarding, and if it becomes necessary sink the ship using all means to save the crew in accordance with directives of the Maritime Fleet.[4]

AUGUST–SEPTEMBER 1962
WASHINGTON, D.C.

On August 22 Central Intelligence Agency director John McCone advised President Kennedy that Soviet SA-2 anti–air defense missiles had been sighted in Cuba. On August 29 a U.S. U-2 reconnaissance flight ordered specially in response to earlier sightings confirmed the presence of eight Soviet-built SA-2 SAM sites in Cuba; two were near sites the navy had selected as possible contingency beach landing sites. The next day, August 30, two Cuban Navy frigates fired on a U.S. Navy S2F ASW Tracker aircraft flying an ASW patrol fifteen miles off the coast of Cuba. The United States lodged a diplomatic protest.

On September 5 another U-2 reconnaissance flight located Soviet SS-2-C coastal defense missile *Luna* sites near the contingency landing beaches. These missiles had already been supplied with nuclear warheads, although at the time the United States did not know it. The same U-2 flight confirmed that operational Soviet MiG-21s were on aprons of airstrips at several locations in Cuba. Based on these sightings, the U.S. Navy deployed a fighter squadron, VF-41, with the newest fighter-bomber, the F-4H-1 Phantom II, to Naval Air Station Key West. The Phantom II was the top fighter in the U.S. Navy inventory.

While on a midterm election campaign, Senator Kenneth Keating, Republican of New York, stated to the press that the Soviets had deployed surface-to-air missiles and regular formations of Soviet troops in Cuba. (These troops we now know were the Motorized Rifle Regiment commanded by the dashing Colonel Dmitry Yazov, who later became Mikhail Gorbachev's minister of defense and ended up in jail as one of the failed 1991 coup leaders.) Senator Keating accused the Kennedy administration of covering up facts from the American people. Republican members of Congress called for Soviet withdrawal from Cuba.

On September 5 President Kennedy revealed that the United States knew that Soviet SAMs and other defensive weapons were already in Cuba, but implied that he could tolerate their presence. Soviet ambassador Anatoli Dobrynin told Attorney General Robert Kennedy that Soviet weapons in Cuba were of no significance. On September 10 Secretary of State Dean Rusk and National Security Adviser McGeorge Bundy argued that the information obtained from U-2 missions was not worth the risk of launching additional photointelligence flights. Against the strong objection of the deputy director of the CIA, General Marshall Carter, President Kennedy directed that future U-2 missions be flown over the sea only and not over Cuba. On the same day aerial photos of the Soviet freighter *Kasimov* revealed a deck cargo of Il-28 Beagle medium jet bombers aboard headed toward Cuba.

As the influx of men and cargoes to Cuba increased in September, the U.S. military leaders began plans for action should the worst come to pass; they updated contingency plans for a joint amphibious and airborne assault against Cuba. They also formed initial plans for implementing an armed naval blockade. By late September the bulk of the surveillance activity of the waves of merchant shipping transporting men and heavy equipment into the island was conducted by navy long-range airborne surveillance aircraft, and over land by air force U-2 strategic reconnaissance. This would later expand to include carrier-based RF-8 tactical reconnaissance aircraft. The U.S. Air Force also augmented naval ocean surveillance coverage with its medium-range reconnaissance RB-47s. Eventually U.S. Navy destroyers, the famed "small boys" of the navy, entered the scene and took up the close inspection and verification of merchant ship cargoes and destinations. These were the celebrated "greyhounds of the sea," the "tin cans" of the navy. During the next weeks the mission of antisubmarine warfare would mushroom into a major effort, since the U.S. Navy correctly assumed the worst case, that the Soviet Union would not possibly undertake this vast movement of arms, troops, and military equipment to an ally in the United States' backyard without at least some armed escort; and in the absence of surface or long-range air assets, those available were expected to include the most advanced submarines in the Soviet naval arsenal.

In addition to the large number of diesel attack submarines known to be in Soviet hands, as a further ominous threat, the Soviet Navy was believed to possess more than half a dozen operational nuclear-powered attack and cruise missile–equipped submarines of as yet unproven effectiveness. It was these invisible forces that the ships and aircraft of the four U.S. East Coast–based ASW hunter-killer groups were poised to confront.

Destroyer USS *Blandy*

SEPTEMBER 1962
NEWPORT, RHODE ISLAND

USS *Blandy* (DD-943) was a Forrest Sherman class destroyer, named in honor of Admiral William H. P. Blandy, chief of the Bureau of Ordnance during the early 1940s, and the brilliant commander of Amphibious Group One during the Pacific island-hopping campaign. *Blandy* was built by the Bethlehem Steel Company in Quincy, Massachusetts, launched on December 19, 1956, and commissioned on November 26, 1957. Mrs. James Lee, the daughter of Admiral Blandy, acted as the ship's sponsor.

Blandy was 418.5 feet long and had a full-load displacement of about 3,960 tons. New features incorporated within the ship included a superstructure made from aluminum, thereby allowing for maximum stability while maintaining a draft of only 23 feet. Another new innovation was the air-conditioning of all living, berthing, and messing spaces. She was among the first U.S. destroyers to have a flared hurricane bow, which gave the ship a rakish look and softened considerably the thunderous hammering of pitching in heavy seas, which was, for many years, the hallmark of destroyer life. *Blandy* was fitted with the newest sonar, the SQS-23, and had a large sonar dome beneath her hull. She incorporated the newest electronics and sonar equipment but was underarmed for antisubmarine warfare, with a main battery of three 5-inch .54-caliber automatic-feed naval guns and two twin 3-inch .50-caliber rapid-fire antiaircraft gun mounts that were designed in the late months of World War II to knock down Japanese kamikazes. Her antisubmarine weapons included old depth charges, two Mark 32 torpedo launchers amidships, and two old Hedgehog rocket launchers used during that war.

Blandy had a complement of 23 officers, 19 chief petty officers, and 350 crewmen. Her main propulsion plant included four D-type Foster Wheeler 1,200-pound-per-square-inch steam boilers with integral superheaters, which proved to be among the most dangerous engineering plants in the fleet.

Blandy's commanding officer, Commander Edward G. Kelley, was a gnarled New Englander from the Massachusetts Maritime Academy who saw service at sea during World War II. He had the reputation as one of the most gifted officers in antisubmarine warfare (ASW) in the Atlantic Fleet.

Although Ed Kelley treated the *Blandy* wardroom officers like his own family and was a kind and understanding father figure sort of captain, on the bridge he was savage and unpredictable. He had moods that varied from serene calm when steaming independently to fits of vicious rage at the height of antisubmarine operations. These spells of heightened wrath usually occurred when the ship was moving in for the final stroke against a submarine, which consisted of a radical turn toward the submerged submarine, to attack by running over the top,

Edward G. Kelley, commanding
officer, USS *Blandy*, shortly after
promotion to captain in 1963
(courtesy Mrs. Grace Kelley)

simulating a depth charge, torpedo, or Hedgehog mortar attack. Once
in a heated moment during an exercise attack, he had been observed
seizing the ship's wheel from a slow-witted helmsman and driving the
ship himself over the contact for a successful simulated depth charge
and torpedo attack, an act that did not endear him to the commodore
on board. Nevertheless, he was a good captain, the officers feared but
respected him and would fight for him, especially against the loathed
staff of Commodore Charles Morrison, the destroyer squadron commander who was usually aboard.

Any ship in the fleet that suffered the presence of a unit commander on board shared the misery of having the commanding officer's
next reporting senior breathing down his back at every evolution. Kind
and gentle as Commodore Morrison was, he brought his staff of ne'er-
do-wells with him—at least they were such in the eyes of the ship's
company. The staff generally kept to themselves, the officers usually
dining in the flag mess and their small enlisted contingent in the mess
decks with the *Blandy* crew. During normal steaming when nerves were
relaxed, things went along smoothly, but as soon as the ship entered
any sort of close formation steaming, or intense antisubmarine or anti-
air operations, the dreaded presence of the staff wore heavily on the
Blandy crewmen and especially the captain. Whether much of Kelley's

gruff and aggressive behavior toward the commodore's staff, and espe-cially the commodore himself, was merely bravado to appear inde-pendent and nonchalant in front of his own officers and crew, we could never really discern, but many of us suspected it was the case. The ship seemed blessed with an extraordinary group of colorful men. I came aboard as a new ensign straight out of Annapolis that July of 1962.

Frank Flanagan, the Bostonian lieutenant junior grade, and combat information center (CIC) officer, had a quick and sarcastic manner with the staff, which soon endeared him to his own Operations Divi-sion troops, mostly radarmen who were known as among the most intel-lectual and operationally adept among all the divisions. Staff officers were careful not to tread on his toes, for the senior lieutenant junior grade had a New Englander's ability of understatement and quiet sar-casm, which he used to intimidate staff officers who occupied their small squadron command corner of Flanagan's empire of CIC.

The running battle of wits between Flanagan and the chief staff officer of Destroyer Squadron 24, Lieutenant Commander Norman Campbell, nicknamed by the ship's company as "Fatty Arbuckle" be-cause of his rotund stature, became a staple of life under way and grew out of all proportion the longer the ship remained at sea. There was great rejoicing aboard when the besieged Commodore Morrison an-nounced that he and the staff would commence a round-robin rotation to the other seven destroyers of the squadron, thus freeing *Blandy* for a period from the constant aggravation of a millstone aboard.

Despite the constant struggle, the presence of the commodore's staff had some advantages. When the squadron pulled into port and moored side by side in a nest, the flagship *Blandy* was always first alongside the pier, making it all the easier to conduct business ashore or aboard the destroyer tender if tied alongside for maintenance. The drawback was the continuous quest for ship's cleanliness. The executive officer (XO), the flamboyant Rodion Cantacuzene, forever harped that "a clean ship is a happy ship," and every spare minute of the day was spent sweeping, cleaning, shining brightwork (brass), chipping, and painting, and, as the deck force called, titivating, a term I at first assumed was another obscure shipboard obscenity, but I soon learned that the cleanliness aboard ship was indeed next to godliness.

During the fall of 1962, as one of the junior ensigns aboard, I served as the ship's electronics materials officer. Much later I became the ship's main propulsion assistant to the chief engineer and then learned about the spirit of the mysterious black holds, as the four engineering rooms in the bowels of the ship were called. The ship's engineers, or "snipes," lived most of their waking hours in the warm bosom of the gleaming engine rooms and fire rooms, which smelled of hot lube oil and strong coffee, polishing their brightwork and deck plates.

After the first month aboard it became clear to me that *Blandy* had a flair for doing operational things extremely well. She was one of the top ships in the squadron in most everything, especially in close order tactical steaming drills called "squadron close order tactics." This event consisted of a number of destroyers maneuvering at close quarters conducting a naval drill that was highly exciting, especially if you were a bridge watch stander. The ships would steam at twenty-five knots in close formation, often with a distance of just a hundred yards between ships, and when ordered by the squadron watch officer, perform on signal—usually signal flag hoists—daring maneuvers such as flanking turns, or column turns called corpens, finally working up to the more complex antisubmarine screen reorientations. These latter maneuvers were conducted when the destroyers formed an antisubmarine screen about an aircraft carrier. The screening destroyers, whose missions were to ferret out submarines, would be forced to reorient their antisubmarine screen formation from one axis, or main direction of submarine threat, to another, while the aircraft carrier turned frequently into the wind for an aircraft launch or recovery.

No maneuver was as exhilarating or at times as frightening as the evolution to take position as plane guard on the rear quarter of, and a few hundred yards from, the aircraft carrier, from a station in the ASW screen ahead of the carrier. The maneuver must be done at high speed, usually at twenty-two to twenty-five knots. The combined relative speeds between the carrier and the destroyer often surpassed fifty knots, and if the maneuver was conducted precisely would bring the destroyer into her plane guard position astern the carrier quickly, turning on a dime using full rudder to match the carrier's base course and speed. The sequence was terribly unforgiving of slow reactions or panic.

On *Blandy* we developed a keen appreciation for relative motion while executing the maneuver. The routine procedure at "darken ship," with no running lights in a total electronic silence, to avoid telltale use of radar, and in a rain squall, could render operations still more unnerving. In reality, the officers standing the officer of the deck (OOD) and junior officer of the deck (JOOD) watches were more frightened of the unexpected appearance of Captain Kelley on the bridge than colliding with one of the darkened forms of other destroyers whipping by at close range. It was a good drill for young men with nerves of steel and daring, but not for the cautious or the faint of heart. Kelley's arrival on the bridge was usually accompanied by a series of vile oaths interrupted by his violent fits of smoker's cough, and a barrage of abuse usually directed at the officer of the deck before the captain vanished back into his dark sea cabin.

The Art of Antisubmarine Warfare

The art of antisubmarine warfare has many variables, all related to the function of the propagation of sound through seawater. Since the primary advantage of the submarine is its ability to hide at various depths in the sea, the best methods of detection are first, by listening passively, and second, by transmitting a sound pulse through the water and timing the echo's return, much like the principle of radar. However, seawater complicates the passage of sound by contorting its flow through that complex medium. The path of sound through water is based on the variables of temperature, depth, salinity, density, and current, each of which causes unique aberrations to sound's propagation. Imagine the sea as a piece of clear glass. Inside the glass are imperfections that each cause light to be refracted at different angles and various speeds. Hence the problem of detecting an object like a submarine in the sea using sound is one of gathering precise knowledge of these changeable characteristics and applying the known principles of conduct of sound through water to determine the most logical depth at which the submarine may be hiding. The hunted submarine also monitors the water conditions and thus chooses the optimum depth at which to take advantage of these sound-limiting factors. The hunter, be it a surface ship, another submarine, or an aircraft, as well as the hunted submarine, frequently sample seawater conditions to determine its most likely advantages. The one who applies the knowledge of the seawater and geography of the sea bottom with greatest accuracy and skill will win, maybe.

The readiness condition on a destroyer while prosecuting a submarine contact during action stations, or general quarters, was in those days called Condition One AS. The position as officer of the deck on the bridge during this condition was a highly coveted job. Under Captain Kelley only the best and most experienced officers could handle that sacred task. The three officers blessed at that time were the cerebral operations officer, Lieutenant Bob Briner—Naval Academy graduate and a prince of a man; Lieutenant Junior Grade Gary Lagere; and the new weapons officer, Harvard graduate Lieutenant Jim Bassett.

Lagere was a tall officer, graduate of the University of Oklahoma, one of the more senior lieutenants junior grade aboard, and in the final months of his naval service. He had become disenchanted with shipboard life, grown tired of the military details, and longed to get back to Oklahoma and work in his field of mechanical engineering. Lagere was one of the few married junior officers. His wife, Anne, a stunning brunette, had been a beauty queen in Oklahoma and was popular with all the officers, who usually begged Gary to bring her aboard when he had the duty in port, so they could enjoy her presence aboard. They were a handsome and popular couple, genuine assets to the wardroom. Lagere was soft-spoken, astute, and quick on his feet, which was a handy asset when standing watch during the excitement of tracking a submarine. Those were the times when Ed Kelley was most violent. One had to learn to stay out of his way, yet be on hand to answer all questions and repair damage sustained by the hapless crewmen who somehow found themselves in the line of fire. Kelley was physical and had been known to actually run over slower crewmen who, unluckily, were in the path of the captain during this key period in the destroyer's life.

Jim Bassett had recently come aboard from another destroyer and graduated from the Atlantic Fleet Engineering School, reputed to be one of the best training establishments in the fleet. His Harvard schooling and prior assignment aboard a destroyer made him one of the most experienced and capable officers on the bridge. He was gifted with a quick mind and an enthusiastic nature.

My first encounter with this complex science and art of locating and tracking a submerged submarine came early in my life aboard *Blandy*. I was standing a four-hour watch as the junior officer of the deck on a quiet afternoon as the ship pulled out of port. The sun shone warmly on the open bridge, and I was enjoying the scene getting to know the bridge, the watch personnel, and the particular way of doing things aboard *Blandy*. I was feeling pleased with myself when I returned to the bridge for the eight-to-twelve watch that evening. Then—suddenly—the sonar

watch reported gaining a submarine contact, and the world came crash-
ing down around my head.

At first it seemed simple, standing next to the 21MC squawk box, a
small, gray box the size of a normal civilian radio with a screen covering a speaker, a line of push buttons for the desired station to call, and
a butterfly handle to press for transmitting. It was pitch dark on the
bridge, only dimmed red lights shone where various electronic equipment purred, and the green strobe of the surface search radarscope
glowed dimly. An excited voice suddenly boomed out on the gray box,
shattering the calm with a jolt. "Bridge, sonar, contact bearing zero five
zero!"

Before I could react by pressing the transmit handle to acknowledge the report, an arm shot out of the dark and hit the switch. "Roger,
sonar, classification?" I was shoved briskly to one side by the same
hand, which I had not yet identified, as violent commotion exploded
inside the pilothouse. I was standing with the officer of the deck outside the pilothouse on the uncovered open bridge, which was the normal location for the watch unless extreme weather forced the deck officers inside the pilothouse. We were separated from the pilothouse by a
line of windows that were normally open during the warm weather, but
closed and dogged in foul weather. We passed verbal commands through
the open windows to the helmsman and to the lee helmsman, who
operated the ship's wheel and engine order telegraph, respectively. In
case the windows were closed, several voice tubes on the open bridge
and inside the pilothouse were available, through which we could shout
commands and the pilothouse could acknowledge them.

In this case the mysterious arm that had emerged from somewhere
on the dark bridge belonged to Captain Kelley. How he happened to
be on the open bridge at that critical moment is a mystery. I soon
learned that whenever there was a hint of a sonar contact, even the
slightest chance that a submarine was within sonar range, Kelley would
somehow materialize on the bridge.

After that moment things began to happen quickly. "I've got the
conn," Kelley roared in his unmistakable growl (indicating he was taking control from the OOD). "Right full rudder, turns for twenty-five
knots. Lagere, set Condition One Antisubmarine."

Under Condition One AS, specially designated men took over specific jobs: the best and most experienced officers assumed the officer of
the deck and junior officer of the deck positions, while the ASW offi-

cer, Lieutenant Junior Grade Brad Sherman, would scurry to sonar, below, on the fourth deck behind the vast compartments crammed with stacks of mysterious humming electronic boxes, which stood in the background in the air-conditioned compartment. These were the holy grail of the ASW ship, the very inner sanctum of the ASW altar. Only those particularly blessed entered these spaces. The extremely talented but at times somewhat strange ASW officer, Brad Sherman, had an uncanny relationship with Captain Kelley, somewhat like a priest with the bishop. Sherman could hold Kelley's attention more than the usual few seconds permitted for most other officers, including XO Cantacuzene.

It was because Brad Sherman operated the heart of the ASW mission of the ship that he enjoyed a special relationship with the captain. Two other very special people in the sonar compartment were the two sonar operators, who usually wore heavy foul-weather jackets to ward off the cold of the air-conditioned space filled with the humming electronics and vital innards of acoustic equipment. One petty officer usually operated the sonar console that controlled the power and frequency of the active sonar transmission, and a second petty officer operated the receiver that filtered the sonar echo and massaged it until it magically materialized on a screen, analyzed in a few seconds as either a false contact; sea life; or, in moments of glory, a submarine. In the latter case the relative importance of these small men, crammed four levels below-decks, was catapulted into a wondrous pinnacle of indispensability.

I learned about all these sonar nuances much later after having had, on this first occasion, the ill fortune of being in the path of Captain Kelley. Somehow, many months later, for reasons I never quite understood then, I was given the job during a Condition One situation for chasing submarines, as the talker, on the sound-powered phone system called the 1JS, on the bridge. The function of this talker was to act as the communications link between the holy place called sonar and the citadel called the bridge, where Captain Kelley drove the ship after the submarine contact. The talker was required to keep a constant communication with the men below and to preclude the captain from having to stay near the 21MC intercom squawk box, or talk on the handset to sonar himself. The job of the 1JS talker on most ships was held by a junior petty officer with some sonar experience and demanded the particular skill of staying with the captain as he bounded around the pilothouse and sometimes out to the open bridge. During some violent occasion in the past, shortly after Kelley had taken command, the job had been assigned to a junior commissioned officer instead of a junior petty officer. The position demanded not only excellent balance and nimbleness of foot but also superb night vision to be able to follow Kelley without getting tangled in the long phone cord. It was not unusual for the captain, when in an advanced stage of excitement, to apply swift physical blows to anyone within reach to emphasize the need for speed, or to punctuate his commands. I suspect it was for this reason that a junior officer rather than an enlisted man was shoved into the breach as talker, as it was unthinkable for an officer to strike an enlisted man but not another officer. It was not seldom that I was pummeled about the upper body by Kelley's ever moving hands or elbows, but no blow was really serious, and one grew accustomed to the process as much as to Kelley's gravel voice.

I acquired a reverential fascination for a piece of equipment on the bridge called the ASW attack director. It was just one of many gray boxes in the pilothouse with an identical repeater on the open bridge where the sonar contact would appear on the dimly lighted dial. This display depicted the outline of the ship showing clearly enough to be discerned in a quick but educated glance of both true and relative bearings of the sonar contact from the ship; it showed as well the arcs defining the limits of where a particular weapon could be fired. The device also depicted the target angle of the contact, which was the orientation of its course relative to ours. A true reverence for that display developed after I had seen Captain Kelley stand for hours staring at the face of the dial. I was always relieved when he stood at the dial because it meant he was not arching around the pilothouse, saving me from the difficulty of staying with him while trying to keep my umbilical cord, the sound-powered phone line, from becoming hopelessly tangled around equipment or other bridge watch standers.

The bridge grew more crowded during ASW operations as extra bodies seemed to appear during these times of heightened tension. Most *Blandy* watch standers were sufficiently hardened through experience to the action on the bridge and knew how to keep out of Kelley's path and to observe the rule of total quiet on the bridge. On the occasions when Commodore Morrison, the squadron commander, appeared in the pilothouse, the captain tried to be courteous but usually ended up being just as gruff and curt as he was with his own men.

As my bridge experience waxed I grew nimble enough to stay with Captain Kelley and avoid his frequent blows, which he aimed at me when I was either too slow or repeated something he did not wish to hear from sonar. The talker on the other end of the 1JS line in sonar was Les Westerman, the first lieutenant who was understudy to Brad Sherman and who had attended the advanced Sonar School in Key West, Florida. That school was the goal of every officer aboard. It was the crème de la crème of destroyer training, and highly sought after by all junior officers. Only the Air Control School, which trained officers and select petty officers in the art of controlling ASW aircraft, drew as much awe as graduation from the Atlantic Fleet Sonar School. Graduates of both institutes were on equal footing, and enjoyed the same level of relative awe on the ship.

Prior to 1962, Soviet submarine presence in the Atlantic was minimal, and their nuclear submarines had seldom deployed. Finding a Soviet submarine in those years took a lot of luck and a great deal of tenacity. Our hunter-killer destroyers worked closely with the long-range patrol aircraft, but finding and locking onto a solid Soviet submarine contact in the 1960s was a rare event.

The real effectiveness of the antisubmarine hunter-killer (HUK) group lay with the modern antisubmarine aircraft. The long-range P2V Neptunes had been the backbone of the long-range maritime patrol family for many years. That ungainly looking aircraft traces its ancestry back to the Lockheed-Vega Hudson, which was a general scouting aircraft of the World War II years. The Neptune enjoyed the distinction of being the only land-based patrol plane designed to hunt submarines. The newer-generation P3 Orion had been designed for other purposes and found to be the ideal replacement in the early 1960s for the aging P2V Neptune. Both these aircraft were used extensively in close coordination with the destroyers and aircraft carriers of the hunter-killer groups.

These aircraft could patrol vast areas of the ocean using a versatile arsenal of disposable sonobuoys, which they dropped in various-shaped patterns in the sea. Most of the buoys were passive hydrophones capable of hearing the sounds of a submarine or a surface ship and transmitting that signal to radio receivers in the aircraft. By laying patterns of these buoys in various geometric shapes they could pinpoint and track an underwater target when an active buoy or a simple explosive charge was dropped into the vicinity. The echo of the explosion would be received and transmitted to the receiving aircraft, which could then triangulate the responses and fix the contact's position and determine her course and speed.

The use of these buoys in this mode in the 1960s was called Jezebel, and the active explosive they dropped was called Julie. Other submarine detection systems aboard these aircraft included the sensitive
high-resolution APS-20 radar, which could pick up electromagnetic
returns from the smallest targets on the surface of the sea; most specifically it was designed to detect the very small submarine snorkel and
periscope in dynamic seas. The third detection system was the magnetic anomaly detector (MAD), which was merely a sophisticated electronic ohmmeter in the aircraft that measured the disruption in the
earth's magnetic field caused by a steel submarine. The early model of
this MAD equipment was effective only if the airplane flew directly
over the submarine at a low altitude, from which it could detect the signal of the aberration in the earth's field. The system improved over the
years to the point that submarines could be detected from as high as a
thousand feet using this equipment.

All three of these detection capabilities were also aboard the smaller
tactical ASW aircraft deployed aboard the hunter-killer aircraft carriers.
The USS *Essex* air wing, for example, had several squadrons of twin-
engined Grumman S2F Trackers, which had similar capabilities, but
the airplane was smaller, with significantly shorter range. Nevertheless,
the presence of the short-range tactical trackers enhanced the detection
capabilities of the HUK because it could rely less on the shore-based
patrol airplanes and more on its own tactical planes. The destroyers in
the HUKs became skilled through training and practice at controlling
these airplanes and advising them where to fly and how and where to
place their passive sonobuoys in a united effort, combining the
destroyer's very accurate sonar with the detection systems of the airplane. According to most Russian submariners of the era, the ubiqui-
tous trackers of the HUK, combined with the long-range P2 and P3
patrols, proved to be the major threat to their covert operations. The
destroyers naturally became dependent on the aircraft, given their capability to cover a greater area to locate the submarine contacts. After
months of working together at sea, the destroyers and the tactical ASW
carriers honed their combined abilities to form a formidable opponent
to the modern submarine, especially to those diesel-powered submarines that were still required to surface or to snorkel to charge their lim-
ited-range batteries. For the lone destroyer to find and track a submarine remained *Blandy*'s ultimate challenge.

My unique window of observation as the ASW phone talker on the
Blandy bridge connected me to the slow, soothing voice on the other

end of the sound-powered phone in sonar. That was the voice of Les Westerman, who had acquired the nickname "Rug" from Frank Flanagan for his head of luxuriously curly brownish-red hair. Westerman was more than six feet tall, and a soft-spoken, kindhearted ensign from Chicago. He was the sort of man who could never inflict harm on any living creature, yet was in charge of the ship's most foulmouthed, uncouth, and hardheaded sailors of the First Division, called the Deck Force. Westerman could magically handle the thugs of his Deck Force. One of his key petty officers was Second Class Bosun's Mate Petit, an older sailor who was routinely reduced in grade by Captain Kelley during repeated appearance at the navy's traditional nonjudicial punishment procedure called Captain's Mast. He made the transition often from senior petty officer back down to third-class petty officer generally because of altercations while ashore and usually while in the advanced stages of intoxication. Petit was a redheaded, freckled, middle-aged man who liked a good fight. He had, I learned later, been aboard the ill-fated USS *Frank E. Evans*, the destroyer that had been sliced in half by an aircraft carrier during night plane guard operations in the late 1950s. The forward half of the destroyer had sunk immediately, carrying seventy-five crewmen to the bottom. Petit had been on watch on the bridge and was fished out of the water by the carrier's motor whaleboat rescue crew. I asked him once about the experience, saying with guarded awe, "Petty Officer Petit, I understand you survived the *Frank Evans* collision with the carrier."

"Yes, sir," replied Petit, without hesitation, "best fookin' thing ever happened to that ship."

I never brought up the subject again.

◈

My first night ASW encounter came late that summer when *Blandy* made a sonar contact in the Ionian Sea. I can still picture the melee that unfolded, still hear the crescendo of shouts and oaths as Kelley swung the ship into a devastating pursuit of the submarine. The *raison d'être* of that type of ship, her primary mission in that day and age, was ASW. *Blandy*'s original three 5-inch .54-caliber gun mounts had been designed as the main armament, but in fact, her main armament became her ASW brains. The strength of the ASW destroyer lay not in her weapons but rather in her skill to gain, track, and maintain contact with the submarine. A destroyer could always call in an aircraft and direct it in for the kill if she was skilled enough to hold the contact.

That night I witnessed the advanced state of ASW readiness when *Blandy* gained contact on a U.S. nuclear attack submarine en route from Naples to the exercise area where she was to play the target for our eight-destroyer squadron. *Blandy* gained sonar contact that night and held it like a determined bulldog for three hours, until the officer in command of the maneuver called the end of the exercise. Commodore Morrison had ordered *Blandy* to break off the contact and allow the submarine to proceed to her exercise area. Captain Kelley did not like to break off the hunt when he held solid sonar contact on a real submarine, and it hurt to the quick to do so.

To gain and hold contact on a U.S. nuclear submarine during training was rare and, therefore, on this occasion holding contact was an achievement of great pride, and Kelley hated to let go. When the commodore ordered *Blandy* to break off, Kelley did so reluctantly, and when the submarine was surfacing after the exercise, *Blandy* was forced to turn to a safety course. To avoid danger, the exercise commander directed the submarine to turn on her running lights. When that occurred, *Blandy* was still right on top of the boat. As Kelley turned the ship to the safety course, he grabbed me by the shirt and in the darkness pointed over the side. There was the submarine with her running lights on at a depth of about fifty feet or more passing underneath us in the clear water—the large, dark form of the submarine like a large whale with bright lights on passing under the ship. That picture remained in my mind for many years.

Those were tense moments on the bridge and in sonar when *Blandy* stood out in the squadron and in fact in the whole Atlantic Fleet. We were good at our primary mission, and we knew it. Ed Kelley prided himself in being a cunning, master tactician in doing battle with submarines. I had heard the story of the famous Barcelona port visit before I came aboard. The wardroom often talked about how *Blandy* had defeated two submarines as the task group entered Barcelona. Captain Kelley was given tactical command for an "opposed port entry" exercise coming into port for weekend liberty. The submarines were two U.S. Navy diesel units assigned the role of the aggressors. *Blandy*'s task group consisted of the ASW aircraft carrier *Randolph* and seven escorting destroyers.

The U.S. Navy in those days had a variety of shipboard sonar, ranging from old but proven World War II directional systems to the new omnidirectional sonars. The newer were more powerful ones operated at a higher frequency. The destroyers *Blandy* and *Barry* and the carrier *Randolph* herself had the powerful SQS-23, which had longer range and higher frequency. The object of the opposed-entry exercise was to get each ship safely into the harbor without being attacked by the two submarines. The submarines could lie and wait just outside the entrance channel when the carrier, with all its aircraft secured aboard, entered the channel, and the escort destroyers followed in single file. The submarines could randomly fire at any ship. The carrier was the prime target. The effectiveness of our entire task group would be severely damaged by its loss. The ASW carrier was a formidable opponent of the submarine because it carried fixed-wing aircraft and helicopters with submarine detection devices and antisubmarine weapons, which were practically invulnerable to submarine attack—except while sitting on the deck of the mother carrier. The destroyer's main task was to protect the carrier. Destroyers were good but not perfect at detection, and as the saying went in wartime, the destroyers could fulfill their mission by marking the submarine's last position with their own flaming oil slick as they went to the bottom.

Kelley's handicap that day was the requirement for the task group to enter port single file in a narrow channel. As the screen of destroyers approached the entrance it had to collapse while each ship ran interference protecting the carrier until she entered the channel as quickly as possible. The submarine tactics were predicable. They would play their strengths—stealth and one big shot. They would lie and wait on the bottom or near an anchored merchant ship to confuse detection and shoot a torpedo at the carrier as it entered the restricted channel. The submarines could quietly listen with sensitive passive sonar. Kelley knew that the submarines probably had a good chance to get off one shot, and that would be at the carrier; he also knew that submariners were very good at listening to the bearing, intensity, and characteristics of the sonars and propeller noise of all surface ships. They could differentiate among the forward screen, the carrier, and its escorts without having to risk detection by looking with the periscope.

As Kelley's task force approached Barcelona's entrance channel and the waiting submarines, the ASW screen was rapidly transmitting at maximum power, attempting to detect the submarines. The two destroyers *Blandy* and *Barry*, because of their powerful sonars, would normally be on either side of the carrier's course, but that day Kelley stationed *Barry* in the carrier's position and the carrier *Randolph* in *Barry's* escort slot in the screen, pinging away with her bow-mounted sonar. By the time the submarines recognized the switch, the carrier was safely in the harbor. Destroyer *Barry* was fresh meat but hardly worth the submarines risking marking their position with a torpedo wake in shallow water for very little reward. The exercise emphasized what everyone knew—that destroyers by themselves were expendable.

Operation *Kama* Departure

SEPTEMBER 30, 1962
SOVIET SIXTY-NINTH SUBMARINE BRIGADE
KOLA PENINSULA

Sayda Bay is a former fishing village snuggled amid the rolling taiga-covered hills of the Kola Peninsula, some twenty kilometers northwest of Murmansk. The water at three small finger piers, used for many years by fishing trawlers before the navy took over, is twenty meters deep, more than sufficient for the Project 641 attack submarine, called the Foxtrot class in the West. Ten kilometers down the pitted dirt road to the southeast lies the port of Polyarny, home of the Fourth Red Banner, Order of Ushakov Submarine Squadron. The squadron in 1962 consisted of the Sixty-ninth Submarine Brigade of four Project 641 long-range diesel attack submarines and the seven-boat Eighteenth Submarine Division of Project 629 diesel-powered ballistic missile subs, called the Golf class in the West. Each of these missile boats carried three R-13, D-2 ballistic missiles. The missiles could be fired at intervals of four minutes, but only when the submarine was on the surface.

The four attack subs of the brigade were the workhorses of the squadron, with their three throbbing diesel engines and three electric motors encased in a black steel hull, with the rounded sail or conning tower squatting midway on the sloping main deck. The lighter-colored shiny panels covering their bow sonar transducers and passive acoustic antenna panels gave the effect of a sneering smile. The Plexiglas window panels of the enclosed navigation bridge provided eyes, making the subs as a group look like four dark, ugly dragons. On September 30 four of these sinister sea monsters sat moored at Sayda Bay's old wooden fishing piers, bound with steel cables, waiting for departure time. The submarines had moved under cover of darkness three days earlier from

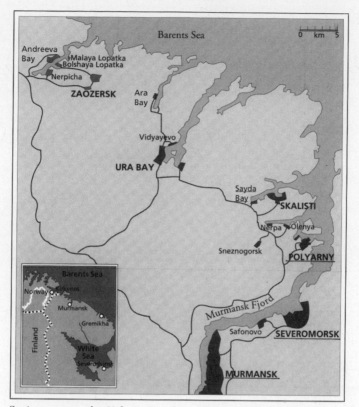

Soviet ports on the Kola Peninsula (courtesy © 1996. The Bellona Foundation)

their usual berths in Polyarny to mask their pending departure from the curious eyes of their families gazing down from the gray-slabbed apartment buildings overlooking Polyarny's harbor. The silent move to Sayda Bay had been made so that the last-minute loading of the special torpedoes could be done in total secrecy.

The special weapons, the nuclear warhead–tipped torpedoes, had never been carried on these submarines, or, for that matter, on any other submarines in the Soviet Red Banner Northern Fleet. These 533-millimeter torpedoes were marked with purple-painted noses to stand apart in the forward torpedo room from the twenty-one regular-warshot torpedoes with gray-painted noses.

Senior Lieutenant Volodya Voronov watched silently in the evening twilight as the floating crane lowered a single torpedo through the forward loading tube into the Compartment One torpedo room of the Foxtrot class boat simply named *B-130*. Soviet submarines were assigned

Sayda Bay: two Foxtrot class submarines and a Whiskey class submarine (left) in icebound bay (courtesy © 1998. Jasper Communications Pty Ltd. Sydney, Australia)

permanent numbers instead of names, by which they were commonly referred to. In the case of the Foxtrot class or Project 641 boats, all had the prefix B—in Russian meaning *bolshoi*, or large. These numbers were not related to the tactical numbers sometimes painted on their sails; these numbers were often changed to enhance deception.

Voronov was commander of the mine-torpedo group. He thought it strange that along with the new torpedo came a single weapons security officer who was clearly not a submariner, although he wore the blue coveralls and black *pilotka* garrison cap worn by submariners. That cap, worn by all submarine officers—the "piss cutter" cap—distinguished the submariners from their surface ship competitors, the "skimmers." This special officer accompanying the special weapon wore a small pistol in a brown leather holster under his blue tunic, signifying his authority. Strangely, over the next weeks he would seldom leave the forward torpedo compartment, where he had a private berth erected above his torpedo in a small curtained area just large enough to cover the torpedo and the officer's bunk, which hung on chains. He would be seen frequently checking the lead seal connecting the ends of a wire that locked the hand plate on the upper front of the purple-nosed torpedo.

The special officer reminded Voronov of a pimp guarding some special obscene instrument. Voronov had noticed that each of the other three submarines in their brigade had received a similar torpedo that evening, accompanied by similarly strange-looking officers who, although dressed like submarine officers, were certainly not qualified submariners. They were too clean and walked in a funny way. Some crewmen had joked that they were KGB officers, but no one dared say so aloud or really cared. The crews just ignored the intruders as if they were not there, and made off-color remarks when not within earshot of an officer.

B-130's commanding officer, Captain Nikolai Shumkov, a dark, solid, muscular officer, swung onto the lower rung of the ladder leading up the main exit trunk from the central command post to the sail of the submarine moored next to the pier. Shumkov paused in the dimly lighted space, pointed to the gauge showing the number one diesel engine manifold pressure, and said, "Viktor, keep an eye on that pressure. I'll be back when I finish getting the send-off kiss."

"Yest, Comrade Commander," the executive officer, Viktor Frolov, snapped. "All departments report manned and ready. Lines singled up at 3:30 A.M."

Shumkov grunted and climbed the narrow ladder, stepped onto the lower level of the sail, and undogged the hatch leading out to the main weather deck. Two sentries stood in the dark, their Kalashnikov assault weapons slung on their shoulders. Their breath formed clouds of steam, which showed in the dim lights on the end of the pier. It was cold, but not as cold as the night before. The ice had thawed around the hull and now shone in greasy, rust-flaked puddles on the pier. Captain Shumkov walked across the brow leading from his boat to the pier, then toward the single-story shed that sat at the base of the pier. As he neared the shed he made out the form of two sentries standing on either side of the door. He observed another figure moving through the dark toward the shed from the second pier. As he drew near he recognized the figure of Captain Aleksei Dubivko from his sister boat, B-36. Dubivko stopped by the two sentries and waited until Shumkov approached. The two shook hands, returned the sentries' salutes, and stepped into the dimly lighted shed. The commanding officers of all four submarines had been directed to gather in the small wooden shed at the foot of the piers to meet at midnight with their squadron commander, Kontr Admiral Rybalko.

At the head of a table stood Rybalko, wearing the dark navy greatcoat and karakul wool senior officers' winter dress cap, called a *mushanka*. Admiral Fokin from the Moscow Main Navy Staff stood to the side. Behind him stood a knot of officers, including Rybalko's chief of staff, who wore a sneer as if he had a nasty smell on his upper lip. The squadron political officer stood like an automaton next to the chief of staff. Admiral Rybalko held himself stiffly and motioned them to seats at the table. He was not smiling. A third submarine commander sat at the table already, and nodded to the two newly arrived skippers. He was Ryurik Ketov, skipper of B-4, the oldest of the four subs. All three captains sat quietly before the formal Rybalko and gazed quietly around the small room. On the wall facing them was a red banner emblazoned with the title of the squadron, Fourth Red Banner, Order of Ushakov Submarine Squadron. There were water stains on the flag, which was surrounded by a gold fringed border. It looked faded on one side and it hung crookedly, hastily placed for the event.

Another admiral sat behind the others, in a straight-backed chair. He wore the two stars of a vice admiral on the shoulder boards of his winter greatcoat, which he also had kept on in the cold room. He was Anatoly Rossokho, chief of staff and deputy commander of the Northern Fleet, and was acting on behalf of the Northern Fleet commander in chief to ensure that the four Kama submarine participants got off on time and without any doubts as to the rules pertaining to the use of their special weapons. Rossokho was not a submariner but had commanded many surface ships, was a noted gunnery expert, and had a reputation as an unorthodox proponent of many special navy projects. If there was a new and innovative idea in the navy, Rossokho was usually involved with it. He was gruff and assertive but an intellectual and even wrote poetry. He had gained fame organizing and leading the early northern sea route convoys from Murmansk though the ice skirting the northern reaches of the USSR all the way to the Pacific. These convoys were extremely dangerous undertakings, and with the advent of nuclear icebreakers Rossokho had pioneered their use in leading convoys of merchant ships and combatants, including submarines that were transferring from the Northern Fleet to the Pacific Fleet. The use of this northern route had been sought for many years as a substitute for the long voyage between the two fleet areas, one of the primary reasons being the ability to transfer warships and submarines from one fleet to the other without foreign observation. Rossokho had a reputation also as an accomplished oceanographer and hydrographer and had twice been named the Soviet state premier laureate for his writing, which included publication of a world ocean atlas and assorted verses of flowery poetry. The presence of the well-known admiral in the bitter-cold room had gone unnoticed until the conversation focused on the question of the rules governing the use of the nuclear torpedoes just loaded aboard the four submarines. Shumkov noticed the admiral first, and nudged his colleague Dubivko.

"Look who's here!" Everything to do with this operation, Shumkov thought, had been cobbled together as if there had been little or no planning for the deployment. The special torpedoes had been awaiting the arrival of the submarines the day before, but the four boats from Polyarny were forced to wait for the floating crane, which for some reason had not left nearby Gadzhievo in time to be ready to load. Regardless of delay, the four commanding officers went about their presail preparations until the barge with crane arrived, six hours late. Now, suddenly, the three officers awaiting the briefing noticed the presence of a man who was more legend than real and who probably was the officer they least expected to see in Sayda Bay that night.

The door of the shed opened again and the fourth commanding officer, Captain Second Rank Vitali Savitsky, arrived, accompanied by the brigade commander, Captain Agafonov, and his chief of staff, Captain Vasily Arkhipov. The three greeted Admiral Rybalko, who was shifting uncomfortably from one foot to the other.

"Let's get started, Comrades, there's little time left," Rybalko said abruptly. The others quickly took their places around the small table. Rybalko began to speak, and the senior admirals, Fokin and Rossokho, remained seated quietly behind him in chairs placed against the wall.

In the corner of the room stood a small coal-burning stove, which glowed pink around the middle and showed glowing fire through its badly fitting seams. The room was filled with the acrid smell of the coal exhaust leaking in through the bent stovepipe. Despite the stove, the room was cold and damp. The floor was ice cold. The admiral stamped his feet and rocked from side to side. Rybalko was now commander of the squadron, which was renamed the Twentieth Special Squadron solely for the Cuba mission.

"Good morning, Comrade Commanders," he began. "I will not discuss the details of your tracks and missions; those are clearly outlined in sealed packages already aboard all your boats." He paused for a fit of coughing, spat into a handkerchief, recovered, and stuffed it in his pocket. "By now you have the general idea of where you're heading. I wish to pass personal greetings from the Northern Fleet commander, and later you may address questions to me and Admiral Fokin, from the

Main Navy Staff, with whom I have had the pleasure of spending the past four days." The admiral paused and looked at the senior admiral. "You all met him during the farewell brief two days ago aboard the tender *Dmitri Galkan*. Again, the details of your mission are contained in the packets, and be sure to read them carefully to your key officers after submerging."

Rybalko paused and looked at each commander, as if waiting to detect any signs of misunderstanding. "Admiral Fokin asked me to emphasize the fact that during this mission each of you carries the utmost responsibility on your shoulders."

The responsibility for preparing the submarines for the deployment had fallen mostly to the Northern Fleet commander in chief, Admiral Kasatanov, and Communist Party Military Council member Kontr Admiral Sizov. However, in fact, the two who had done the most to prepare the four submarines, and had taken direct action when they ran into difficulty filling requisitions for extra spare parts and provisions, had been Admirals Fokin and Rybalko.

As the admiral droned on in his high-pitched voice, Shumkov glanced at the other commanding officers, all looking attentive but tired. The past week had been hectic. They had taken on a large quantity of fuel and stores, which took up almost every centimeter of free space in each of the subs. Shumkov watched as an orderly opened the stove front and noisily poured in a can full of hard coal pellets. The stove door slammed, interrupting the admiral.

"Arkhipov, clear this space of working staff."

The chief of staff jumped to his feet and scurried over to the two orderlies and pushed them roughly toward the door and then out into the pitch-black morning air. Then he returned to his seat.

The admiral continued. "You each possess the capability of inflicting lethal damage to American forces, but I urge you to use discretion. It is considered highly unlikely that American ASW forces will be any more than at their usual state of alert, which isn't much of a threat." He coughed again. "Study your missions closely, they are outlined in great detail."

Shumkov looked at Dubivko, who smiled, then rolled his eyes slightly, indicating he had heard all this before. The two were close friends, and had served aboard several boats in earlier years. They were viewed as two of the most efficient commanders in the squadron, and tops in the brigade. Neither suspected what their missions were, but they knew from the arrival of the special tropical uniforms that they were to be deployed for a long period and that it was somewhere a great deal warmer than the Kola Peninsula. Both looked forward to the adventure, but knew that the less adventurous skippers, Savitsky, the "sweater," as they called him, and Ketov, the "cautious," were not enthusiastic about the idea of an extended deployment. Both Shumkov and Dubivko thrived on the mystery and unknown aspect of their mission.

The admiral wound up his talk. "Each of you has in your hands the potential to start the next world war, and so, Comrades, do try to keep us out of war. Now"—he paused as if he were looking for words— "good sailing, and keep seven feet beneath the keel." The old Russian naval saying, much like the "may you always have fair winds and following seas" send-off in the West, was used for more friendly and less formal farewells; it seemed a little out of place here. Rybalko seemed visibly moved, apparently by the import of their impending mission. "Are there questions?"

There was a long, silent pause. Shumkov looked around the table and saw Captain Ketov suddenly rise to his feet.

"Comrade Admiral, I know our orders are detailed in the sealed packets already aboard, but we're all concerned about the rules governing the use of the special torpedoes. What exactly are we to expect? How and when may we use them?"

There was another long, silent pause. Then Admiral Fokin stepped forward. Rybalko looked relieved and stepped back slightly, coughing again briefly.

"Comrade Commanders," Fokin began, "we are still not fully prepared to address that issue, but to be sure . . ." Suddenly the Northern Fleet chief of staff, Vice Admiral Rossokho, who had remained seated behind the group of seniors, rose and came forward. He looked over the group and paused as if awaiting a stage cue. All four submarine commanders looked in awe at the famous figure. He had sharp features, which distinguished him from most other Russian officers. He looked more like a Greek statue than a Russian admiral.

Rossokho looked at the four officers and then in a loud, clear voice responded, "Comrade Commanders, enter these words in your logs when you return aboard: Use of the special weapons is authorized under the following conditions: first, in the event you are attacked with depth bombs and your pressure hull is ruptured; second, if you surface and are taken under fire and hit; and, third, upon orders from Moscow."

There was another long pause as all the admirals turned to look at the tall, slim, but barrel-chested Rossokho. His chin jutted forward and he stood as if waiting to be attacked. No one said another word about the rules. Ketov stood, looked back at Admiral Rybalko, then at Admiral Fokin, and seeing that neither was going to add to those remarks, sat down. Rybalko then asked again, "Questions?" There was none.

The officers rose together and one by one shook hands warmly with Rybalko, saluted the other admirals who stood a little to the rear of Rybalko, deferring to the junior admiral who was the operational commander of the four submarine commanders, and made their way toward the door. Outside it was still pitch black, and a swirling fog had set in, making the darkness an even more menacing wilderness. The four skippers and the brigade chief of staff stopped to light cigarettes, then stood together in silence a few moments as their eyes adjusted to the dark.

"What do you think brought Rossokho to this godforsaken place? Is the operation some new experiment in naval science?" Ketov broke the silence.

"Beats me," Shumkov said. "All I know is that we have more caviar and canned meat than I've ever seen aboard a submarine in my whole career."

"Yes, and some weird-looking short khaki trousers to wear," Ketov answered. "Did you ever see Savitsky's knees in shorts down on the Black Sea? You haven't lived yet. Looks like a crane."

"Well, Comrades," Chief of Staff Arkhipov spoke, "let's get moving. Good luck." They shook hands all around.

"Oh, Comrade Dubivko," Shumkov said with a mocking voice, starting to walk down the pier, "remember, I'll be right behind you in this soup, so don't stop or I'll run up your stern."

"That's normal for you, Nikolai," Dubivko said with a smile. "You brown-noser, you know the brigade commander will be watching from Ketov's boat, so you'll be showing off the whole time." They smiled in the darkness and walked down the pier. Shumkov reflected on the past six months. Although they had learned of Operation *Kama* only two months ago, their commands had actually been in preparation for more than six months. All four boats had been in the Rosta yards outside Murmansk since January for extended overhaul and repair. The four skippers had anticipated that they were due for a long and arduous patrol, and they would probably be together, since the yard overhaul had been a change in schedule for all four submarines, but none of the

Left to right, commanding officers: *B-36*, Dubivko; *B-130*, Shumkov; Chief of Staff Arkhipov; *B-4*, Ketov (courtesy Ryurik Ketov)

crews had any inkling that the extended deployment was intended to include a change of their home port. Since April rumors of all kinds had flown around the homes of the submariners in Polyarny. Many of the rumors had been close to the truth. The wives had been passing the story that they were expecting to be flown or transported by ship to new ports in some faraway land with a tropical climate. Many of these rumors had been dismissed as wishful thinking, especially in the months when the elusive spring had always seemed just around the corner and the persistent frost and snow on the Kola Peninsula continued to dampen the spirit until the brief summer came in July. Life in the Northern Fleet was not easy, but there was always the golden prospect of a vacation at the fleet recreation centers in the Black Sea for the whole family. These vacations were usually taken at the end of a rigorous patrol and gave the stoic wives and families something to look forward to. The added responsibilities had caused curtailment of the length of some of these vacations because for the commanding officers there always seemed to be a long list of unfinished business, personnel problems, training cycles, and material problems to solve. As the submarine commanders walked the length of the pier toward their submarines and waiting crews, their morale soared at the prospect of a new and as yet uncertain adventure. It would be some time before all four skippers would be ashore together, and they would be a great deal more seasoned when that time came.

❖

At 4:00 A.M. on October 1, 1962, the day following the loading and just hours after the admiral's send-off, the diesel attack submarine *B-59*, commanded by Captain Second Rank Savitsky, cast off all lines and twisted away from the pier. The brigade's chief of staff, Captain Arkhipov, stood behind Savitsky in the small cockpit atop the sail in the swirling fog and light snow. Behind them *B-36*, commanded by Captain Second Rank Aleksei Dubivko, quietly slipped her mooring lines and left her berth at Sayda Bay, cutting through the dense fog into the black channel heading north to the Barents Sea. She was followed by Shumkov in *B-130*, and thirty minutes later by the remaining *B-4*, with Captain Ketov commanding and carrying the brigade commander, Agafonov.

The four submarines sailed completely darkened, running lights off, and steamed on electric power until clear of the channel when they started their three loud, throbbing diesel engines, which began to kick out clouds of foul-smelling exhaust fumes. Total secrecy had been ordered, although they all knew that in the darkness and fog anyone who happened to be in the vicinity couldn't have seen them had they tried. However, the orders were clear. Captain Nikolai Shumkov in *B-130* had caught a glimpse earlier of the package of charts taken aboard in Polyarny from the fleet headquarters duty officer. The huge pile of charts had covered the entire North Atlantic and Caribbean, with the last chart in the pile that of the approaches to Mariel, Cuba, a small port due west of Havana. Shumkov had put 2 and 2 together when the boxes of summer tropical khaki shorts and short-sleeved uniforms came aboard; he was certain they were headed to Cuba. His sealed orders were already aboard, locked in Senior Lieutenant Cheprakov's communications office safe, and would be opened only after their first dive in the Barents Sea as they began the first leg of their journey.

OCTOBER 1, 1962
CAPTAIN NIKOLAI SHUMKOV
COMMANDING OFFICER, *B-130*
BARENTS SEA

Lieutenant Volodya Voronov, the mine and torpedo officer, sat at the radar repeater in the enclosed conning bridge of the sail and watched the dim green glow as the illuminated sides of the channel swept by on his screen, the sub as the center dot from which the green sweep circled. Voronov whispered the recommended course changes softly to Shumkov, who was leaning on the cockpit railing above him in the cold night air. Voronov, the young, blond officer from Khimki, in the northern suburbs of Moscow, was the best watch officer aboard, and Captain Shumkov always felt a sense of relief to have him working on the watch as they left the channel in the impossible visibility. He would depend on him often and deeply throughout the deployment.

The visibility was no more than three meters in swirling fog. It was the perfect night for getting under way covertly, for no one could make out the submarine even if standing on the pier; the dark forms merely evaporated into nothing. It was a good night to run aground, too, thought Voronov as he stared at the green outlines painted on his radar repeater by each sweep, then fading until repainted by the next. He concentrated on the radar navigation picture until his eyes burned.

Lieutenant Cheprakov was head of the submarine's Radio and Electronics Division, *BCh* Four, and was responsible for operation of all the ship's communications and radar equipment. (Soviet ships are organized into departments called *Boyovoi Chesti*, abbreviated with the term *BCh*.) Cheprakov knew that without his three warrant officers, called *michmen*, he was as good as useless, for he was new to the job and still could not disassemble and repair any of the equipment by himself. A serious officer, Cheprakov had been entrusted to command the group of five English-speaking radio intercept operators. These men were responsible for intercepting and monitoring the U.S. voice radio traffic whenever the submarine was near enough the surface to deploy an antenna; most of all, they were men trusted for sensitive material. The entire crew wanted to be able to listen to U.S. radio, and these men were able to tune to the long-range shortwave Russian-language Voice of America programs, which they all knew played the best jazz in the world. However, it was prohibited to do so—but, of course, it was done regularly yet discreetly by Lieutenant Cheprakov's men.

"Right standard rudder," Shumkov said softly but firmly into the voice tube, "come right to course zero four zero, turns for ten knots."

"Aye, Comrade Commander," the helmsman repeated over the voice tube, "rudder is right standard, coming to new course zero four zero. Engine room answers turns for ten knots."

"Very well. Next course, Voronov?"

"Next course change in eight minutes, right to zero six five degrees, sir," Mine and Torpedo Officer Voronov whispered. He was no doubt squeezing his buttocks as if it would help the ship ease through the narrow channel lined on both sides with rolling, snow-covered brush of the taiga. He had navigated the same channel a dozen times before, but never in a shroud of total fog with zero visibility, and never at night.

Communicator Cheprakov sat below in his cubicle off the central command post, waiting. He knew that as soon as they entered the open water of the Barents, and the sea bottom fell beneath them to more than one hundred fathoms, they would submerge. Then he would bring to Shumkov the sealed envelope from the communications safe. The captain planned to open it and read the operation order to Cheprakov and the XO, called the *starpom*, and, of course, in the presence of the *zampolit*, political officer.

Astern of Shumkov, at two thousand meters, crept Ketov's *B-4*, carrying the brigade commander, Captain Agafonov. Dubivko and Shumkov were lucky not having senior staff officers embarked. No one liked the confining presence of the staff. Although *B-130* carried the staff engineer, he turned out to be a helpful officer. Shumkov also knew that Dubivko carried the staff navigator, an innocuous young officer, but these additions posed no problems for the rest of the ship's company.

B-130 had entered service in September 1960, making it a few months less than two years younger than the other submarines. The boat had suffered a long history of mechanical troubles, and had a flaw in its numbers one and two main diesel engine auxiliary drive gears. Minuscule, hairline cracks had appeared in both gears, but repairs had been deferred for the next scheduled yard overhaul, and the submarine pronounced seaworthy by the fleet engineering staff. This was a strange reaction, given the importance of the pending operation. Because the flaws had been discovered after the unscheduled yard periods, the staff thought it more prudent to ignore the cracks rather than risk being found guilty of an infraction of methodical planning. These types of situations often occurred in a central planning system, and although most knew the process was indeed flawed, no one of senior rank had the courage or the gumption to do anything about it. The diesels worked fine, but Shumkov knew the cracks were there and worried that someday, under pressure of extended steaming, they might worsen and become a major casualty. The thought haunted him constantly, but he knew his engineers were good, and they certainly did not wish to miss this deployment. It promised to be a most exciting time, and Shumkov craved adventure and action. He also knew that despite the complaints and warning by his chief engineer, the careful Senior Lieutenant Viktor Parshin, their batteries had exceeded their normal life and were due for replacement. If Shumkov had followed the engineer's demands that they be replaced, the boat may have been knocked out of the deployment and substituted for by another of the same class. So Shumkov had taken the chance. Keeping the older batteries meant the electrolyte ran hotter during recharging and was a potential fire and explosion hazard. Shumkov understood his engineer's careful ways and trusted that the deployment could be made without fear.

The silhouettes of the four darkened submarines proceeded silently in column at six knots, each separated by two thousand meters despite the fog and poor visibility, until passing the entrance to Aral Bay. Shumkov remained frozen at his station in the navigating cockpit of the open bridge as the soupy fog swirled about his head, giving him the appearance of a spooky figure gliding along at the top of a blackened monster. Sea conditions were abnormally calm; the lack of wind kept the thick fog wrapped around the Kola coastline like a pale shroud.

A Project 641 Foxtrot class submarine is nothing more than a steel cylinder whose vital innards are compressed within a strong steel pressure hull shaped like an expensive Cuban cigar. The diesel engines, electric motors, batteries, living spaces, and weapons are concentrated inside this steel tube in a dizzying maze of piping and plating. Since the pressure hull is heavier than water and alone would sink, an outer hull made of weaker material encases the pressure hull and provides its necessary buoyancy. The outer hull increases the total volume of the submarine without adding significantly to its weight. The space between the outer casing and the pressure hull is divided into cells that hold fuel or fresh water, and into ballast tanks that hold air when the submarine is surfaced, or controlled amounts of seawater when the boat submerges. While on the surface only about a seventh of the submarine's pressure hull is above water level. When the boat dives, its total buoyancy is reduced by flooding the ballast tanks with a controlled level of seawater. If the boat is stationary when submerged—that is, without headway—it would sink immediately, since no neutral or suspended state can exist. The submarine retains its desired depth using a combination of speed provided by electric motors, and lift provided by movable diving planes fixed to the bow, which when tilted upward or

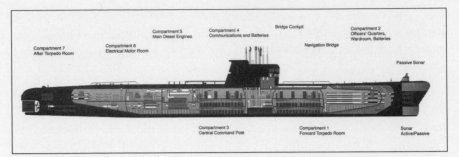

Project 641 type, Foxtrot class long-range diesel attack submarine cutaway schematic (courtesy © 1998. Jasper Communications Pty Ltd. Sydney, Australia)

downward drive the boat to or away from the surface. Since the submarine is designed for cruising underwater, it has very little reserve buoyancy when on the surface; the slightest damage may prove fatal. A surface ship displacing the same twenty-five hundred tons as the Foxtrot class submarine enjoys considerably more reserve buoyancy and can absorb considerable damage, even taking aboard water up to her total weight before sinking. A surfaced Foxtrot submarine, however, can only ship aboard about a fifth of her weight, or five hundred tons of seawater, before sinking. Since the submarine's fittings, engines, batteries, and equipment are compacted within the severely limited space in the pressure hull, repairs of any kind are extremely complex. Whereas a surface warship like a destroyer can be saved from extensive battle damage by repairing the hull, a submarine with the slightest pressure hull damage is usually doomed to a crushing plunge to the depths of the ocean. Life aboard a submarine is precarious at best.

The executive officer, or *starpom*, Captain Third Rank Viktor Frolov, climbed the ladder from central command, quietly opened the hatch leading into the upper conning tower, and stepped carefully onto the open bridge, taking care not to disturb the group gathered there. He stood motionless next to Shumkov for a few moments. Then he ventured a whisper: "Comrade Commander, it's time to look at the orders and plot the track. I have all the charts laid out below in the navigation plot."

Shumkov didn't respond immediately, and by not doing so made the exec think he was in a trance.

"Comrade Captain," the exec began again.

"Understand," Shumkov tried to answer calmly, "time to dive." He turned and looked down the short ladder leading into the conning station inside the sail to find Frolov's alert eyes. Then Shumkov nodded quietly to him.

Frolov immediately stood and barked into the voice tube, "Prepare to submerge, all hands clear topside." The command center watch quickly began the well-rehearsed routine of making preparations to take the boat down, choreographed in a smooth-running ballet. The only music was the sound of the light seas slapping against the steel hull as water surged in and out of the horizontal and vertical vents in the hull called limber holes. As the dive preparations proceeded, Shumkov scanned the empty space around the cockpit; absolutely nothing was visible. The radarscope had shown no contacts as Frolov slid deftly down the ladder rails into the central command post, called the CCP, and unsnapped his warm *kanadka*, the fur-lined foul-weather jacket. The sound of the rapid unsnapping cracked the silence as ten men went silently about their tasks in the dim blue light of the complex central command. This was the brain of the submarine, while two compartments aft of it were the heart—one of which was the engine compartment, the throbbing three diesels that drove the three shafts that extended aft through the remaining three compartments and passed through the hull via the magical shaft bearings, which allowed rotation but excluded water by virtue of the high-pressure air-inflated stern tubes. The three screws turned at an even rate just below the cavitation speed of nine knots.

The boat began to settle slowly as the ballast tanks flooded, forcing air to bubble and hiss through the limber holes. Shumkov stood aside as the last lookouts dove through the hatch into the pressure hull beneath; he was the last man left topside. Shumkov took one last look and inhaled the moist, cold air, then climbed down a few steps and closed the main trunk, spring-loaded hatch with a clang.

Shumkov always demanded total quiet and smoothness in his central command post. All hands had learned the hard way that their captain, soft-spoken as he may have been, was intolerant of any noise or confusion in the CCP, and would resort to the most drastic disciplinary methods to punish noisy watch standers. He once had two conscript seamen who had made the mistake of talking during preparations to submerge sent to a shed near the pier in Polyarny, where they were required to remain beating on a tin trash can with metal pipes for two hours, at which point they emerged nearly deaf from the din. They had not made the same error twice.

Once the boat had settled at the submerged depth of 120 meters, steaming straight and level due west at 9 knots, Shumkov walked to the curtained-off navigation cubicle in the CCP. There he found the navigator; his second in command, the *starpom* Frolov; political officer Saparov; and communicator Lieutenant Cheprakov, standing in a ring around the chart table, which was piled with cases holding the charts, more than five times the normal number for a routine patrol. The four officers stood quietly while he looked at each of them in a purposely slow-motion gaze, checking each as if inspecting them in the dim light. The charts had been the brunt of jokes for days, ever since the Brigade Staff navigator, Captain Third Rank Igor Lyubichev, had distributed the chart packages to each of the four boats. The Main Navy Staff had, in their wisdom, ordered that so as not to divulge the ultimate destination of the submarine brigade, a complete set of worldwide charts was to be distributed. The packages were so bulky that it took the navigator three trips to each submarine to carry the classified charts. The presence of these charts had given each navigator the feeling he was going on a voyage the length of that of Jules Verne's *Nautilus*. The effort to cover the entire operation in total secrecy had grown from tedious to ridiculous, especially given the fact that practically every officer's wife in Polyarny was looking forward to a trip to the Caribbean, and some had even begun to study Spanish.

"Very well, Cheprakov, open the safe and bring the sealed envelope."

The communications officer reached up to the small, rectangular safe, which hung on the bulkhead in the corner of the space. He spun the dials and opened the safe in a flash, reached in, and removed the thick manila envelope. He removed the outer envelope and handed it to the exec, who laid it on the chart table. It was also sealed and had wide red stripes, marking it as secret material. Shumkov nodded again, and this time Frolov picked up the package, slowly opened the inner envelope, took out the bound booklet of orders, and handed it to the captain. He paused and scanned the cover, opened, and began to read.

The orders were titled *Kama* in large, dark print—the code name of the naval portion of Operation *Anadyr*. Many of the officers had already heard of *Anadyr*. It was the code name that in itself was a *maskirovka*, a cover, which was the mythical large-scale defense exer-

Project 629 type, Golf class diesel-powered ballistic missile submarine (courtesy U.S. Navy)

cise to be taking place high in the northern latitudes of Siberia, hence the name of one of the most northern rivers in Siberia. The *Anadyr* movement of ships to and from Cuba, which had begun in earnest in July, was so massive that when the transport of the military personnel and equipment began, the Soviet-flagged merchantmen had to turn over their transport duties of the other aid material to their allied Warsaw Pact merchantmen. Thus merchant bottoms from East Germany, Poland, Bulgaria, and Romania picked up the nonmilitary cargoes, while the Soviet merchants hauled the more sensitive military material. It was a huge effort, and once in full swing was difficult to mask as mere routine trade support for the fledgling socialist brotherhood of Fidel Castro.

Shumkov quickly scanned the orders further, then began to read aloud: "The mission of the submariners in Operation *Kama* is to reconnoiter the approaches to Mariel, to accurately log the acoustic conditions in the outer approaches, and to enter Port Mariel to make preparations for the arrival of the seven ballistic missile submarines from the sister division of Polyarny's Fourth Squadron. Upon the arrival in Mariel the new organization would be designated the Twentieth Special Squadron." The plan called for later deployments of Northern Fleet surface supporting units, including the submarine tender *Dmitri Galkan*, acting as flagship with the squadron commander, Kontr Admiral Leonid Rybalko, aboard. Other surface combatants would join, including two old all-gun cruisers, two missile-equipped destroyers, two all-gun destroyers, and a division of twelve seventy-ton, twenty-five-meter missile boats of the Komar class, each carrying twin R-15 cruise missiles, called the Styx SS-N-2 missile in the West.

The captain continued reading aloud from the larger mission of Operation *Anadyr*: "The overall mission of the internationalist intervention on behalf of the Socialist Republic of Cuba is to equip the country with sufficient Soviet armed support to deter further aggression

by the anti-Soviet bloc led by the United States of America, and to further thwart a repeat of the ill-fated invasion of Cuba, which was
attempted in 1961 by antisocialist, anti-Castro lackeys supported by the
American CIA and Navy." As he read, Shumkov quietly wondered why
the defense of Cuba called for the installation of intermediate- and
medium-range ballistic missiles, but kept these thoughts to himself and
read on from the operation plan.

Shumkov paused for dramatic effect, then looked up and repeated
the words written on the inside of the package, the same words they
had heard from the briefing by First Deputy Chief of Main Navy Staff
Admiral Fokin, held two days before departure aboard the submarine
tender *Dmitri Galkan* in Sayda Bay—"Comrades! Our brigade is poised
to take part in a special mission for the Soviet government: upon completion of our secret transit across the Atlantic you will be stationed permanently in a friendly country. Our assignment is vital and filled with
great responsibility. Of uttermost importance to the success of the mission is that we maintain the secrecy of our deployment. The Sixty-ninth
Brigade of long-range diesel attack submarines will make best speed,
while remaining undetected, arriving as soon as possible in Mariel,
Cuba, after October 20. I wish you happy sailing and the successful
accomplishment of your mission."

Quick mental calculations made it obvious to Shumkov that they
would have to make a maximum submerged speed of nine knots, surfacing to snorkel at night while still evading the U.S. fixed hydroacoustic arrays known to be deployed in the North Atlantic guarding
the Iceland/Shetlands/Faeroes gap and off the Azores before being able
to hide beneath the warmer layers of the Gulf Stream. The task, to
make such high speed and yet remain undetected, was nearly impossible. This was, of course, to be done with the normal presence of U.S.
antisubmarine warfare ships at sea. That was, also, barring any contingency or exercise that might place more than the usual U.S. hunter-
killer antisubmarine warfare groups at sea. At the normal state of readiness, which was Condition Four, one ASW carrier HUK group would
be deployed in the North Atlantic at all times.

Shumkov looked at the exec, who was thinking along similar lines.
Then the captain continued to read aloud the rules of engagement, a
lot of words that basically said that the special nuclear-tipped torpedoes
could be used only if attacked by U.S. forces. Here again he paused
and looked at the *zampolit* Saparov, who started to speak, then stopped.

Shumkov looked again at his communicator, Cheprakov, realizing that the success of this covert transit would weigh heavily on the shoulders of this young officer. Among his other duties as ship's communicator and electronics materials officer was the radio intercept officer. He and his group of five English-language-trained intercept operators would monitor all high-frequency and UHF communications of the Americans to help the submarine avoid contact. It would prove a tough mission indeed.

The next portion of the package contained a sheet with a red border around the edge, the rules of engagement. Shumkov read them first to himself and then aloud:

1. Weapons during transit will be in combat readiness for use.
2. Conventional weapons to be used as directed by the Main Navy Staff except may be used in the discretion of the commanding officer in case of attack against the submarine.
3. Torpedoes with atomic weapons may be used only as directed in instructions from the Ministry of Defense or the Main Navy Staff.

Those statements were considerably at odds with the words all four commanding officers had entered in their logs on orders of the Northern Fleet chief of staff, the impressive Vice Admiral Rossokho, after the send-off briefing on the pier.

OCTOBER 2, 1962
KONTR ADMIRAL LEONID RYBALKO
ABOARD THE SUBMARINE TENDER DMITRI GALKAN
BARENTS SEA, 150 KILOMETERS NORTHEAST OF POLYARNY

What a mess! thought Rybalko as he recalled the last two chaotic days during which the Soviet Northern Fleet had scrambled to get four long-range diesel boats ready for sea. What kind of navy do we have? he asked himself and mused. We were better off in the height of the war; at least we had trained crews to put to sea. There was certainly something wrong with the state of the fleet, and he thought he knew what. The system was just full of falsehoods, lies, and exaggerations. Rybalko thought back to the last-minute change of command made to his brigade of attack boats now en route to Mariel, Cuba. Just days before sailing, after all the emphasis on the preparations of the submarines, the brigade commander of the Sixty-ninth had turned up in a hospital in Severomorsk, suffering from nervous collapse. Rybalko had been forced to get approval by telephone for his nominee, Agafonov, from navy commander in chief Gorshkov, which had been tough enough. But getting the nomination through the entire chain of command from Northern Fleet headquarters, the political section of the Party's Naval Council, the Personnel Directorate of the Main Staff, and then from the nominee's own wife! There was an old tradition that a newly appointed commander of a high position was required to have verbal approval from his wife that he take the command. Agafonov had been approved all the way up the line. Rybalko wondered what he would have done if Agafonov's wife had said no. That never happened, and little importance was ever placed on that ancient custom. Nevertheless, it had cost him two precious days of work in the busiest period of the pre-sail preparations. He squinted out over the swells, now blowing with the early October scud, and a few flurries blew against the pilothouse windshield. Rybalko turned and looked around at the officer standing next to him in the wind.

"Comrade Admiral, the noon position report, sir." The young senior lieutenant stood with a wet piece of paper in his outstretched hand.

"How can I read that? It's soaked."

"Sorry, sir, I'll get another copy." The young officer turned to go back inside the pilothouse. If the bastard wouldn't stand in the bloody rain I could give him a dry copy, the young officer thought just as Rybalko caught his arm.

"Here, give it to me, you have better things to do." He took the soggy paper from the young officer. "How far are we from the Sarich point?" He smiled and thought better of taking out the past few days' frustrations on the young officer.

"Sir, point QQ bears 268 degrees at 50 miles. At this speed if the weather remains the same, we'll be there at 15:30." All times aboard were computed in Moscow time, even though they were two time zones west already.

"Very well, Comrade Navigator, see to it I'm informed of any deviation in ETA at the point; we're expecting to pick up four Zulu boats there, coming from the south out of Gadzhievo." The additional submarines would join the group only for the trip to North Cape, masking the departure of the Sixty-ninth Brigade of attack boats, a deception effort to throw some confusion into the game. No other long-range 641 boats were ready, and the four Project 611 boats, called Zulu class, were included to make the Americans think there were more submarines in the main group if they picked up the contacts. What a disgracefully meager force, Rybalko intoned to himself. The assistant navigator saluted and turned, spray flowing off his raingear. He reentered the pilothouse and lost hold of the hatch, which blew shut behind him with a loud clang.

Rybalko watched the three ancient *Skorry* class destroyers escorting the ad hoc task group west through the Barents. The destroyers would leave them just off North Cape, because they had neither the range nor the training to deploy all the way with the submarine brigade. What a ridiculous situation, he thought. A blue-water navy, offspring of the new strategic thinking of the Main Naval Staff, a fleet in being, and they couldn't even muster up a full-strength brigade of diesel boats for an important deployment! And on top of that, the load-out of nuclear torpedoes in Polyarny had not gone well. As a result of ill-fitting torpedo hatch scuttles, they were late loading one of the tactical nuclear-tipped torpedoes. That concerned him, because none of the four boats had ever trained to launch these weapons, and if they were ever to fire the nuclear-tipped fish, he fully expected the boats to blow themselves up along with the surface targets. But he knew, or hoped, that it probably wouldn't ever come to that. There had been considerable concern among the four commanding officers about carrying the atomic warheads that they had never trained to use. They had been assured by all the staffs that the officers accompanying the weapons were trained in nuclear safety and would ensure that no harm would come to those weapons.

In any case, the ridiculous insistence that the brigade be issued khaki, short-sleeved shirts and shorts because they were deploying to the Caribbean was another foolish order and held up their sailing from Sayda Bay for six additional hours as the boxes of khakis were flown up from Moscow. They certainly could have used more *kanadki*, the World War II foul-weather jackets, so named after several Canadian-flagged merchant ships made it through German convoys with their holds full of these excellent jackets. The submariners were the first to draw them, and they were far superior to any Russian-made foul-weather gear. Now only about half the brigade had them, and, instead, in this freezing October weather, they were deploying in the driving snow with impractical short-sleeved khakis! Another stupid decree from the political section of the Northern Fleet Staff to show solidarity with the Cuban people.

Rybalko walked back to the pilothouse hatch, opened it, and smiled in spite of himself at the sight of the entire bridge watch, which snapped to attention, all clad in short-sleeved khakis and short trousers.

"Admiral on the bridge." He shut the hatch and strode across the bridge to the charthouse cubicle, where the assistant navigator was hunched over, working on the charts, still dripping wet from delivering the noon position report in the rain and spray.

"What's the weather report, Comrade Navigator?" He asked in a kinder tone than he had used out on the bridge wing in the howling wind.

"Looks better, sir. Winds should veer to the south and decrease in a few hours, and a clearing front will pass by the time we reach QQ; visibility should improve." The navigator smiled, as if the improved weather report would improve his superior's disposition, too, somehow.

OCTOBER 3, 1962
CAPTAIN SECOND RANK ALEKSEI DUBIVKO
COMMANDING OFFICER, B-36
SOUTHBOUND IN THE NORTH ATLANTIC

Aleksei Dubivko was an aggressive commanding officer. He was excited about the deployment when he was first told about it in Polyarny the August before. He had pushed the officers and men of B-36 until they had achieved the position as one of the most combat-ready submarines in the Northern Fleet. He had scored the highest grades in all the operational and engineering competitions but had been outscored in weapons readiness by his good friend Nikolai Shumkov in B-130. Shumkov had the extra experience in weapons, which had put him just slightly over the otherwise perfect B-36 of his friend Dubivko.

Having come from the Far East, where he graduated from the Vladivostok Higher Naval School and served first in surface ships, Ukrainian-born Dubivko was a newcomer to the Northern Fleet. However, he was quick to fit in with the other submariners. In 1953, at the unusually junior grade of senior lieutenant, Dubivko had picked up command of a medium-range diesel submarine fitting out in Gorky on the Volga. He had thought it somewhat strange to be ordered to the center of the vast Soviet Union in the landlocked central Gorky Region just west of the Ural Mountains, to take command of a seagoing diesel submarine. He was well aware that many oceangoing ships and submarines were constructed there ever since the days of the Great Patriotic War, when entire shipyards and factories were moved east en masse to escape the advancing German armies. As a result, the shipbuilding yards in Gorky continued to launch surface warships and submarines throughout the post–World War II Soviet building spree. Nevertheless, Dubivko still thought it strange to be ordered from the naval city of Vladivostok to Gorky, pick up a submarine, and ride it inside a huge floating dry dock through the vast inland waterway system via the Volga River all the way to the Northern Fleet. There he took his new boat to one of the many home ports that were springing up in increasing numbers like mushrooms in the deepwater fjords along the Kola Peninsula.

Dubivko had been so successful with his first command that he was ordered to another new construction submarine, this time B-36, a long-range Project 641 boat just out of the building ways of Leningrad's Sudomekh construction halls. After fitting out he had taken the submarine through its workup and fleet acceptance trials. Then, in the operational readiness competition, he had won all awards for excellence except the weapons firing, which his competitor Nikolai Shumkov had taken hands down. Dubivko was somewhat jealous that his friend had completed a special weapons training course and actually fired two live atomic torpedo warshots from a special submarine into targets off the Novaya Zemlya Special Weapons Test Facility.

When Dubivko's B-36 crew were loading the torpedoes in Sayda Bay a few nights before they sailed, he had watched from the navigation bridge in the late September afternoon. Then he noticed three officers from the weapons facility come aboard. They had been watching the loading operation. One had a briefcase and wore the Northern Fleet headquarters staff emblem. Dubivko's watch standers on the main deck pointed up to the top of the bridge, where he was observing. He had no idea what the three officers wanted. He watched them enter the confined space of the cockpit a few moments later. A large staff officer, a captain first rank, was out of breath and puffing heavily—he obviously needed more such exercise.

The staff officer introduced himself and stated that he had come from the Northern Fleet Special Weapons Directorate. Dubivko wondered what this was all about. The staff officer then introduced a young lieutenant to him; his name was Alexander Pomilyev. He said that Pomilyev would be riding with B-36 on the mission as a special weapons expert. Dubivko was surprised. He felt that he didn't need any special weapons experts aboard; they were quite well trained in all their weapons systems. Then the staff officer explained that the next torpedo they would load was a special torpedo with a fifteen-kiloton atomic warhead. Dubivko was astounded. This was the first time he was told of such a weapon being loaded.

"What am I supposed to do with this? Take it to Mariel and give it to the Cubans?"

"No, of course not." The staff officer grew indignant. "Your special handling instructions and rules of use of this weapon are contained in your sealed orders. You will read these when you are at sea. Lieutenant Pomilyev is an atomic weapons specialist and will take care of the weapon from today until your arrival in Mariel, will be available to monitor the condition of the warhead, and will help you load it. The weapon will be kept as a ready service torpedo in the forward torpedo compartment, and loaded into tube number two only when you cross the Iceland/Shetlands/Faeroes gap and are in waters heavily patrolled by American and British antisubmarine aircraft."

"What is the purpose of having this weapon aboard?" Dubivko asked. "Are we expecting to go to war soon?"

The staff officer refused to answer. He just grunted and said that the lieutenant would take care of all matters regarding the special torpedo; Dubivko was expected merely to follow instructions. He got the feeling the staff officer was in a hurry and wished to be on his way. Dubivko looked at the lieutenant. "Are you a qualified submariner?"

"No, Comrade Commander, but I am familiar with your forward torpedo room and will get on-the-job training to familiarize myself with the other duties of submarine officers when under way."

Dubivko was astonished at such a situation, but only wanted to get the loading completed and ready to sail. He thought it strange that they were carrying a weapon they had not trained with. Dubivko had a feeling something was under way, and that they were not being told some very important information. He let the matter go and intended to ask the brigade commander, Captain Agafonov, more about that weapon at the presail meeting that evening.

Dubivko watched as the heavy staff officer struggled down the ladder, out to the main deck across the brow, and waddled down the pier. He turned to young Lieutenant Pomilyev. "Welcome aboard the B-36. Take your gear below and report to Lieutenant Zhukov for your berthing and special watch assignments." The captain smiled at the young man, who look frightened. "We'll make you a first-rate submariner, but above all I want you to take care of that weapon—we don't want anything to happen to that."

Dubivko watched as the young man, who looked a little confused, climbed down through the main hatch into central command, following on the heels of the seaman escort. Dubivko looked out and watched the remainder of the torpedoes being loaded. He was not able to discern which was the special weapon; it was already too dark to notice any telltale different color scheme. He understood later that the special torpedo had a special paint on its blunt nose.

❖

When Dubivko's *B-36* was selected among the other top long-range diesels as a member of the Polyarny Sixty-ninth Brigade of the Fourth Red Banner, Order of Ushakov Submarine Squadron and began preparing for the special deployment, he had taken extra steps to ensure that his crew was in top form. Realizing that the upcoming operation was likely to include an extensive time at sea, Dubivko concentrated on making sure his assigned ship's medical officer was prepared. He arranged for his doctor to be assigned to Severomorsk Naval Hospital on special duty under instruction in emergency surgery and related trauma handling. This extra training would pay off later.

The first week of the deployment was routine until they passed through the Iceland/Shetlands/Faeroes gap and encountered a severe storm with seas more than ten meters high. During the storm one of Dubivko's sonarmen was afflicted with acute appendicitis. After initially trying to treat the infection with massive doses of antibiotics, the submarine's medical officer decided he must have emergency surgery. The boat was making seven knots submerged and, in accordance with their orders to remain covert, surfaced to charge batteries only at night. It was impossible in such heavy weather to conduct surgery even at periscope and snorkeling depth. For hours they steamed at snorkel depth to fully charge the batteries for their next submerged leg and to be able to go deep enough to evade the swells, which could be felt as deep as twenty meters below the surface. It was a formidable battle.

The weather was atrocious; the Atlantic sea conditions deteriorated to a force-eight gale. Dubivko was forced to surface completely to charge batteries rather than run with only the snorkel above the surface. Their

Project 641 submarines were improved versions of the German World War II–type XXI U-boats, the first to successfully employ the snorkel concept. To remain covert during their transit and yet fulfill the requirement to charge batteries about every forty-eight hours, they preferred to use the snorkel. When extended from snorkel depth, which was about eleven meters, their stainless-steel air induction mast protruded approximately one and a half meters above a calm surface to provide air for the diesel engines. Two diesel engines were required to run during charging, one for propulsion to drive the boat, the other to charge the batteries, the third standing by. However, in turbulent seas the flapper valve in the snorkel would often slam shut when dunked below the surface to prevent flooding in the air intake. When this occurred the powerful diesels sucked air violently from inside all the submarines' compartments, causing the most horrendous vacuum. Then would follow a vicious belching of exhaust, which often sent the crew coughing and vomiting from their stations. So powerful was the suction that their eyes would bulge and their ears pop painfully. Dubivko had known that filling amalgam was sometimes wrenched from sailors' teeth during these conditions. Therefore, despite the increase in chance of detection by enemy radar, they were forced to run on the surface in these storms. With two diesels running on the surface they generated considerably greater noise and were much more vulnerable to detection by radar and sonobuoys. Conversely, the surface background noise caused by the stormy turbulence helped mask them from search aircraft. Nevertheless, the foul weather made their transit extremely uncomfortable and physically dangerous. While they rolled and bounced, the stores, which had filled the boat on departure, often broke loose and caused bedlam below. Hams and sausages, which had been stowed hanging from the overhead between torpedo tubes, broke loose, and boxes of canned meats came adrift. The danger of being injured by flying food was great. Imagine a submarine commanding officer having to inform a mother that her son had been killed in the Atlantic in the line of duty by a flying smoked ham or a case of canned sardines!

The submariners had no other alternative. At one point during the severe weather, as they continued to charge batteries, Dubivko observed a U.S. P2V Neptune long-range patrol aircraft. They had initially been warned by their electronics support measure (ESM) watch.

"Sir, we have an American airborne radar and some communications showing there is a P2V out of the Naval Air Station Keflavik heading our way." In these seas Dubivko was certain the planes could not detect them even with their sail awash; there would be too much sea clutter on their radar. Their sonobuoys also would be practically useless with all the surface noise caused by the storm. So Dubivko continued heading into the seas on the surface to charge fully. It was frightening at times, and in the back of his mind he feared what could happen if for any reason they lost power. Granted, they had three diesels, but it was not unheard of to have a contaminated fuel tank and with water in the fuel to lose one or even two diesels. It was too terrible to imagine, so Dubivko blotted it from his mind. He trusted his chief mechanic and was certain he would not allow any kind of accident that could endanger the boat. Dubivko considered that they were lucky that only one of the watch officers was injured, having suffered three broken ribs when he fell against the bridge cockpit. The seas were so heavy it was like being thrown to the heavens on top of a huge swell with nothing in sight except wind and scud-streaked sky in all directions, before plummeting downward into a trough with seas on all the horizons. It was terrible!

The submariners watched the U.S. P2Vs fly over several times, always heading generally southwest, as if they had known of the boat's track. The submariners all thought the Americans must have had fore-knowledge of their transit; otherwise how would they know to follow the general direction of their track? It was a continuing battle trying to charge batteries in the storm with the boat pitching and rolling like a cork. They finally were able to submerge with sufficient charge to remain below the teeming turbulence for the next day. The doctor conducted the appendectomy on the wardroom table. Within three days the sonarman was back on his feet. Oddly, when the patrol was over, the Northern Fleet Medical Service awarded the sonarman a medal for bravery for having survived the operation. The doctor received nothing for his superb work.

OCTOBER 3, 1962
CAPTAIN VITALI SAVITSKY
COMMANDING OFFICER, B-59
NORTH ATLANTIC

Author's note: Senior Lieutenant Vadim Orlov was assigned to B-59 as the onboard head of the Radio Intercept Group. Born in Vladivostok, he completed the Leningrad Higher Naval School in 1959 and became a navigator aboard surface ships in the Baltic Fleet for several years. He later attended the Radio Intelligence School and was assigned to B-59, his first submarine as head of the supersecret Radio Intercept Group. His post was the intercept cubicle set up in the petty officers' mess in compartment four. Neither the commanding officer, Captain Savitsky, nor the brigade chief of staff, Captain Arkhipov, survive today, so Orlov gives his description of the events during their deployment as part of Operation *Kama* in October 1962.

❖

Orlov knew from rumors about B-59's coming deployment roughly two months prior to departure. He heard that they were to be permanently stationed in a foreign country with a division of ballistic missile boats also from Polyarny. He guessed it was going to be Cuba.

Orlov was only superficially acquainted with his skipper, Captain Second Rank Savitsky. The commanding officer had been ordered aboard just a few weeks before they were due to depart on the special *Kama* mission. The crew weren't sure why their former commander was replaced, but they thought it was all part of tightening up the brigade. The new commander, Savitsky, was a good man and highly qualified, but the brigade chief of staff who was on board was more accustomed to the work of a radio intercept officer. He knew better than Savitsky how to apply the work Orlov did to the tactical situation. Notwithstanding the discomfort of having a senior officer embarked, Commander Savitsky did well.

The departure and transit were normal. When they first submerged they gathered around the captain in the navigation vestibule and opened the sealed orders. It was quite a dramatic moment as they found out about their assignment. Orlov was surprised that they had been ordered to make the transit arriving in Mariel, Cuba, by October 20, and to make it covertly. It would be nearly impossible to make the required speed of advance submerged while surfacing only after dark to charge batteries. They could make a maximum of seven knots submerged, while their speed on the surface depended on the weather. Lieutenant Orlov had made only one patrol in the open Atlantic and knew that during this season the Atlantic could be quite rough.

The crew were highly spirited and at the time thought themselves capable of any challenge. What excited them most was the prospect of living permanently in Cuba. Their orders even stated that their families

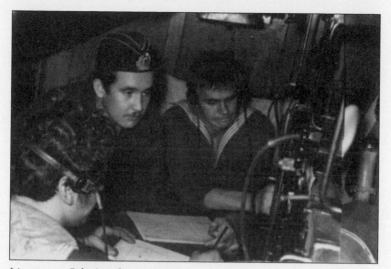

Lieutenant Orlov's radio intercept detachment, *B-59* (courtesy Vadim Orlov)

would follow later by transport and would live in accommodations in the town of Mariel. Anyone who had experienced life in Polyarny during the long, bleak winters would understand their excitement at the prospect of living with their families in Cuba. The crew had little knowledge of what was brewing in the Caribbean at the time. Orlov was surprised that there were to be seven ballistic missile boats of the Project 629 type (NATO name Golf class) also stationed in Mariel. He wondered how the USSR had worked out the diplomatic details on that issue.

B-59 made it as far as the Faeroe Islands covertly, and after that, from what Orlov was intercepting in the U.S. long-range air patrol base communications, it became obvious to him that they were expected. The American chatter indicated that they were already looking for what they thought were half a dozen Soviet long-range diesel attack submarines. At the time Orlov reckoned they had been compromised by some intelligence source in Polyarny. He had no knowledge of the U.S. underwater hydrophone system. Orlov's radio monitors began to detect the U.S., British, and Canadian long-range antisubmarine air patrols overhead periodically. However, as far as they could determine, the fliers didn't come close, although they planted sonobuoy fields all over the main routes. *B-59* merely went deep and avoided contact. They took great care to surface to recharge only in the night hours and only between the frequent air patrols.

October Fury

OCTOBER 1962
AT SEA

On October 2 the U.S. Atlantic Fleet Amphibious Command conducted a multiple Marine Battalion Team amphibious landing exercise with Amphibious Squadrons 8 and 12 at Vieques Island, off Puerto Rico. The objective of the exercise, as stated to the press, was to oust the Orange dictator Ortsac (Castro spelled backward) from power. On October 3 the musical *Stop the World—I Want to Get Off*, starring Anna Quayle and Anthony Newley, opened at the Shubert Theatre in New York. Its hit song was "What Kind of Fool Am I?"

On October 7 the newspaper voice of the Soviet Ministry of Defense, *Kraznaya Zvezda* (Red Star), stated that Soviet armed forces were on strategic alert. On October 11 Atlantic Fleet command deployed the attack aircraft carrier USS *Independence* with the aircraft of Air Wing 7 aboard from Norfolk with destroyers USS *English*, *Hank*, *O'Hare*, and *Cory* as escorts. On October 13 the Second Marine Air Wing deployed elements of Air Groups 14 and 32 to the naval air station at Key West. The U.S. Army and Air Force prepositioned supplies to bases and ports in the southern states. The air force moved selected squadrons and consumables to Florida bases. The Tactical Air Command began to accelerate training.

On October 14 a U.S. Air Force U-2 mission revealed Soviet SS-4 *Sandal* medium-range ballistic missile sites under construction in Cuba. These missiles had a range of 1,020 nautical miles. A total of forty-two were deployed in Cuba with two- or three-megaton warheads. The U-2 flight also found SS-5 *Skean* intermediate-range ballistic missiles—four launchers and eight missiles per site, with a range of 2,200 nautical miles.

On October 15 all six U.S. Polaris ballistic missile submarines based in Holy Loch, Scotland, deployed to wartime stations. The Polaris boat USS *Abraham Lincoln* shortened her overhaul and deployed from Holy Loch along with two others from New London.

OCTOBER 15, 1962
CAPTAIN NIKOLAI SHUMKOV
B-130, OFF THE AZORES

"Comrade Frolov, take us up to periscope depth," Captain Nikolai Shumkov barked loudly for all in central command to hear. "Time for our next support broadcast in twelve minutes."

"Bow planes up twenty degrees, stand by to raise HF antenna at twenty meters."

The command center grew quiet as all eyes watched the depth gauge. The deck sloped gently upward as the depth gauge began to swing counterclockwise. "Passing fifty meters, sir." The planesman was center stage. The captain stood in his usual spot behind and between the helmsman on his left and the planesman on his right. Frolov, wearing the blue-and-white duty armband, was the watch officer, and stood next to the captain.

The command center began to creak as the pressure decreased. This was an exciting feeling, Shumkov thought; the feeling of going to periscope depth after long hours submerged was always exhilarating, even though he knew they would only be at communication and snorting depth. The ocean surface lured the submariner as a sign of hope and excitement. There had been no communication from Northern Fleet headquarters since they had departed Sayda two weeks ago. The only communications the submarine had received were the daily radio checks at designated hours on the UHF net from Brigade Commander Agafonov, who insisted that each boat acknowledge by a coded clicking of the transmission key on the circuit as each boat in succession came to periscope depth to charge batteries, and then pass the brigade signal to the next sub to come to snorkel depth. This routine had been devised by Captain Agafonov to ensure that no more than two of the quartet were near the surface at a given time, even briefly, to pass on the radio check before descending back to their steaming depth of sixty meters.

"Passing thirty meters . . . twenty-five."

"Stand by to raise antenna." Shumkov liked to give commands that resulted in their equipment being deployed. It gave him a sense of pride to realize that all hands in the command center were aware that their equipment was peaked and working.

"Twenty meters, sir."

"Raise HF antenna, open main induction. Engine control, start diesel engines. Conduct battery recharging."

Exec Frolov turned to Lieutenant Volodya Voronov, the oncoming watch officer, and they went through their carefully choreographed routine for relieving the officer of the watch. The ceremony complete, he returned Voronov's salute, then pulled off his armband and handed it to the younger officer. "I'll be in radio watching the broadcast."

Shumkov stood still watching the planesman, and deep in thought, stood for a few more moments before following the communicator into the radio cubicle. Shumkov was anxious about receiving the broadcast but didn't want to show it. It was a sign of weakness to be too anxious about anything. He would try to keep his composure at all times, although he was concerned that there was a lot transpiring in the world that he knew nothing about. That was normal for the military, and specifically for the submarine force. Nonetheless, his appetite for information was almost all-consuming. It was the way of the Soviet system that information was closely held, especially operational information. It was for those with the need to know and then sometimes withheld from them until the last possible moment. There was always the chance of miscalculation, for secrecy spawns more secrecy and the tendency to err on the side of doing nothing when something needed to be done.

Shumkov watched as the communications officer stood before the teletypewriter, peering at the line of type representing the radio carrier tone, with the type carriage moving repeatedly from left to right, printing the series of identical unintelligible four-letter groups. "Nothing yet, sir, just the continuous tone."

The communications officer, too, tried to hide his eagerness to receive news, an order, anything. It was standard procedure for the fleet broadcast to come up on the low-frequency schedules to provide brief periods of communications support for submarines in midocean. Maybe ten minutes at the most. The massive low-frequency antenna farm southeast of Moscow was sending nothing to them—at least nothing more than the carrier tone—to tell them that their equipment was functioning. The low-frequency broadcast had always intrigued Shumkov, although he was a well-educated radio technician. The thought that the low-frequency waves actually propagated through the surface of the earth and into the depths of the oceans, reaching out tens of thousands of kilometers around the globe, fascinated him. The thought that his equipment was tuned and provided the key card to read an encoded message at these great distances was still a magical, almost religious aspect to him personally. Suddenly, as communicator Cheprakov's eyes glared at the teletype paper—as if trying to bore through the mechanism—it began to print out a line of different four-letter groups.

"The test line, sir." He could barely contain his excitement. "This is the test line to synchronize on." He leaned forward, watching as the groups of four letters typed an unintelligible message. Cheprakov counted aloud to ten, then pressed the encryption button, and magically Cyrillic script began to print out on the paper. The two officers stood mesmerized as the full text formed. It ran for several minutes, then stopped and returned to printing the meaningless carrier lines again. Cheprakov reached out and tore off the message, and handed it to the captain, who read it slowly, then walked out into the central command and over to the navigator's plot. The exec stood awaiting an order or a hint at least to what was going on.

Shumkov always enjoyed holding his officers in suspense. "Break out the charts of the southern end of the Bahamas and the Sargasso Sea." He scanned the message header as the navigator thumbed through the pile of charts until he found the right one, carefully pulled it out, and pinned it on the plot over their current track chart. They smoothed the chart out and then focused at the plot, which showed the string of the Bahama Islands stretching in a chain to the east from the coast of Florida: Grand Bahama, New Providence, and Eleuthera. The chain was then interrupted by the narrow Caicos Passage. The chain continued to the southern extreme and the Turks Island Passage, the waterway between Turks Island and Hispaniola, the island consisting of Haiti and the Dominican Republic. Shumkov felt a thrill as they looked at Miami and the Florida coast. Each man knew there were U.S. antisubmarine forces based on the Florida coast at the naval air stations at Jacksonville, Mayport, and Key West; but to see the chart where their new orders were taking them was a thrill beyond imagining. For a Soviet citizen to be out in this environment away from the prying eyes of the Party and away from the cold streets of Polyarny, in this tropical paradise, was almost too much for them to absorb, even though they were beneath the surface of the gleaming sea.

Shumkov thought of his friend Dubivko in his sister boat B-36, and tried to imagine his face as he read this same message. It was enough to give his spirit a significant lift despite the growing heat and discomfort of the submarine's close atmosphere. He handed the message to the exec. "Here, read it aloud to the others."

Frolov took the yellow teletype paper. It was marked "Operational Secret. Modification of Orders."

"The Sixty-ninth Brigade of Submarines will modify track from . . ." There was a series of page and paragraph numbers referring to the original orders, which they had first read after submerging two weeks earlier. "The brigade will deploy in a barrier due north of the entrance to Turks Island Passage and take up combat positions in the Sargasso Sea."

Frolov paused and looked at the captain. What didn't they know? Something was obviously missing. Their previous orders had directed them to make a covert transit to Mariel, Cuba, and make reconnaissance and a hydroacoustic survey en route. Suddenly they were being ordered to combat patrol guarding a narrow sea passage. What was going on? What didn't they know? Shumkov was growing concerned and pondered the chart.

He suddenly had an idea, straightened up, and beckoned to the communicator, Cheprakov. "Come with me to my cabin." The two men walked out of central command down the narrow passageway and stepped into the commanding officer's small stateroom. Shumkov sat down at his desk but didn't invite the younger officer to sit. "Cheprakov, what have your English-language monitors heard lately?"

"Nothing, sir; we haven't been at a shallow enough depth to have an HF antenna up very long."

Shumkov pondered this for a moment. "I want you to violate regulations. I'll keep us at this depth for an extra few hours. Have your men scan the American commercial broadcast frequencies, pick up what they can, and then report back here." He handed a small piece of paper to the communicator. "These are the Voice of America Russian- and English-language broadcast times. Tune in this afternoon and begin to monitor."

Cheprakov was startled. "But sir—"

"I know it's against the rules, and our beloved *zampolit* should report us. But I figured a way to do it: We'll have him listen in with us, tell him its operationally required to know what the hell is going on. This is too serious, to be running blind. We have a nuclear-tipped torpedo here and we've been ordered on a combat patrol. At whom and when do we shoot? We need to know more. Get it?"

The younger officer was astounded, but happy that his commander had taken him in his confidence and ordered him to do something against regulations. He grew excited.

"Aye, Comrade Commander. I'll go aft now and get them on it."

"Good, let me know when you have some Russian language on the Voice of America and I'll summon the *zampolit* and we'll come back to your spaces. Get enough headphones for all three of us to plug in; I don't want the sound to go out on the speakers. Got it?"

"Yes, sir." The young officer disappeared down the passageway. He entered his radio intercept space and with his men surrounding him tuned carefully to the Voice of America shortwave broadcast. Cheprakov put both hands to his earpieces as if to contain the English from spreading too far—and reaching unauthorized ears. He listened intently: An American announcer's voice came in clearly: "Today, the sixteenth of October 1962, the New York Yankees won the fifty-ninth World Series by beating the San Francisco Giants, four games to three!"

MID-OCTOBER 1962
USS *BLANDY*
NEWPORT, RHODE ISLAND

Frank Flanagan read the intelligence summary aloud in radio central. Jim Bassett and I listened. On October 16, Art Lundahl, director of the National Photographic Intelligence Center, briefed President Kennedy on the discovery of the SS-4 missile sites in Cuba. On October 17 navy photoreconnaissance flights revealed SS-5 missile sites west of Havana. The chief of naval operations, Admiral George Anderson, replaced the commander of the Second Fleet with Vice Admiral Alfred G. Ward. Admiral Horatio Rivero replaced Admiral Ward as commander of the Amphibious Force Pacific. On October 18 President Kennedy met with Soviet ambassador Anatoli Dobrynin and Foreign Minister Andrei Gromyko; the latter assured the president that no offensive missiles were in Cuba nor would any be deployed. Kennedy later called him "that lying bastard."

Frank put down the message board, and we filed out of radio central, heading for the wardroom and the evening meal. The stewards had turned the radio on. An announcer read the news: "On 19 October the navy deployed photoreconnaissance F8U-1P Crusader jets to Key West. Attack aircraft carrier the USS *Enterprise* deployed from Norfolk with aircraft from Air Wing 6 aboard." The announcer stated that the carrier was getting under way to avoid Hurricane Ella, but no other ships left Norfolk.

OCTOBER 20–22, 1962
HEADQUARTERS, ATLANTIC FLEET
NORFOLK, VIRGINIA

On October 20 the navy activated Task Force 135, consisting of the attack aircraft carriers *Enterprise* and *Independence* and an underway replenishment group. Shore-based Fleet Air Wings 11 and 32 were flown into Naval Air Station Roosevelt Roads, Puerto Rico. The Atlantic Fleet commander ordered A-3J heavy attack squadrons from Air Wing 6 to be replaced by Marine Corps A-4D Skyhawk Squadron 225, a light attack unit. The Air Force's Air Defense Command deployed several squadrons of F-104 fighters to Key West.

At 3:30 A.M. on October 21, ASW aircraft carrier USS *Essex* departed Guantánamo Bay, Cuba, and activated Hunter-Killer Group Bravo. Her destroyer escorts were ordered to prepare to depart from Newport, Rhode Island.

OCTOBER 20–22, 1962
CAPTAIN ALEKSEI DUBIVKO
B-36, NORTH ATLANTIC

Shortly after sending the signal on the fleet scheduled broadcast for the four submarines of the Sixty-ninth Brigade to curtail the transit to Mariel, the Moscow Main Navy Staff ordered Captain Dubivko to take his *B-36* through Caicos Passage on October 20. Dubivko realized the transit was extremely dangerous, with shallow waters on both sides and U.S. ASW patrol aircraft and destroyers probably covering the entrance and egress routes of the busy passage. Dubivko chose to make the transit using a surface ship for cover. He would lie to and lurk in the side of the narrows to await a large merchant ship and then duck underneath.

Dubivko received word that a large tanker was heading toward the entrance of Caicos Passage, and was relieved to be able to concentrate on placing *B-36* beneath her wake to make the transit masked from acoustic detection. It was a very dangerous tactic, for if they miscalculated at all, they could run smack into the propellers or hull of the tanker. Dubivko and his watch team would be at periscope depth for the entire transit.

Dubivko carefully moved just north of the passage, then eased off to the eastern approach, where he put *B-36* in slow hover, a state of near-neutral buoyancy at periscope depth and waited. Several hours later he detected the ten-thousand-ton tanker approaching Caicos Passage from the north. They used a technique learned from the Northern Fleet covert transit exercise book, which they had practiced during maneuvers but never under real conditions.

Dubivko turned *B-36* onto an intercept course and speed and gently approached the tanker so as to slip ten meters under her to make the entire passage in the turbulence of the tanker's wake. This maneuver guaranteed that the sounds of their screws were masked by the loud cavitation of the tanker's propellers, and helped their own navigator verify that the depth was adequate, trusting in the tanker's choice of the deepest channel. Dubivko and his men realized that the transit of this passage was full of risk. They had already been pursued by several Neptune and Tracker patrol aircraft from the U.S. antisub hunter-killer groups, so he chose this method to make the passage—in the safety of the merchant ship's wake. He took the submarine to a position just north and slightly east of Caicos Passage and settled at a good depth just below the slight temperature thermocline, and waited. The most nerve-racking part of any patrol is waiting when you're not busy. As they sat there, Dubivko began to imagine all the things that could go wrong. What if they were detected by one of the aircraft and pursued by one of the many destroyers they heard over the past weeks? There were hundreds of them around, and they had not expected that. Dubivko had his radio intercept operators monitoring the U.S. traffic, but all they learned was that there was a huge operation under way and that the Americans were very alert and active. Not very encouraging! Dubivko could not fathom what had transpired to cause such a large reaction. Had one or more of their submarine brigade been detected and already forced to surface? Were they already at a state of war? Why had there been no information on the regular submarine communication broadcast schedule from Moscow? Dubivko was full of questions and began to fear for their safety for the first time.

"Range to the contact?"

"Three thousand meters, sir, bearing zero five zero."

"Course and speed?"

"Course two two zero at twelve knots."

"Very well, give me an intercept course at nine knots."

"Aye, sir, intercept course two six zero will cross his track in twenty minutes."

"Very well, we'll make the intercept at sixty meters depth, then ascend to fifteen meters, and take station on her stern, matching her speed."

The night was calm and the visibility good. Dubivko grew tense and noticed that the rest of the watch also had a serious but relaxed look.

"Zhukov, take control for the intercept; I'll take us up for the transit." Dubivko remembered during the training exercise in the Barents that one of the boats from another brigade had slid under the hull of a merchantman, followed for several hours, and for some reason drove right into the merchant's propeller, which had sliced neatly into her sail, causing a near-disastrous flooding into central command. The boat had managed to return to Polyarny, but only after emergency repairs at sea. Had the weather been worse, they may not have made it. Dubivko shuddered at the thought. They were more than five thousand miles from home waters, and if they were to suffer a casualty, he wasn't sure where they could go for assistance. They knew there were no support ships yet in Mariel, and it was a long steam home.

"Range to the tanker, fifteen hundred meters; time to intercept, twelve minutes."

"Zhukov, take us in and I'll take over at a thousand meters." Dubivko went to his cabin, took his foul-weather jacket off a hook, and washed his face quickly with tepid water. The water situation aboard was grim. Their distillers had a very limited capacity to make freshwater. They kept the distillers on the line whenever they could, but at times when silence was necessary, they had to secure the loud plants. When they snorted they kept them on the line, but could produce only about five liters per hour. That wasn't much, and since the sea temperature was so high, their freshwater was always lukewarm and foulsmelling. It was pure enough to drink, but hardly refreshing. Although the temperature had cooled down after dark, it was still hot and humid in the boat. The temperature inside had been one of the worst factors ever since they had passed south of Bermuda into the Sargasso Sea. The only times they could get the temperature down was when running on the surface with the main trunk hatch open, and if calm enough, with the after hatch in compartment seven and all the connecting hatches open, a breeze would surge through the boat. It was strictly against regulations to steam with so many hatches open, since watertight integrity was sacrificed, and any sudden swells could wash into the after torpedo room very quickly, shorting out the electrical circuit boards. This patrol, however, had been replete with unorthodox actions, and in these unusual conditions Dubivko relied on common sense and pure ingenuity to survive.

Zhukov stood calmly watching the depth gauge and glanced at the small plot being kept on the small sheet of Plexiglas by the assistant navigator. The plot showed that two contacts, both heading on slightly southwesterly courses, were slowly merging. Every few minutes Zhukov ordered a single sweep with the surface search radar on low power. In these conditions it was possible to paint the target at short range while still risking electromagnetic detection by the U.S. destroyers and aircraft. Once they arrived beneath the tanker, the only check would be the sound of the tanker's screws, which, at that range, would be very loud and show up as a wide wedge of sound on the sonarscope. The only really accurate measure would be visually through the periscope, which Captain Dubivko would monitor himself from the first level inside the navigation bridge above the central command in the sail.

"Range to tanker, one thousand meters, sir, coming to fifteen meters depth." Zhukov spoke smoothly, which gave the captain a great amount of pride and confidence.

"Range, eight hundred meters, sir, bow planes up ten degrees come to fifteen meters. Stand by the main trunk hatch."

Two seamen darted up the ladder, one on each side toward the first hatch. They put their hands on the wheel to undog the hatch when they heard the command from Zhukov.

"Passing thirty meters, sir . . . twenty-five . . . twenty." At twenty meters the seamen began to turn the hatch dog wheel, and water cascaded into the command center. Despite the fact that they all expected the water to spill in, it was always a shock when it began. Water pouring in from any source, expected or not, was an unnerving experience aboard any submarine.

The water subsided to a drip, and the two seamen darted up through the trunk. There they stopped and made ready to spin the next hatch wheel open. They paused until they heard the depth readout by the planesman as fifteen meters, then spun the wheel and disappeared into the wet navigation bridge. Dubivko then followed the two seamen up the trunk; behind him followed the assistant navigator and another lookout. Zhukov came last and passed the control to the captain.

"Range?"

"Directly above us, sir," the sonar operator sang out.

"Roger, turns for eleven knots."

The helmsman repeated the order. They all watched and waited for the contact to pass overhead as they gradually increased speed to match the tanker's speed. At this rate they should slip neatly beneath the large hull within seconds. Dubivko knew there was a tendency to be sucked a little too close to the hull because of the vacuum caused by the surface effect of the water passing beneath the hull of the tanker, so he was careful to maintain the submarine's distance just below that level so as not to bounce upward toward the hull.

Now he could hear the thrashing of the tanker's propeller without earphones. It sounded directly overhead. Dubivko waited, watching Zhukov. Then as the latter heard that the range had opened to a hundred meters, he nodded to the captain and gave the signal. Dubivko responded by depressing the switch on the periscope handle engaging the servomechanism, and it began to rise. He swung the scope to look forward, squinted while gently swinging the handles in a semiarc, while searching for the tanker's stern light. The light would be shielded, so as only to be visible through the prescribed arc for navigation accuracy, so if they were positioned too far to either side of the cone, the light would not be visible.

Dubivko stared through the optics but saw no light. He tensed. It had to be there! They were at exactly fifteen meters depth, and the ship was ahead—he could see the white foam of the wake in the periscope, but still no stern light.

"Right five degrees rudder," he called out, his voice no doubt revealing the growing tension. He watched carefully as the submarine's heading swung slowly to the right on the gyro repeater. Still no light! Dubivko paused, then quickly ordered, "Shift your rudder."

"The rudder is left five degrees, sir."

The bow swung left, and he shouted, "Steady; meet her!" He spotted the glow of the stern light just ahead at a level about three meters above the waterline. The whole relative picture then came into focus. Dubivko could see the ship's main deck, the white stern light on a stanchion on center of the stern, and the top of the propeller just breaking the surface. The tanker was not fully loaded; hence the screw was breaking the surface causing an increased turbulence, even better to mask the signature of the submarine. In this position a patrol aircraft would not be able to detect B-36, either acoustically with a sonobuoy, due to the noise of the turbulence, or magnetically, because of the larger electromagnetic signature field of the steel tanker. The odds were that even a destroyer at close range would not be able to detect their periscope, since it was protruding through the wake so close to the tanker that it also would be masked.

"Steady on course two two zero, turns for twelve knots."

Now all Dubivko needed was that the tanker steer a steady course and keep the same speed; any variations would make it necessary for him to adjust accordingly. So far it looked good. The merchant ship appeared to have a steady helmsman and hadn't varied more than a degree or two each side of his base course; but he could at any time.

Dubivko was pleased. It had gone well, but he was still uncertain of the identity of the ship, although it didn't really matter. For all he knew it might be an American, but it was immaterial. It was still before midnight local time and they had plenty of time to complete the transit prior to first light, provided the tanker did not slow, or worse, stop. That would be a setback. They could still lurk beneath the hulking tanker, but the sound masking would not be nearly as complete. If they slowed too much an aircraft or a surface ship might be able, with active sonar, to detect them beneath the tanker—but not likely. Dubivko would hope for the best and play it by ear.

In the meantime, the stress of keeping the submarine stationed in the tanker's wake was a good way to make the time fly. Dubivko was exhilarated by the feeling of accomplishment, and felt more secure each time he looked out at the stern light winking in the spray.

Then suddenly, when all seemed to be going perfectly, the tanker slowed. Dubivko first noticed the sound of the screw beat slowing. "What the devil? . . . Turns for ten knots, eight . . . five." B-36 slowed to match the tanker's speed; then suddenly the stern light began to swing to the left. The tanker was turning abruptly.

"Zhukov, quick, anything on the plot to cause a left turn?" Dubivko sounded tense again, although he tried his best never to give away his doubts and fears through the tension in his voice, but it was extremely difficult to remain cool in such a situation.

"No, sir," Zhukov answered, "we're still in the passage, but she can't proceed long on this easterly heading or she'll run aground."

"What's the depth?" Zhukov had the sonarman take a fathometer reading.

"Sir, depth matches the chart, two hundred meters, nearest shoals two thousand meters to the east. If she stays on this course and speed she'll go aground in four minutes."

Dubivko thought quickly. They were about to lose their cover. If the tanker was pulling to the side of the passage for repairs he would have to anchor, and that would leave B-36 with nowhere to go. They'd either have to risk detection or stop and sit below the tanker on the bottom and wait until she got under way again. Suddenly they heard a loud staccato sound.

"What's that, sonar?"

"Sir, she's dropping anchor. Depth to the bottom here is now is less than fifty meters. She's probably going to make some repairs."

Dubivko swore softly. It was near midnight and their covering shadow was now stopping for some reason. "All stop," he ordered.

They watched and listened. "Zhukov, check the zenith navigation scope and watch for aircraft." The zenith scope, also called the navigation periscope, was below, in the command center. Zhukov slid quickly down the ladder into the center, raised the scope, and took several scans of the heavens.

"No aircraft lights, sir. No electronic emissions."

"Roger, Zhukov. Take us down to the bottom. We'll just sit tight in the mud and listen."

They studied the chart of the passage. Not half a mile from the tanker there was shallow water of about twenty meters. They quickly calculated the tide and then climbed back up to the navigation bridge. They could sit on the bottom at that depth, shut down, and observe all around by scope while their escort did whatever she was doing, and they would be relatively safe. The long vigil began.

B-36 still had nearly a full charge on the batteries. Ninety percent, the chief had responded. They were actually shallow enough to snorkel from this depth, but it would be a dead giveaway. The tanker crew might detect their exhaust fumes. They waited.

The long hours ticked by. Zhukov, the exec, and Dubivko spelled one another at the periscope. How fortunate, Dubivko thought, to have officers he trusted as not only superb communicators and second in command, but also as equally good ship handlers. He trusted Zhukov as a son, and sometimes wondered what he could have done without him.

Zhukov was at the periscope. It was about 3:00 A.M. local time. It was still too early for the first signs of dawn, but suddenly Zhukov stiffened. "Sir, a contact directly to the south. Two faint white lights." He waited. "Sir, it's approaching the tanker."

"Bridge, sonar, hydrophone effects bearing one eight zero, twin screws, sir."

"That's the contact," Zhukov whispered. Dubivko looked through the scope. He was torn between getting off the bottom and making some movement. He felt helpless sitting like that in the mud, but he restrained himself. Why not stay this way? Minimum sound, no telltale machinery noise. They could hold where they were.

As the contact grew closer they were able to positively identify it acoustically as a destroyer, certainly American. Perhaps they were checking out the tanker. Why would a ten-thousand-ton tanker just suddenly stop and pull to the side of Caicos Passage? No doubt the U.S. ship was curious, too. They watched as the destroyer came within a mile of the tanker, then slowed. As they watched, a signal lamp began to blink on the U.S. destroyer.

"Alpha, Alpha." Zhukov read aloud softly. Dubivko marveled at how fast the communicator could read flashing light, in this case the U.S. signal for "What ship?" They were using the international code of signals. It was easy for Zhukov to read. Dubivko also knew Morse code but not nearly at the speed of his communicator.

"Watch, sir, there'll be a response soon." It was difficult to observe the tanker from their position. All they could read was the destroyer's signal light. The tanker's signal lamp was on the upper level behind the bridge, but they could just make out the glow of the lamp as it slowly beat out an answer. It was unreadable from their position. Then feeling despair settle again, Dubivko wondered what would happen next.

Just when he was beginning to feel lost, Zhukov began to translate a long, deliberate message on the light sent from the destroyer. "They're giving them a radio frequency, 343.8. That must be UHF." Quickly Zhukov called the radio intercept station in compartment four and passed his intercept operators the radio frequency assignment picked off of the U.S. destroyer's flashing-light message. Within a few minutes they called back.

"Bridge, radio, the American has come up in clear voice on the frequency. The tanker is a Norwegian bound for Galveston. They suffered a boiler casualty and are in the process of lighting off a spare boiler. The American requested to know if the Norwegian needed assistance. The tanker said no, thank you. It appears the destroyer is pulling away."

Dubivko was relieved; they watched as the U.S. destroyer circled and then retired to the north through the passage. B-36 remained aground on the sandy bottom until around noon the next day, when the tanker began to belch black smoke.

"Bridge, sonar, tanker is taking in her anchor. She appears to be getting under way." Dubivko watched as the tanker swung back to the south.

"Stand by to get under way. All ahead slow, turns for three knots." *B-36* swayed slightly as they worked free of the mud. Dubivko retracted the periscope; they were now relying solely on following the hydrophone effects of the tanker. As the tanker slipped out into the main channel, Dubivko drove the submarine to fifteen meters and nudged gently into the wake and gradually matched the speed of the tanker. He was satisfied to take a visual sweep on the periscope every few minutes just to confirm they were on station and still following the tanker precisely. When they were about 150 miles north of Haiti, they broke off, turned west, and slowed. They would wait out the remainder of the daylight and surface to charge again after dark.

"By the way," Dubivko asked Zhukov, "what was the name of the Norwegian?"

"Sir, I heard the American mention the name *Gretel* before they left. Could be the ship was called *Gretel.* In any case, it was fun hiding under her skirt, wasn't it, sir?"

After his careful and tedious transit of the passage, Dubivko was directed to reverse course immediately, retransit Caicos Passage to the north, and proceed to a patrol station to the northeast and remain covert, conducting surveillance of U.S. fleet units while avoiding the U.S. hunter-killer ASW groups. The patient Dubivko, unhappy after his long and suspenseful transit south, waited for another chance and then repeated his transit, this time northward beneath a Polish-flag refrigerator ship.

"Might as well make full use of the Warsaw Alliance," Zhukov said.

While patrolling in the Sargasso Sea in their assigned area, *B-36* ran on economy electric drive by day, and at snorkel depth on two diesels by night to recharge batteries. They crept to an area about two hundred miles south of Bermuda, where they operated for about twelve days. Several times in this area they detected hydroacoustic signals from U.S. destroyers and ASW aircraft, but managed to evade detection by running silently, dodging their search patterns, and sitting quietly as the hunters sped past. Dubivko's agile hydroacoustic technicians and radio intelligence intercept operators were able, working at various depths, using a mix of different antennas, to detect and identify most of the surface ships while they searched in vain for *B-36.*

All the while *B-36* was evading U.S. naval forces, Dubivko was under the impression that his good friend Nikolai Shumkov in *B-130* was just a few miles to the west of his assigned area, conducting similar

Captain Dubivko and Lieutenant
Zhukov in Polyarny, September
1962 (courtesy Yuri Zhukov)

maneuvers. The Main Navy Staff orders to them on October 20 had assigned Shumkov's *B-130* a sector just to the west of Dubivko. There had been no orders from Brigade Commander Agafonov since their entry into the broad Atlantic area.

The communications officer, Lieutenant Zhukov, was showing extraordinary initiative and often spent hours and days without sleep in the stuffy confines of the radio intercept cubicle in compartment four. He had achieved remarkable success reading the tactical voice communications of the U.S. hunter-killer destroyers and aircraft. By carefully triangulating their radio transmissions, Zhukov, Dubivko, and the other watch officers were able to keep tabs on the destroyers and remain on the edge of the hunters' search patterns. The sonar conditions were so good for the hunters, with no layer to conceal Dubivko, that *B-36* operated mostly at fewer than a hundred meters, often ascending to thirty meters to put up an antenna for Zhukov to use his valuable skills to keep them undetected. The greater the depth, the less effective their radio intercept and hydroacoustic analysis was for predicting the Americans' search patterns.

ASW aircraft from the carriers *Essex* and *Randolph* had been difficult adversaries, and Dubivko worried whenever the S2F Trackers and sonar-dipping Sea King helicopters flew nearby. To *B-36* the long-range patrol aircraft were the most serious threats, especially the newer P3 Orions, which dropped precise patterns of sonobuoys and monitored them for hours. Several times Dubivko had been astonished when coming to periscope depth for a peek, thinking a P3 had departed the area after laying several buoy patterns more than twelve hours earlier. He was astounded to observe the same P3 still orbiting over his pattern with two engines feathered, at times remaining on station for an incredible thirteen hours. He had argued with Zhukov that he must have been mistaken and that no turboprop aircraft could remain over water for such a long period, but Zhukov proved himself accurate by identifying the call sign from the patrol squadron out of Jacksonville, Florida, as the same P3 that arrived a full thirteen hours earlier.

Zhukov also noticed that U.S. pilots were extremely careless with their communications, and often in the heat of prosecuting a possible submarine contact they departed from the lightly coded terminology and returned to uncovered, clear UHF and VHF voice communications, which Zhukov and his radio intercept operators copied without difficulty. Zhukov found that the aircraft carriers *Essex* and *Randolph* were the worst offenders of radio discipline, and resorted often to clear communications. When they were launching or recovering airplanes, talkers on the carriers prattled on and on in barely disguised conversation. Zhukov rotated his men when operating near the carriers so each had the opportunity to listen to the chatter on the crowded nets, which were used for directing the aircraft in landing and holding patterns. It was amusing for the Russians to hear the pilots using nicknames and their abbreviated call signs to conceal their identity. Any half-witted intercept operator could easily pick out the various pilots by listening to their talk. Some of the Russian operators, after listening to the same voices for days and nights on end, placed bets among themselves on which pilots were flying in which aircraft, based on their unique voices and communication techniques. It was great sport and kept their minds from stagnating during the many hours of continuous watch standing.

Zhukov and his operators also tuned in to regular high-frequency and shortwave radio broadcasts, including Voice of America and BBC, which they monitored attentively. Not only was the music terrific, but also they were able to fill in the information gap that existed between the curt orders received sporadically with little or no explanation or background from the Moscow Main Navy Staff on the VLF fleet broadcast schedules. These orders merely told them in abbreviated and highly encrypted text to proceed here, patrol there, and curiously to curtail their covert transit to Mariel. Dubivko often went aft himself to compartment four to listen directly to the more aggressive Russian-language programs broadcast by Radio Liberty and the Voice of America. These newscasts and analyses were filled with vitriolic language and propaganda. Zhukov and his operators enjoyed the antiquated Russian language used by the Voice of America announcers, who were obviously of Russian or Ukrainian origin and who had been away from the current language in use in the modern Soviet Union. These broadcasters frequently used phrases long obsolete — and provided a welcome source of amusement for the Russian monitors aboard the boat.

By piecing together the news broadcasts, Dubivko came to realize that the Americans had reacted sharply to Operation *Anadyr*, and to the stationing of strategic weapons in Cuba. According to some broadcasts it was apparent that U.S. armed forces were making serious preparations to conduct landings in Cuba. They also heard that Soviet special envoy Anastas Mikoyan was in Cuba and then Washington, carrying out negotiations with the Americans regarding the possible compromise of the secret plan *Anadyr*, and to ease the rapidly accelerating tensions between the two countries.

Zhukov mentioned to Dubivko that he heard the Americans were setting up camps in Florida to receive Soviet prisoners of war. "It would surely be better weather there than in Polyarny this winter," one of the intercept operators commented. "These khaki shorts and tropical shirts will go nicely in Florida." The political officer quickly told him not to utter such unspeakable things.

The entire B-36 crew was now aware of the U.S. naval blockade, and came to realize that probably 85 percent of the U.S. Atlantic Fleet was arrayed above them on a wartime footing.

OCTOBER 20, 1962
CAPTAIN RYURIK KETOV
COMMANDING OFFICER, *B-4*
NORWEGIAN SEA

Captain Second Rank Ryurik Ketov was an experienced submariner, the submarine *B-4* already his second command. His first had been the medium-range diesel submarine Project 613 (NATO Whiskey class) *S-200*. He had made two patrols off the western coast of the United

Kingdom aboard that submarine after a fleeting-up promotion from executive officer to commanding officer. Later he was selected to take command of one of the newer long-range diesels of the Project 641 (Foxtrot class) boats. *B-4* was commissioned in 1961 and had the unusual honor of carrying a name, *Chelyabinskaya Komsomolets*. No one really knew the significance of that name, but no doubt it was in honor of some Party event in that eastern Siberian town. Ketov only knew that it was a great privilege to be selected for that command.

On October 20, when all four submarines from Captain Agafonov's brigade received the orders to curtail their transits to Mariel and to take combat patrols in the Sargasso Sea, Ketov's *B-4* was just due west of Dubivko in *B-36*. *B-4*'s transit from the north had been uneventful until they ran into the leading edge of Hurricane Rose.

The waves were incredibly high. Ketov had followed the procedure of running submerged by day and on the surface at night to charge the batteries and vent the boat. It soon became so rough it was a real challenge to be on or near the surface at all, but they continued as ordered like good sailors. One night during the height of the storm *B-4* received a distress signal in Russian from an unknown source.

"Comrade Commander," Radio Intercept Officer Vladimir Pronin called from his cubicle in compartment four, "we have one of our merchant ships calling for help!"

"Where?" Ketov asked.

"From the signal strength he's quite near. But his bearing is all over the place. It's so rough I'm having trouble getting a good cut on his signal." It was well after midnight local time and they were bouncing around as usual, trying to charge batteries with two diesels on the line. Ketov's exec came up to the bridge cockpit, where the commander was strapped in with the watch officer and one lookout. It was almost impossible to climb the ladder from central command without getting bashed on the hatch or the inside of the trunk. Part of the time the men crawled on all fours; part of the time they hung by the ladder rungs.

The exec was in a panic. "Captain," he said, "we've got to do something; we have a Morflot ship due east of us who has lost power and is wallowing. I reckon he's about six miles east." He looked at Ketov as the waves crashed over the cockpit, eyes wide and looking disturbed. It was all they could do just to hang on and steer south; the seas were beating them from the northeast.

"I know, I heard Lieutenant Pronin's report. But I'm afraid there's not a lot we can do," Ketov said. The exec looked at him, shocked.

"But sir, surely we must move in close to see if we can help them. If they abandon ship in this they won't stand a chance."

Ketov looked out at the waves as they rose to the crest of a huge swell, then shuddered at the top and began to descend into the trough. The scud blew from the top of the waves, cutting the visibility down to just a few meters on all sides. "If we got close to him we'd be in great danger of hitting him. I have very little control over our heading at this slow speed. There is absolutely nothing we can do!"

The exec was silent; he just stared out into the spray while he held onto the sides of the cockpit. He was a sensitive man, and Ketov knew it cut him deeply to hear the distress signal and not respond. "Sir, at least we can come around to the east and let them know we are here, fire a flare or something, so if they abandon ship we can pick them up."

It was out of the question. Ketov did not want to be short with his *starpom.* There was no way out of the dilemma; he recalled the words of Admiral Fokin during their briefing aboard the submarine tender *Dmitri Galkan* just days before they sailed. It had been the most memorable thing he said; covert transit was the most important item of their mission. Ketov wasn't sure he understood why, but there was certainly a good reason. So somehow he had to console his exec.

"I've thought about it already. We're prohibited by our orders from calling any attention to ourselves; we must remain silent. We can do nothing; our transit must remain covert."

Ketov figured it was a merchant ship not too far away that was apparently taking on water and in serious trouble. It was agonizing to listen to the SOS and not be able to help. Remaining covert prohibited them from going to anyone's aid. Even if they had been allowed to assist, it is doubtful they would have been able to do a thing, the surface was so rough. They were barely able to keep their footing even during the periods they were at snorting depth. It was an awful storm. The height of the waves, Ketov recalls, reached seventeen meters. The swells were hitting them on the port beam from due east now at a period of roughly seven to nine seconds, which is about as bad as it could be for the submarine's length and beam. They were rolling like a cork.

The exec was silent and merely gazed out into the scud. After a few minutes he bolted below, mumbling something into the wind. It hurt a great deal to keep steaming past countrymen who were in distress, but

Ketov would not only have been hazarding his own boat and crew, but also would have been in violation of his orders to keep their transit secret. They were even prohibited from sending the ship an answer on the distress frequency. Ketov was in a quandary and felt sick to his stomach. Then he had an idea.

He picked up the sound-powered phone and dialed the CCP. "Get me the exec!"

There was a pause, and the exec came on the line. "Look," Ketov said, "get back there with Pronin, tell him to relay the distress call on our own high-frequency fleet common—send it two or three times and then get off the air. It's the least we can do. The chances someone will get a cut on our transmission are slight. Do not repeat it more than three times."

"Aye, Captain." The exec was greatly relieved and satisfied that they were at least doing something. It was a terrible feeling to just go on their transit without lifting a finger to help. Ketov was violating his orders but knew that chances were no one would ever know who they were, and they would be submerged and well on their way out of the area in a few hours. So they did it, and all felt better. The code of all seamen, to render assistance in time of danger, was a code that meant a great deal to them, and they would take a calculated risk to render some assistance. They never learned the identity of that ship nor whether the crew survived. They only hoped that their small sacrifice was not in vain. Ketov never heard a word against his action and, of course, never entered it into his daily log; to do so would have invited an investigation and no doubt censure for risking the compromise of their transit. In retrospect, Ketov is glad he did it, even if it had been a foreign ship, and not Soviet. He said he would do the same again tomorrow under identical circumstances.

While *B-4* ran on the surface charging batteries, the heavy waves damaged the weather hatch over the after torpedo room, and they began taking a great deal of water into the hull. Ketov was in the cockpit with a lookout and signalman and the watch officer. They were all strapped in, so as not to be swept away in the swells. At one moment the waves crashed overhead, thrusting the sail completely underwater, then seconds later flung them upward, so high they could see nothing but the gray clouds. Then they fell back again in the foaming scud. It was certainly the worst weather Ketov ever saw, but they continued on.

For a while Ketov was forced to change course to the east to diminish the heavy rolls they were taking. He feared that the water they were shipping through the sprung hatch aft might cause an electrical short that could ultimately lead to a total loss of power, and that would have been a disaster.

The hours seemed endless as they tossed and corkscrewed through the foam and the swells. Finally, after nearly six hours of the constant bashing, the watch officer informed Ketov that the chief mechanic advised that they had 98 percent charge, and in half an hour they could submerge into relative peace and calm. The minutes dragged by and finally Ketov gave the order to clear the bridge. They submerged despite the leaking outer hatch. Their damage control party did some shoring work on the hatch, and it stopped shipping water. However, they had to continue at no deeper than thirty meters depth; any deeper and the hatch immediately began leaking again. At thirty meters depth the swells were barely noticeable, and they were able to rest.

The storm continued for about three days, during which their advance southward was slowed considerably. Ketov would try to make up the distance later. As soon as they steamed south of the Iceland/Shetlands/Faeroes gap, they began intercepting long-range patrol aircraft communications from the U.S. patrol squadrons based at Keflavik, Iceland. They found it rather simple to follow the communications of the P2V Neptunes as they came out looking for them. Ketov was somewhat of a cynic, but he was certain that the Americans had advance warning and knew their track. It became obvious when the long-range American P2Vs and sometimes the British Shackelton surveillance aircraft patrolled up and down their projected base course, which was exactly 225 degrees true. Their track took them directly toward the Antilles. It seemed to Ketov that they had been detected far earlier; he guessed by the U.S. passive acoustic arrays he knew were planted in the northern Atlantic. He had no idea how accurate they were.

As they continued through the Sargasso Sea the conditions changed drastically. While hiding below the thermocline layer from the ever-present aircraft, they noted that the outside water temperature rose significantly. As a result their limited air-conditioning systems failed and the temperature rose and became unbearable in many compartments. The temperature reached 37 degrees Centigrade in the engine room, while in Ketov's cabin it reached 40 degrees. The only officer who slept in the forward torpedo room was the special security officer for the atomic torpedo, who slept right next to the weapon. The others who normally berthed there sought other bunks throughout the boat despite the heat; they just did not like sleeping with that weapon.

Ketov's chief mechanic tried to retain three and a half to four tons of freshwater aboard, but their desalinization plant was poor. They rationed the drinking water to one glass a day per man, plus one glass of red wine at evening meals. Due to the high seawater temperature, they were able to distill only about ten liters of freshwater per day, and the bulk of that went to preparation of meals. With seventy-eight men, three toilets, and two showers aboard, the personal hygiene problems were horrendous. The health of all crewmen was seriously impaired by the constant heat and humidity, and continuous exposure to poor air and diesel and chlorine fumes. Most of the crew developed open ulcers and painful rashes on their skin.

When they were on the surface the crew used the toilet and salt-water shower in the sail between the navigation bridge and the central command post. In calm water Ketov allowed the crew to bathe in the sea a few at a time, but only under strict supervision, since they were on constant alert to submerge quickly on the detection of aircraft. Although *B-4* could hold thirty-six tons of freshwater on board for cooking, drinking, and washing, they rarely reached that level. The single freshwater shower was in compartment six, with a second toilet. A third toilet was in compartment three, for the central command post watch standers and officers only. The freshwater shower was used as sparingly as possible; by the book each man was allowed two freshwater showers per week, but that was unrealistic in these latitudes. The ship's medical officer dispensed disposable towels daily until he ran out; then each morning he made the rounds and gave out cotton balls doused in alcohol for a refreshing wash. Many crewmen chose to suck the alcohol out of the cotton instead of washing, which was ridiculous. Ketov and the chief mechanic had washbasins in their cabins, and there were several other such basins—in sick bay and in the galley—but those were guarded closely so no one abused the rationing of freshwater. When the freshwater ran low they used seawater for cooking. Potatoes, for example, were not bad cooked in seawater, but there was the danger that the use of salt water would increase thirst considerably and merely worsen the water situation.

A crewman of Ketov's *B-4* preparing to bathe in the sea (courtesy © 1998. Jasper Communications Pty Ltd. Sydney, Australia)

Except for those men on watch, when they were on the surface, one additional person was allowed in the open bridge cockpit for fresh air or a cigarette, but given the austere conditions, Ketov relaxed that to an additional three off-watch personnel. Eventually, when conditions aboard worsened, the captain expanded that number to five additional men aloft at any time in addition to the watch.

As the situation grew more tense, Ketov felt they should ascend to copy broadcasts every four to six hours, in case Moscow would send them new directions regarding the rules of engagement or the use of the special weapon. They had been ordered that in special circumstances they should be ready to copy new orders for a change in the operation order and the rules of engagement. Naturally, to steam so shallow opened the possibility that they might be detected, tracked, and perhaps attacked if they went to a shooting war, so they had to comply. The times of the broadcasts were at midnight and noon Moscow time, or 5:00 A.M. and 5:00 P.M. local time. If the readiness conditions changed, Moscow would change the timing of the broadcasts, so the submarines were obliged not to miss one of the regularly scheduled broadcasts during which headquarters would post the new times, if they increased defense readiness.

B-4 continued to track southward and made up for the time lost due to the heavy weather in the North Atlantic. Despite a few close calls with U.S. patrol planes, they remained undetected.

October 22, 1962
USS Blandy
Newport, Rhode Island

The pleasant autumn nights ashore for USS *Blandy* crewmen ended abruptly on Monday, October 22. *Blandy* had been out in the local Newport operating area conducting gunnery calibration and a swing ship drill to compensate the ship's compass. We steamed in and were alongside Pier One by 3:00 P.M. Liberty call went an hour later. For some reason Bob Briner and the XO had made all officers, chiefs, and leading petty officers leave their recall telephone numbers with the officer of the deck on the quarterdeck before going ashore. The ship had a formal recall bill, but it had not been updated in months. It turned out that the two officers had been farsighted.

Flanagan and the usual group were planning to go ashore after dinner. I was at the Servmart with two of the electronic technicians from my division, picking up spare parts for the SPA-4 radar repeaters in the combat information center and the open bridge. The Servmart was a huge supply center for off-the-shelf consumable spare parts and was up the hill from the destroyer piers. The lady behind the counter in the large hangarlike building was logging our purchases when the phone rang. She picked up the receiver and looked stunned.

"Okay, I'll make the announcement." The clerk walked over to a mike in the large room and announced, "All personnel from the destroyers at Piers One and Two are directed to return to your ships immediately as ordered by the duty officer of the Cruiser Destroyer Command."

"Okay, Chief, tally up and let's go."

The three of us left the store and jumped into my blue 1959 VW Beetle and drove down the hill to Pier One. "Can't park on the pier, sir," Chief Tyler said. "The shore patrol ticketed me yesterday for leaving my car for ten minutes just to pick up some laundry for the base cleaners."

"I'll risk it. We'll bring the parts to the ship and I'll move the car back to the parking lot later." I drove to the end of the pier where *Blandy* was moored inboard in a nest of four Destroyer Squadron 24 destroyers. One advantage of being flagship is that it gave us the pier-side berth. I left the car parked hastily at the end of the pier with the keys in the ignition. The three of us filed across the brow onto the ship.

Aboard the ship, chaos reigned. The XO was arching all over, stores were expected in half an hour, and the fuel barge was alongside the nest, already topping off all the destroyers with fuel. Two wives of M Division engineers pulled up in an old Chevy as I walked up the brow. They looked in a panic. I recognized Peggy Cardwell, leading Chief Cardwell's wife. She got out of the car and came over to the brow. Just as I turned to ask if I could help her, I saw Captain Kelley's car, his orange-and-white Edsel, driving down the pier. Kelley's wife, Grace, was driving; she stopped, and the captain got out.

The quarterdeck ship's bell rang: Ding-ding, ding-ding, "*Blandy*, arriving," sang out on all topside 1MC speakers. I walked quickly up the brow and watched the captain. He kissed Grace, who was sitting in the driver's seat, then walked over to Chief Cardwell's wife. There was a conversation I couldn't hear; then I saw the captain reach for his wallet. The chief's wife shook her head. Then I heard Kelley bellow up to the quarterdeck.

"Get Chief Cardwell to the quarterdeck on the double, his wife needs the car keys!"

It was typical Kelley. He cut his farewell time short with his wife, Grace, and concerned himself with the problem of one of the crew wives. Two months later, when we returned, my VW was still there, covered with a coating of black soot; on the windshield flapped a parking ticket so badly weathered by the months of rain, wind, and snow that it was barely readable. The keys were still in the ignition.

Ensign Dan Davidson, junior ensign aboard, was at home after the ship had returned from the local operation area, when the call came. Just married, Dan was planning to cook his first meal for Edie, who was still at school, teaching. Dan worked hard at his stuffed peppers, setting the table and getting candles ready. It was an important first for their marriage, and he enjoyed the new domestic life. Just as Edie walked in the door, thrilled at the sight of the table set, the smell of the stuffed peppers giving their new home a comfortable and cozy feeling, the telephone rang.

"Yes, this is Mr. Davidson. Oh, good evening, Commander Lester." It was the exec.

"Return to the ship immediately, Dan, we're on two-hour notice to get under way."

"Yes, sir, ah . . . we were just sitting down to dinner, sir. Could I eat first and then be right down to the ship?"

"Godamnit, Davidson, when I tell you to do something, you do it now, understand?"

Dan left the house, and didn't see Edie for more than a month. He never got to eat his stuffed peppers.

❖

That evening the crew listened to President Kennedy's address to the nation at 8:00 P.M. We watched the president on the TV set in the wardroom while stores were being loaded aboard *Blandy*. His words hit us like lightning.

MONDAY EVENING
OCTOBER 22, 1962
THE WHITE HOUSE

President John F. Kennedy began:

> Good evening, my fellow citizens. This government, as promised, has maintained the closest surveillance of the Soviet military buildup on the island of Cuba. . . .To halt this offensive buildup, a strict quarantine on all offensive military equipment under shipment to Cuba is being initiated. All ships of any kind bound for Cuba from whatever nation or port will, if found to contain cargoes of offensive weapons, be turned back.[5]

OCTOBER 23, 1962
USS *BLANDY*
NEWPORT, RHODE ISLAND

The crewmen who had left the ship earlier the day before on liberty had been recalled, and we had struggled to get supplies aboard as fast as possible. There had been a mass of activity on the pier, and Commander Lester had tried his best to keep it organized.

Our squadron sortied shortly after 9:00 P.M. Monday evening with sister ship USS *Sperry*, whose officers, having come directly to the ship from a formal mess night at the officers' club, still wore their mess jackets, black ties, and gold navy cummerbunds on the bridge. We steamed out of Newport, past Block Island, and into the black Atlantic night, turned south, and proceeded through the darkness, feeling uncomfortably tense.

We did not know exactly what we were to do other than what we heard the president tell us just before we sailed. The next morning at quarters the XO told us that a top-secret operation order was coming section by section over the teletype; as acting communications officer I was responsible for decoding the missive letter by letter in the close and confined crypto operator's compartment. In those days, such decoding was a slow process. The operation order consisted of a large volume of material more than two hundred pages long. The high classification made it impossible to send to the fleet on the normal secure teletype system, so I spent the next days in the tiny room poking out the text word after word as the world around me spun in an ever-spiraling crisis.

The ship had not been provided any interim instructions about what we were expected to do on a blockade. Thus, typically, we formed our own plan: While proceeding to Cuban waters we would screen all ships we encountered, determine their destination, and if bound for Cuba stop and search for contraband. On board *Blandy* we manufactured our own method of identifying contraband, based simply on our interpretation of what materials would assist a Cuban war effort. The effort dominated our wardroom conversations. The XO listed guns, tanks, missiles, and explosives as clearly contraband. Oil, gasoline, diesel fuel, and police uniforms were questions. Frank Flanagan wanted to stop and seize all ships carrying sugar and rum. Then the exec exploded, claiming we weren't sufficiently serious about this matter, and stormed out of the wardroom. Meanwhile, I typed away at all hours of the night and day in the stultifying confines of the tiny crypto shack as the long op order finally took form.

Our business at hand was to prepare for searching ships we would encounter and possible seizure of weapons. The weapons officer, Jim Bassett, was in charge of forming and preparing the boarding party that would execute the search-and-seizure operations. Les Westerman and I were each to lead one of the two parties onto the merchant ship being inspected. We were all issued sidearms and spent some time on the fantail checking out the weapons.

At the noon meal we sat around the wardroom table discussing how our homemade plan was coming together. Captain Kelley insisted that unless otherwise directed he would shoot the rudder off any freighter

USS *Blandy* and USS *Essex*, part of Hunter-Killer Group Bravo, October 1962 (courtesy Bill Bangert)

that resisted. We even talked about using a system of signals from the boarding party when they were aboard a freighter and encountered resistance, to have *Blandy*'s five-inch guns train on some part of the ship to intimidate the master and the crew. Preparations continued through the rest of the day. That evening after dinner I went up to the torpedo deck. The two Mark 32 torpedo launchers on each side held the three acoustic homing torpedoes whose safeties had been removed earlier that day. The six torpedoes were ready to have their launchers cranked forty-five degrees outboard and manually fired into the water; as they left the tube the arming wire would be pulled out of the detent to arm the detonator. The torpedo would then dive to about fifty feet on a predetermined course and time, and turn on its active sonar to search. While actively pinging, the torpedo is programmed to turn in wide circles until it receives a solid echo. It then turns directly toward the returning echo until it hits a solid object or until a magnetic sensor detects the closest point to a large ferrous object, such as a close passing submarine. It would then detonate its warhead of TNT.

As I stood on the torpedo deck pondering my thoughts, the lookout reported a sighting to port showing one white light. This was the first high-seas contact since leaving Newport. Eventually the signalman got a response to his flashing-light signal of long, short, long, short—Alpha Alpha—"Who are you?"

The answer returned, "Norwegian freighter."

We asked, "What is your destination?"

"Panama Canal." That was good, and we checked it out. His position and course were consistent with going to the Panama Canal.

Then he flashed back, "Who are you?"

We answered, "U.S. Navy warship."

Then he flashed back a response. The bridge watch officer asked the signalman what was he saying. The signalman answered, "Sir, he sent, 'Godspeed.'"

OCTOBER 22, 1962
NORFOLK, VIRGINIA

Late that night a large number of U.S. Navy destroyers and cruisers sailed from Norfolk, Virginia. Among them were the USS *Charles P. Cecil (DDR-835)* and the USS *Cony (DDE-508)*. These destroyers also turned south after passing through Thimble Shoals. *Cecil's* mission was to join the attack carrier USS *Enterprise*; *Cony's* was to join the USS *Randolph* hunter-killer group in the ring of the blockading force.

OCTOBER 22, 1962
COMMANDER CHARLES ROZIER
COMMANDING OFFICER
USS *CHARLES P. CECIL (DDR-835)*

Commander Charles Rozier was lucky to have command of the fine ship USS *Charles P. Cecil*. It had an excellent crew. The ship was sometimes referred to as just *Cecil* or occasionally as *"old Charlie P."* Her home port then was Norfolk, Virginia. It was a good port with a lot of activities for the crew. The contribution of the navy to Norfolk was widely recognized by the locals, and the sailors found it a pleasant place to live. With its southern background, however, segregation lingered, and it wasn't great for all navy personnel. The community was looking forward to becoming a city, and already had taken steps reflecting that new status. The Norfolk public schools were mediocre, but Norfolk boasted an excellent public library, a zoo, and a fine symphony and chorus. The streets were well maintained and clean. There were a number of good restaurants along the main drag, Denby Avenue, and the signs stating "No dogs or sailors" had mostly disappeared from the windows.

Cecil was a radar picket ship in Destroyer Squadron 26, which was a part of Cruiser Destroyer Flotilla 8. *Cecil's* division within the squadron had returned from a Mediterranean deployment in August that year and had spent most of September in Norfolk. *Cecil* was equipped with the sophisticated SPS-37 long-range air-search radar, and the SPS-8 height finder radar, which put the ship in a unique air defense category. Plotting and tracking air contacts was its specialty. Submarine hunting was definitely its secondary mission, since it still had the antiquated World War II–vintage SQS-4 sonar, which, although responsible for detecting and tracking many German U-boats, was no match for the more sophisticated and longer-range sonars on most ships of the Atlantic Fleet. Notwithstanding the old equipment, the *Cecil* crew had proven themselves capable of holding submarines and carrying out ASW attacks in exercises, but they had never tracked a real live Soviet submarine since Commander Rozier had been aboard.

Lieutenant John Hunter was the navigator aboard *Cecil.* The navigator's job was a stimulating experience and one that had been influenced heavily by the personal supervision of the commanding officer, Charles Rozier. As a young man, when he was a year away from achieving an arts degree at Emory University, Rozier had transferred to the Naval Academy and for the four years there was always ranked at or near the top of his year group. Along the way he picked up an electrical engineering degree from Rensselaer Polytechnic Institute and a master's degree in engineering administration from the Massachusetts Institute of Technology. Rozier was an exceptional ship handler and was renowned throughout the squadron for the precise maneuvering of his destroyer.

Commander Rozier often let other officers take the ship into and out of port and alongside the fleet oilers or carriers when refueling. Once, when the ship's electronics technicians couldn't fix their complex IFF (identification friend or foe) equipment, Commander Rozier quietly went below and did the job himself. Only once did he seize control of the ship from his navigator, John Hunter, and that had been when Hunter was taking the ship alongside a fleet oiler to refuel. Hunter had approached the oiler too closely and had not allowed for the suction caused in the area near the large ship's hull. Commander Rozier relieved Hunter in such a gentle way that the young navigator knew he could never make the same mistake again.

Cecil had returned to port from its local operations off Norfolk. In the recent squadron competition it had clearly earned the reputation as the best anti–air warfare destroyer in the fleet and had a lot of fun achieving it. Commander Rozier and the executive officer, Lieutenant Commander Arthur Hasler, believed in working smarter rather than harder. There was wonderful teamwork aboard *Cecil* at sea and warm camaraderie in port. John Hunter's toughest job as navigator was keeping his awkward but lovable chief quartermaster out of trouble with the shore patrol and the local police in every port.

Late in September *Cecil* had been exercising at sea in the local Virginia Capes operating areas. On Saturday, October 20, Charles Rozier was with his wife, Claire, and their three children, having lunch at one of their favorite barbecue restaurants in Norfolk called Fat Boy's North Carolina Pit Barbecue. The commander was astounded when a navy shore patrol truck pulled up. A young shore patrol petty officer came up to Rozier and asked if he were Commander Rozier, commanding officer of USS *Cecil*. The Norfolk Fifth Naval District shore patrol had been told at noon that day to find all destroyer sailors in the area and tell them to return to their ships and to be ready to sail by 4:00 P.M. The two shore patrolmen were assigned to find all crew members from the USS *Stickell* and *Charles P. Cecil*, both of Destroyer Squadron 26. It must have been an impossible task. Rozier found out that they had gone to his home looking for him and, when they saw he was not there, asked neighbors where he might have gone for lunch, and they had guessed correctly.

The authorities were attempting to get all navy men back to their ships without making announcements on the radio or in public so as not to alarm the populace. The sole method of identifying sailors by their ship was to read the small blue-and-white tags on the shoulders of their uniforms, a challenging task at best.

That Saturday afternoon Hunter had played a round of golf at Naval Air Station Oceana, and was on his second martini with his girlfriend at Virginia Beach when one of his junior officer roommates called. The excited officer said that the ship had phoned their bachelor pad and said they were getting under way. Hunter hurried into Norfolk and, sure enough, they were due to get under way at 4:00 P.M. They finally sailed the next day at 2:00 A.M., following astern of their squadronmate USS *Stickell* (DDR-888). Neither *Stickell* nor *Cecil* had enough men aboard to sail by 4:00 P.M. Sister ship *Stickell* got under way at

8:30 P.M. while 75 men short. Commander Rozier finally got *Cecil* under way with only 200 of his crew, out of 350, aboard. However, he had a mix of 100 extra crewmen from other destroyers, whom *Cecil* borrowed for the deployment. The crew departed Norfolk not certain of their assignment. Their only orders were to turn south.

Because *Cecil* left many crewmen behind in the rush to sail, for a while the ship had to borrow men to fill the watch bills. Several days later the officers sorted out the crew manning shortage off the Carolina coast, and then transferred the 75 men who had missed the sailing in a prolonged highline transfer with *Stickell*.

The officers of *Cecil* knew that the crisis had to do with the situation in Cuba, but they did not know exactly what. On that deployment Hunter was the combat information center officer, so Commander Rozier shared the newly received, highly classified Atlantic Fleet contingency operation order with him and the operations officer. The operation order assigned *Cecil* to a role in the fleet air defense portion of the U.S. invasion of Cuba. Since they were a radar picket destroyer, DDR, they were being sent north of Cuba to control the U.S. aircraft that would, under the contingency plan, be attacking targets in Cuba.

On October 22, when *Cecil* was east-northeast of the Bahamas, they listened to President Kennedy's speech, which the captain piped on the 1MC loudspeakers throughout the ship. *Cecil* was ordered to go south of Haiti with squadron sister destroyer USS *Adams* and ammunition ship USS *Wrangell*, and to wait for further orders. The men of *Cecil* waited and waited while watching the blockade screen take form around Cuba, but as a radar picket ship they were not part of the actual blockade. *Cecil* was finally ordered to proceed to a screening station for the USS *Enterprise* carrier group.

OCTOBER 23, 1962
USS *BLANDY*
NORTH ATLANTIC

The day after sailing, *Blandy* joined up with the other ships of the squadron and the ASW Hunter-Killer Group Bravo. We were one of eight ASW escorts of one of three hunter-killer groups assigned to the ASW command of the Atlantic Fleet. We formed a bent-line ASW screen oriented south and turned together toward Cuba and new adventure.

United States ships were ordered to fire a first round across the bow and the second into their rudders to disable any ships that failed to stop as ordered. The electrifying words in the secret operation order showed clearly that the hunter-killer task group was heading for a real-war situation. The description of actions to take against Soviet ships that failed to stop were glaring.

While steaming south, running to and from the ASW bent-line screen, back to plane guard station behind *Essex*, life took on an exciting flavor, something more than the routine days, weeks, and months spent training in ASW operations. There was something in the wind, and for once it was real.

"Okay, Duck, get your ass in gear," Frank Flanagan muttered to me in his broad Boston accent. "You and Dan are standing bridge watches now, one in three. During general quarters, Duck, you'll be 1JS talker on the bridge. Dan, you'll be with me in CIC."

Flanagan was acting officious now; gone was his lighthearted and fun-loving attitude of the days on the beach in Newport. Once the ships of Destroyer Squadron 24 had sortied that dark night, the thoughts of nights in the tavern with the girls from Salve Regina on Cliff Walk had faded from the daily wardroom talk. All was business now, and the demands of the XO were real and threatening. The wardroom had an air of seriousness. No more joshing at lunchtime or poking fun at the mess caterer, Steve Jackson, who was missing. He had not been called back from leave and would begin a long and tortuous trip back to the ship, transferring from an oiler to an ammunition ship to the carrier and finally back to his home in our wardroom.

Steaming alongside *Essex* was a routine event, done normally every second or third day provided the carrier wasn't launching or recovering aircraft, and the seas were not running prohibitively high. Refueling while eighty feet off the beam of the carrier while steaming at twelve or fifteen knots was another function that did cause the tensions on the bridge to run higher than normal. While at that distance, with lines passed between the fueling destroyer and the carrier, the slightest variation from the carrier's course or speed could cause major, even disastrous results. Stories of horrible accidents haunted the captains of every destroyer. Loss of steering control due to mechanical failure or a careless helmsman could turn a routine refueling into a major catastrophe in seconds. The maneuver was the sort of final exam for the officers of the deck, but after six months in the Mediterranean we had all become proficient.

Captain Kelley liked to have all his officers, regardless of position aboard, qualified to bring the ship alongside the carrier. Even the supply officers Jackson and Eilberg had taken their turns, and the chief engineer, Bill Bangert, had, after much swearing and obfuscation, performed brilliantly.

"I'm a goddamn engineer, XO, not a ship driver, supposed to be in the hold supervising the fuel transfer," said Bangert.

"Shut up, Bangert, get up to the bridge. Kelley wants you up there and qualified."

While taking on fuel and stores, mail and spare parts, large groups of deck force personnel and engineers were topside on the weather decks working the lines between the ships, which required constant manual tending. It was a time of high spirits as mail, bullets, missing personnel, and chow came aboard. Captain Kelley always ordered the signalmen to break out the *Blandy* house flag, which was the "go to hell" flag and flew high from the inboard halyard. Sometimes the *Essex* band would muster on the hangar bay playing music. It was a time all hands enjoyed.

Engineers, however, had the critical task of ensuring that the proper valves were open to take the tons of navy special fuel oil, the syrupy, black NSFO, coming aboard in two gigantic eight-inch hoses, which resembled elephant trunks. These would be sent across from the carrier and manhandled into the two open fueling trunks of ten-inch diameter into which the hoses were inserted and then tied by hand by bosun mates, who possessed a magical ability to do these things like trained ballet dancers. The whole scene was a pleasure to watch, provided that all was going well.

There had been one disaster several months earlier in the Mediterranean when we were alongside the carrier USS *Randolph*. For some reason the two ships parted slightly, causing the forward refueling hose to be yanked from the trunk. It was a sight to behold as the hose slipped out of the trunk, then poised like a cobra waving back and forth, spewing black oil all over the spotless side of the ship. What had been particularly awful was that *Blandy*'s laundry was on the main deck port side and had its porthole open to cool the hot space. A rack of newly pressed dress white uniforms, belonging to the staff on board, was standing just inside the porthole. The hose poised a few moments as if taking aim, then spurted black fuel through the porthole, practically flooding the space before the hose was yanked back under control by bosun mates of the deck force. It took nearly a week to clean up the ship's sides and the laundry. All the uniforms had to be thrown out.

The event would have been funny had it not been just short of a more serious accident—and nobody was injured. When Frank Flanagan began repeating the story of the laundry mishap with staff officers present in the wardroom, the exec had finally banned the topic to prevent a fistfight between Frank and the staff communications officer, Lieutenant Robert Gillies, who naturally suspected subterfuge and couldn't understand why that laundry rack held only staff whites and none from the ship's company.

The highline transfer, by which personnel were moved to and from the carrier on a series of lines, was another dramatic procedure. The bosun chair was hauled across by lines and blocks attended very carefully by crewmen handling the in-haul and out-haul lines. In rougher weather those being transferred in the bosun chair, which dangled between the ships above the churning seas, were subject to high excitement. We had seen near misses, when the ships rolled in opposite directions and the hapless man in the moving chair was first dumped into the drink, then snapped like a projectile from a slingshot when the ships recovered and again rolled, flinging the chair and the transferee aloft in a thrilling carnival ride.

Transferring the squadron chaplain on Sundays was always a favorite, especially since we all knew that Chaplain Ahrensbach, a genial fellow, although always a little in awe of what was going on around him, hated the highline transfer almost as much as the Sunday "holy helo"(helicopter) ride. The holy helo was a helicopter sent from the carrier to pick up the chaplain and take him around to each ship for services, and was sometimes used instead of the highline transfer. *Blandy* and most other destroyers had no helicopter landing pads, which required the chaplain to be picked up and winched to the helo on the end of a cable, also a thrilling experience. Ahrensbach dreaded Sundays, the only day he was required to do much more than sit in the wardroom drinking coffee. He had been dunked on the highline more times than he wished to remember, and the helo transfer petrified him. Nevertheless, he went about his rounds each week without protest. The ship's laundrymen claimed Chaplain Ahrensbach turned in a full week's supply of shorts to the laundry each Monday, exactly equal to the number of highline transfers or holy helo lifts he had made the day before. This was all part of life aboard destroyers.

Blandy was blessed with a superb deck force of professionally talented bosun mates who knew their duties and carried them out flawlessly, albeit they always seemed unable to behave ashore in liberty ports. For some reason these talented seamen rarely rose to be senior petty officers, usually stumbling into Captain's Mast and reduction in grade due to fighting or displaying less than exemplary behavior ashore, but they could not be topped at sea.

Disbursing officer Steve Jackson finally returned to the ship after circuitous rides on more than five ships. He returned to his seat at the end of the long wardroom table, in the spot reserved for the serving mess caterer. The seat, as if by design, was fittingly too low to appear at the normal height of the other officers.

"Get a phone book and sit on it," Flanagan chided. "How the hell can we see you to complain how shitty this chow is?" Jackson blushed red, as he did often, peering through his thick glasses, which were always so soiled we wondered how he could possibly see through them. The glasses enlarged his eyes so they appeared unnaturally big, giving his face an unbalanced look. "You look like Elmer Fudd down there—" Flanagan was abruptly cut off by the arrival in the wardroom of the executive officer, Lou Lester.

"Sit up, Westerman," the XO chimed in his affected accent; he had graduated from the Naval Academy but sounded British at times. The closely knit company of junior officers knew better than to mock him within earshot. Lester had a fierce temper, and was known to fly off the handle in brief bursts of emotion, which some officers suspected was feigned. We unkindly nicknamed him "Bollard Head," since from the rear, the back of his pate resembled the shape of the bollard that ships moored to on the side of a pier.

As mess caterer, "Stonewall" Jackson was required to be at the late setting with the XO and the captain. Jackson hated it since he was always the brunt of not only the junior officers' hazing but also the captain's constant complaints about the poor quality of the food. This was followed by Lester's blasts, usually following the meal, of the imperfections of the presentation and the decorum of the mess.

"This won't do," scolded Lester. "I've seen better table manners in the service quarters of the Harvard Club in New York. At least there the diners don't swill their food and try to flee; they eat like proper gentlemen." Then Lester would invariably begin to recite words of John Paul Jones: "It is by no means enough that an officer of the navy should be a capable mariner. He must be that, of course, but also a great deal more. He should be as well a gentleman of liberal education, refined manners, punctilious courtesy, and the nicest sense of personal honor."

Flanagan rolled his eyes and Les Westerman snickered, while Stonewall Jackson gawked through his thick, stained glasses as the XO continued to berate him for all the shortcomings of the meal just past—after Captain Kelley had returned to the bridge and as the wardroom was emptying before eight-o'clock reports.

We continued steaming south, and gradually the atmosphere of uncertainty dampened the usually high-spirited life aboard. Flanagan collared me. As electronics material officer, and as acting communications officer, since Bill Morgan had been transferred by highline to the carrier to go ashore to get our new crypto cards and communications key lists, I was struggling with three radar repeaters out of commission and a score of radios not functioning properly. I was nearly overcome by the responsibilities I had not yet mastered. The communications equipment on a Forrest Sherman class destroyer of the 1960s was a nightmare, almost like the engineering plant. The Forrest Sherman class destroyers had emerged in the late fifties as the replacement for the overworked and aging Sumner class 692 and improved 710 class destroyers built near the end of World War II. But the new Forrest Shermans, like *Blandy*, *Edwards*, and *Barry* in the squadron, were hermaphrodites, neither efficient ASW platforms nor good gunnery platforms. Worse, they were strapped with the new and highly dangerous twelve-hundred-pound-per-square-inch steam plant, which killed more men in accidents than any destroyer propulsion system before them. The steam in those systems was all superheated, and as a result, terribly difficult to control should leaks appear. It was a deadly business belowdecks.

PART II

Spies and Diplomats

On Monday morning, the same day President Kennedy announced the naval blockade of Cuba, with Captain Agafonov's submarine brigade now on combat patrol in the Sargasso Sea off the Bahamas, Captain Third Rank Lev Vtorygin, the assistant naval attaché at the Soviet embassy in Washington, D.C., strode into his chief's office.

"You called, sir," the handsome naval officer spoke in the hushed tones used most of the time in the Belmont Street annex to the embassy in Northwest Washington. The Russian officers spoke in low volume because they assumed the Americans were listening on electronic monitoring devices. After all, it was normal practice for the Soviets to bug Western embassies in Moscow; the practice was taught in the Military-Diplomatic Academy, the Moscow charm school for all military and naval attachés.

Vice Admiral Leonid Bekrenyev turned a switch, and heavy symphony music cut into the room from four speakers to mask their conversation. Lev Vtorygin knew immediately that his boss, the senior attaché, had some sensitive operational matter to discuss. Bekrenyev motioned for the young officer to sit at the small table in a corner alcove surrounded by heavy red curtains, which set it off from the rest of the room. The interiors of Soviet diplomatic buildings were decorated in the same style worldwide. High ceilings with tall windows, covered in dusty-looking chintz and framed by heavy dark red drapes, which were generally pulled closed when the room was in use. The furniture was modern with highly polished surfaces, which at first

Senior Lieutenant Lev Vtorygin
in 1953 aboard destroyer *Surovy*
(courtesy Lev Vtorygin)

glance looked of high quality, but, like many things Soviet, on closer inspection revealed cheap, laminated wood. Even in Romania and Yugoslavia, where craftsmen still existed with the proud tradition of cabinetmakers, they had succumbed to the numbing effects of state ownership. Ostentatious crystal chandeliers lighted the inevitable color picture of Lenin hung somewhere looking soulfully down at the clustered diplomats.

"Lev, things are heating up. Moscow fears the Americans are overreacting to the situation in Havana, and may be taking precautionary measures for intervention. You're aware of the military exercise they just completed on the island of Vieques last week? The one briefed by the press as staged against the Caribbean dictator called Ortsac—Castro spelled backward?"

Vtorygin nodded. "You don't really think they're—"

The admiral cut him off. "We don't speculate, we observe and report what's going on. Now listen carefully." The admiral opened a wall map and assumed an officious tone in his voice. "You know the terrain well, and have done this before. Take Polikarpov in the Land Rover, begin at Camp Lejeune, take Route 95 south to Moorhead City, and observe traffic in the loading areas, and on the rails and highways."

The admiral carefully laid out the planned trip on the large map, which he unveiled from behind a white screen. Two security officers had silently eased their way into the cubicle. The late Indian summer warmth made the room stuffy and close, and the air conditioner never worked. Vtorygin suspected it had been cut off for security reasons, because it was another place to hide eavesdropping equipment. He began to get excited—this was the kind of road reconnaissance he loved, and the freedom to operate away from the stifling confines of the embassy and the prying eyes of the security staff. They were everywhere and watched everything; he suspected that even when he went to the bathroom, someone watched his every move.

Diplomatic assignments in Western countries were highly sought-after posts, and no one was beyond the scrutiny of the security staff—too many Soviet embassy officers had defected in the past, and the scandal of navy captain Nikolai Artamonov was still hanging heavily over the Soviet Navy. Artamonov, skipper of a Skorry class destroyer assigned to the Baltic base of Riga, had disappeared in 1959 and shown up in the United States with his Polish girlfriend, leaving his wife and son behind in Leningrad. Artamonov, using the alias Nick Shadrin, had become a live trophy for the CIA, the Defense Intelligence Agency, and the Office of Naval Intelligence, and was paraded at U.S. military installations in forums for officers as a sample of disgruntled Soviet leadership. In September 1960, while wearing a disguise, Artamonov testified before the House Un-American Activities Committee. Admiral Bekrenyev and Captain Vtorygin observed the hearings in which Artamonov gave a critical assessment of the Soviet political system and a dark prediction of future military adventures abroad planned by the USSR.

Vtorygin had been a shipmate of Artamonov and was especially nervous about his past association with the defector, a fact the security people had apparently not yet picked up. Vtorygin kept his mouth shut, a good practice in this business, but he expected at any moment that this coveted job in Washington could be terminated because he had known the defector intimately. They had gone ashore from their mine-sweeper together, drank and chased skirts together. Nevertheless, he kept this all to himself. The inner workings of the KGB were not as efficient as their reputation was scary.

Admiral Bekrenyev outlined the track Vtorygin was to follow up and down the East Coast—Norfolk, the Little Creek Amphibious Base, Naval Air Station Oceana, Jacksonville, Charleston, and as close to Key West as he could get. "What about the hunter-killer antisubmarine groups from Newport and Quonset Point, Rhode Island?" Vtorygin asked, noting they were not included in the outline of the mission.

"Closed to our travel now, in retaliation for us closing Murmansk and parts of Leningrad to the American attachés in Moscow." The admiral looked alarmed and glanced at his watch. "I want you to leave today, since I anticipate they will close more of these military areas shortly just to prevent us from getting in close for observation. In any case, I'll file the request for your travel now, and you get on the road with Polikarpov immediately, so we can feign ignorance if they close more areas. This way you'll be on the road and we'll claim we didn't know in time to brief you. You will attempt to enter each of these areas, marked in red, even if you are stopped. You will have surveillance, but you know how sloppy, unaggressive, and lazy the Naval Investigative Service and FBI can be. If you move fast you can hit most of these areas before they get their defenses up. Go quickly, do not speed or violate traffic laws, don't attract attention." The admiral slapped the tabletop for emphasis. "And, if you are caught taking photos in restricted areas, remember we will deny you were acting officially and you will be on your own."

Vtorygin looked stunned. "You mean, sir, we will be kicked out without support."

"Exactly, Now get moving; your vehicle will be gassed and ready in the motor pool. You will draw your cash for expenses at the budget and fiscal office; they have an envelope for you and Polikarpov. And Lev"— the admiral smiled and shook a finger at the young captain—"no extracurricular adventures. Do you understand?"

Vtorygin was surprised, then saw the hint of a smile in the admiral's eyes, "Why, of course, sir." He spun around and made for the door. So the admiral remembered his short liaison with a waitress in a Holiday Inn the last time he had made a road surveillance trip outside the Washington, D.C., area; he was sure his travelmate, the army assistant attaché, had ratted on him. This time he was traveling with navy assistant Boris Polikarpov, whom he knew he could trust. The pressure of this trip probably meant they wouldn't have time for such dallying.

Polikarpov was loading a small brown suitcase into the Land Rover when Vtorygin opened the door to the motor pool garage and stepped into the vast maintenance area. The workers were Russians, imported as embassy laborers, unlike the U.S. embassy in Moscow. There was not one local American working inside the Soviet embassy compound. Vtorygin always marveled that the Americans were so blindly trusting and hired hundreds of local Muscovites to work in their embassy. Locals did everything from teaching the Russian language and driving the U.S. diplomats, to arranging their travel. Consequently they knew every step the State Department Foreign Service officers made, even serving as nannies for their children, cleaning their embassy apartments, and working in the embassy snack bar.

Strangely trusting, these Americans, and very naive, thought Vtorygin as he strode to the bathroom and gave his Adidas sports bag to the six-foot-tall assistant. Polikarpov had served in Ottawa as the assistant naval attaché before coming to Washington, and his English was superb, but he had gotten thrown out of Canada for getting caught taking classified material from a Canadian Ministry of Defense secretary, whom he had managed to bed several times. But the Royal Canadian Mounted Police, the counterintelligence version of the FBI—Vtorygin thought the Canadian term quaint—had caught the couple red-handed in a motel bedroom in Toronto. Polikarpov had been declared persona non grata and sent home. He was usually more careful than that—Vtorygin had chided him that his good looks had gotten in the way of good craftsmanship, and he had become more careful. Vtorygin liked to travel with the tall, good-looking officer, who was quick at the wheel and wonderfully alert for surveillance.

The gray Land Rover slipped quietly out of the garage through the high embassy gates and down Massachusetts Avenue, heading for Shirley Highway south. They would enter the major highway, check for surveillance, and, if followed, would pull off at a gas station near Quantico and try suddenly to lose them by lurching onto Route 1 at Stafford, Virginia, and doubling back to cover the railheads at the marine base in Quantico.

OCTOBER 22, 1962
DEFENSE ATTACHÉ OFFICE
U.S. EMBASSY, MOSCOW

"Another special collection tasking, sir." The harried army warrant officer handed a piece of teletype paper to air force colonel William F. Scott, U.S. Air Force attaché and senior multiengine pilot. "Seems Washington is already uptight."

"I've never seen anything like it in all my twenty-two years of service. Looks like we're ratcheting up this situation into a full-blown crisis, almost as bad the Berlin face-off last year." The tall air force attaché read the message and handed it back to the warrant officer. "Call all the principals for a meeting in the bubble in half an hour. I'll tell the front office what we've been ordered to do."

Colonel Scott walked to the narrow, dusty staircase leading from the embassy tenth-floor military attaché office down to the seventh, where the ambassador and deputy chief of mission had their somewhat more luxurious offices. Scott had been in Moscow for two years and had just been extended for a third; he was weary of the stifled existence, living and working in the drab embassy chancellery, a mere several floors separating the highly secret workplace from his ornate, high-ceilinged flat. It wouldn't have been bad had he not been constrained on his travel outside the building by constant surveillance and frequent harassment by the Soviet goons from the foreign diplomatic security branch of the KGB. He and the other fifteen officers in the embassy attaché office were under routine observation while moving about the capital and when traveling outside Moscow. It wasn't so bad initially, but after two years on the job it caused a special tension to build among the men and their families, which, although not noticeable initially, built up until sleep became difficult and a nervous reaction came to all the personnel. Only when out of the USSR on rest and recreation or on home leave did it become obvious how uptight they were in Moscow, especially when sleep and relaxation came and they realized how tired and burned out they were.

Colonel Scott entered the deputy chief of mission's office. "Mike, we have some tough heads-up tasking from the Pentagon."

The DCM, a longtime career foreign service officer, with four tours in Communist countries under his belt, looked up from his cluttered desk, reading glasses perched on his lower nose. "Shall we go into the conference room, or can you write it out on the blackboard there?" Embassy officials in Moscow avoided discussing sensitive materials by scribbling on the many chalkboards placed in most offices in the secure portions of the embassy, as it was assumed all spaces were under electronic surveillance.

"We'll need to cut the ambassador in, too, since our orders will place most of my officers at considerable risk of compromise."

"Wait here," the DCM said, then rose and left the room, crossing into the ambassador's officer. Several moments later he poked his head back in. "Come on, Bill, the boss is already on the way to the conference room." The two walked down the hall and stepped into a cramped, old-fashioned elevator built for three persons but able now to hold only two due to the weight limitations of the old elevator. The elevator as well as the whole embassy chancellery was built by German prisoners of war still in Moscow in the early 1950s.

"This is beginning to look like the real thing."

The DCM nodded. "I'm really concerned that we've caught them in a severely embarrassing act, and that's not cool for the Soviets. They don't take kindly to losing face."

They met the ambassador just outside the conference room. The three middle-aged men entered the enclosure, which was a plastic bubble-shaped room shrouded by dirty blue drapes. A small table was surrounded by half a dozen chairs. The air was close, and it reeked of cigarette smoke. An air conditioner came on as the DCM shut the hatchlike entrance. Soft music began to play to counter any attempts to intercept their voices.

Colonel Scott began in a subdued voice, "Mr. Ambassador, the navy just reported photographing Soviet missile sites in Cuba, around the Cienfuegos area and outside Havana. The analysts say they are for surface-to-air and intermediate-range ballistic missiles. CIA and DIA have reported that half a dozen more large-hatch Soviet merchant ships carrying what appear to be IRBMs and Il-28 aircraft are converging on Havana. The president is scheduled to address the nation tonight Washington time about our reaction. Our attachés have been ordered to commence round-the-clock surveillance of all key Moscow and Leningrad military targets, like we did last year during the Berlin blowup."

The ambassador nodded. "And what does that mean?"

"Sir, that means all defense attaché personnel, including the non-commissioned officers, will be on the road twenty-four hours a day, making the surveillance rounds according to our notional plan."

"Will you be doing overt acts that may cause incidents?"

"Yes, sir, we're required to obtain discreet photography of any unusual movements by the normal alert units, such as the airborne guards, the Taman Division, and naval deployments from Leningrad and Murmansk, wherever our navy and air force folks can get near to the key bases. It also means we routinely check the Ministry of Defense, navy, ground force, and strategic rocket force headquarters for signs of increased alert."

The ambassador looked at the DCM, then at Colonel Scott, shook his head, and sighed. "We cannot afford incidents at times like these. I understand your orders, and the importance of your missions, but do impress on your men that they will take utmost care to avoid incidents, especially your cowboy navy attachés. When they're up in Leningrad and Murmansk I want no unnecessary risks taken. Remember last time, when things got tense, two of your sailors got caught photographing submarines on the Neva and got knocked down and their trousers removed by the goons. I will not have that again; they will not take such risks. Things are tight enough as they are." The ambassador lowered his voice. "Understand, Scott?"

Earlier in October an assistant U.S. naval attaché had been declared persona non grata; a second member of the U.S. embassy staff had been so named on October 12.

"Yes, Mr. Ambassador." The colonel's face reddened as he recalled the humiliating aftershocks when his naval attaché, a captain, and assistant attaché, a marine major, called from the Leningrad consulate reporting how they had been forced to walk bare-assed through the crowded streets of Leningrad during rush hour after being bushwhacked by Soviet surveillance men on Schmidt's Embankment while they were trying to count submarines tied to the quay across the Neva River. It wouldn't have been so bad had the Russians not published photos of the two officers running through town with only their shirts on and camera bags hung over their shoulders, the white buttocks glaring on the front page of *Izvestia*: "American Military Spies Exposed in Leningrad."

That had been in the middle of the most recent Berlin flap, when U.S. and Soviet tanks were facing off at Checkpoint Charlie in Berlin. Colonel Scott had had a difficult time reporting to Washington exactly why his two naval attachés had been caught literally with their pants down. It had not been funny at the time. Ivan could be cold and ruthless, but he did possess a sense of humor at times.

The ambassador stood, opened the hatch, and began to exit the conference room. He suddenly turned to the speechless colonel: "And Bill, for Chris' sake, no more Hollywood car chases by your attachés. They are not here to play 'shake the goons.' Have them take the Metro or walk as much as possible. I'm tired of admin having to respond to reports of traffic violations by the Moscow traffic cops, GAI, by your officers. Tell them to grow up; they're here to do a job, and they can't do it while playing cops and robbers." The colonel reddened again until he saw the glint of a smile in the ambassador's eyes. "I wish all our embassy sections had the spirit and morale your defense attaché office has, Bill, but do keep them in check. This is serious business now, not a bloody circus."

The ambassador left the two in the conference room. The DCM looked at Colonel Scott. "I guess he's a little more attuned to your actions than we thought. He always appears so spacey. He really doesn't miss much, does he?"

Scott looked bewildered. "We've got a job to do that depends on being unobserved; that's a difficult task in the environment of this police state. Our guys are under terrific strain, and yet it seems like they are playing around. Never mind; we'll get the job done regardless." He stood, and the two senior diplomats left the bubble.

Within two hours four U.S. military attachés in civilian clothes left the embassy building, two by the front entrance and two by the side vehicular gate; the two teams immediately jumped onto two different city buses. The gray-uniformed KGB guards in the tin guard shacks immediately picked up their telephones. The game was beginning all over again, and the stakes were higher than ever.

Travel in the Soviet Union by U.S. diplomats was complex, difficult, frequently boring, at times downright dangerous, but always challenging. Western diplomats were permitted to travel in fewer than 1 percent of the total Soviet land area. U.S. embassy policy was to have junior foreign service and military officers travel as often as possible. It was impossible to form accurate notions of life in the USSR by remaining inside the capital or inside the embassy ghetto complex. From the outset, a trip to some city in the far-flung hinterland of the USSR was a formidable bureaucratic process. The embassy officers had to file in writing with the Soviet Diplomatic Service Directorate, called by its Russian acronym, UPDK—itself a formidable force of obfuscation and constipation that thwarted all attempts of Western diplomats to organize travel outside the capital. For the military attaché the complexity was compounded by the additional layer of the Ministry of Defense Directorate for Foreign Military Diplomats, called the UVS. This singularly stuffy office was second only to the UPDK for finding methods of obstruction to normal commonsense procedures for traveling from point A to point B in the USSR. Once all the work was done preparing for a trip, train or airplane tickets in hand, and permission from the UVS and the UPDK to leave the capital, the diplomat or attaché could be unceremoniously blocked from his trip at the last minute by a phone call terminating his permission to travel—as simple as that, and resulting in several weeks of preparation suddenly wasted.

For military diplomats the travel was further complicated by the ever-present surveillance, which began at the moment of departure from the embassy, including aboard the trains and aircraft, to preclude diplomatic misbehavior en route and continued at the town of destination, often through the constant presence of the Intourist employees who ran the accommodations approved for diplomats, and the inevitable city tours that the attaché routinely took not only for orientation and planning but also for genuine intellectual purposes. During these stilted and propaganda-filled tours the traveler learned of the heroic struggles of the local populace against the Nazis in the Great Patriotic War, and spent hours gazing at grotesque monuments to the victory of socialism over fascism—huge structures of such immensity and deformity that one was reminded of horrible fever dreams. In any case, the Western diplomat endured the tours, if only to gain his orientation for further forays for reconnaissance purposes and to meet and talk to local citizens when possible to obtain a sampling of local feeling and attitudes—or as the State Department said, "getting the pulse of the land." Meeting locals was more difficult than appeared on the surface, especially for the military diplomat. When a local discerned that the attaché spoke Russian with a foreign accent, the local was immediately on guard, since Western tourism by individual tourists was largely nonexistent. Then the fact that the traveler was a diplomat would inevitably come out, causing the Russian even greater cause to be alarmed. If he was determined to be an American, the Russian would withdraw politely; if a U.S. diplomat he began to retreat quickly; a military diplomat caused him to bolt, eyes ablaze with fear lest he be accosted by security and questioned, or severely beaten, or, worse, face charges of complicity with foreign spies.

The unfortunate diplomats, whose job and sole purpose of travel to these obscure and often desolate towns was ostensibly to feel the country's pulse, found themselves in a quandary on how to find someone to talk to. Any overt attempt to meet in private with a local only exacerbated the issue and complicated the local's life. Often it was easier to confine attempts to contact locals to the grim prospect of chatting up the Intourist guides or taxi drivers who were authorized to deal with foreigners but who contributed little beyond their approved script to the knowledge of the diplomat. There were, of course, exceptions, but it depended on the period in the Cold War, whether the brief periods of thaw or limited détente of the Khrushchev period determined whether one might obtain a few stilted lines of human warmth from the approved contact. Any further attempt to meet covertly with locals was dangerous to the local and to the continuing longevity of the diplomat's stay in his post—as any aberrations of normal behavior, the sterile life in the Intourist hotel, dinner in the approved restaurants for foreigners, and the occasional visit to a museum or cultural performance, would result in the filing of the dreaded AKT, a report of undiplomatic conduct, and the diplomat might find himself on his way home as having been revealed to be involved in "conduct unbecoming a diplomat" and would face the inevitable expulsion.

There were moments, however, of high humor and the occasional reward of a major intelligence collection coup. There was the time when two naval attachés, one British and the other American, returned to their hotel room in Odessa after hours of slogging by foot through the desolate industrial wasteland of the dock area observing the chance maritime target. With time to kill before the only restaurant available to serve foreigners was ready to open, one attaché filled the tub in anticipation of a hot bath. While waiting for the tub to fill, both officers fell fast asleep on the couch and bed. In half an hour both were awakened by a frantic knocking on the door, which was opened by a hotel floor guard with a passkey—each floor had a guard, usually a female of considerable girth. The tub had overflowed, leaking water downstairs to the dining room and shorting out the lights in the ceiling, resulting in a sound berating by the guard. Making matters even worse, when the sputtering guard left the room, slamming the door in the wake of her large behind, the ceiling, made of substandard water-soluble plaster, collapsed in a dusty heap in the first-floor dining room. The attachés were forced to sign a charge sheet and then evicted from the hotel and sent back to Moscow, and the inevitable AKT was filed.

Sleep in the hotel rooms was often interrupted at any hour, especially when two officers traveled together, by an airy female voice offering to come to the room to give full body massages. In any case, the travel was required, and for the enthusiastic officer, at least it got him out of the stifling capital and the never-ending rounds of diplomatic dinners and receptions, which not only threatened his sanity but his health as well. It was a tough life.

During the thirteen days of the Cuban missile crisis from October 18 to 31, 1962, the U.S. Defense Attaché Office would log more travel miles than they had the previous six months, day and night through the darkened streets and alleys of Moscow and the desolate waterfronts of Leningrad, Riga, Murmansk, and Archangelsk.

After Kennedy's address to the nation on October 22, Soviet television and radio blared out hourly assaults on the "criminal intentions of the enemies of peace" and the "high-handed American aggressors." However, there was no mention of Soviet troops or missiles in Cuba. During that week, the Red Army held its usual night rehearsal for the annual November 7 military parade in Red Square commemorating the Bolshevik Revolution. The attachés noted that the arms displayed that year were identical to those exposed during the parade the year before. The Soviets held their cards close to their chests.

While the Soviet public never knew it at the time, the integrity of their own internal security was shattered that month. On the same day that President Kennedy announced the blockade of Cuba, Soviet security forces arrested Colonel Oleg Penkovsky, a highly placed spy. His apprehension implicated senior members of the secret police and Soviet military intelligence in a major intelligence scandal. He was later executed.

OCTOBER 22, 1962
SOVIET NAVAL ATTACHÉS VTORYGIN AND POLIKARPOV
SOUTHBOUND ON ROUTE 95 FROM WASHINGTON, D.C.

The two Soviet attachés sped south along Shirley Highway. They were driving a customized Land Rover, which had been modified with an option to switch off its tail and brake lights to assist in dodging surveillance at night. The car was equipped with an enlarged fuel tank carrying sixty gallons, reinforced suspension, and sun shades in all windows to mask the interior. Generally it was their policy not to try to evade surveillance if they acquired it, simply because that antagonized the FBI or naval counterintelligence people. They understood that the Americans were professionals trying to do their jobs, and merely wanted to complete work on time and go home to their families at the end of their day or night shifts. By evading surveillance the attaché merely sharpened opposition and often led to their reinforcement and more aggressive behavior. They found when dealing with government employees that it was best to lull them into a sense of false security by making them think that they were on perfectly innocent missions, by letting themselves be followed. However, when engaging in some compromising activity, such as servicing a dead drop or meeting with an American they had recruited, they had to be sure they could surge away from the known surveillance, do the deed, and quickly return to their charges, victims merely of heavy traffic and confused city driving. Ideally, the Soviet attachés chose remote country roads with long, visible approaches where they could observe their surveillance and had enough time to drive away and be sufficiently clear of the area not to be caught.

Lev smiled as he thought of the ground rules and of how often he and Polikarpov had nearly been apprehended while carrying out some of their clandestine missions. Americans, Lev found, were terribly naive and trusting. They just did not possess the sinister mentality of constant suspicion that every Soviet citizen had, by dint of decades of self-preservation under regimes where each and every friend, neighbor, and even family relation might compromise your personal actions. Soviet citizens lived in a perpetual state of fear and doubt.

Polikarpov turned off at the Quantico exit; so far they had not spotted any surveillance. They were happy to be on the road and away from the daily tensions of the embassy, where every move was under watch. This mission was a joy for them, since a road reconnaissance was much more relaxed than working clandestine agent operations, which were tense and nerve-racking. The Soviet attachés enjoyed the relative freedom to travel around the country while merely observing and occasionally taking discreet photography, but that was not their major focus. The American open press, vast proliferation of open source material on defense equipment, provided sufficiently detailed information for their analysis. The growing tension over Cuba had made it necessary to have rapid and reliable reporting from the ground of U.S. intentions. The Soviet attachés were sent out to determine if the U.S. armed forces were in fact loading out marine amphibious forces, or placing the 82nd Airborne and 101st Airborne Divisions on alert. These events would be difficult to hide from the public, and consequently also from probing Soviet attachés traveling around the country with impunity. It was welcome work.

Polikarpov drove down Route 1 past the Quantico main gate and then turned off at the small town of Three Corners, which was tucked in between the base and the Potomac River. The attachés would not be able to linger there, but a quick incursion might pass without notice. As soon as they came to the rail line they noticed it was blocked by a train. As far as the eye could see, olive drab Marine Corps vehicles, tanks, trucks, and artillery were loaded and tied down on the flatcars. Polikarpov did a quick U-turn as Lev Vtorygin counted and took notes rapidly on a small notepad. Still no sign of surveillance.

Suddenly the blue car of a Virginia state trooper with flashing blue lights appeared in the opposite lane. Polikarpov immediately assumed the worst and pulled off on the shoulder, while Vtorygin immediately hid his notepad. The police car crossed the centerline and pulled up behind the two attachés, its siren now shrieking. Polikarpov stopped and waited for the officer to come forward. Vtorygin sighed, convinced that they had been sighted and reported in the area of Quantico. When the officer came to the driver's window he saluted and asked for their papers, then suddenly looked again at the Land Rover's plates. The officer blushed and realized they were diplomats, but for some reason did not appear to be aware that the code on their license plates indicated the Soviet embassy. He was very young; he apologized and waved them along. Polikarpov was relieved, but Vtorygin knew better.

"He knew who we are. He was just slowing us down and confirming."

Within twenty minutes a black Ford sedan pulled out of a busy side street in Stafford and attached to them for the rest of the day. Polikarpov drove back to Route 1 and then back up to I-95, heading south. They turned off at Fredericksburg, got on Route 17, and took the long, scenic route south to Newport News. Just as they approached the bridge crossing the York River into Yorktown from Gloucester Point, they pulled off and checked into a motel. It was already dark. Vtorygin knew they would have close surveillance from here into Norfolk, and he chose to stay what was for the opposition uncomfortably close to the Camp Peary complex, which they knew was a CIA training ground for their special personnel. Vtorygin had no intention of going anywhere near that bastion of security, which he knew was just across and up the York River in the vast old army camp with the secluded buildings and short airstrip conveniently cut off from view from any public vantage point. It would be a bad night, for their surveillance team would lose sleep just keeping a round-the-clock watch on the two Soviet diplomats. The Americans would be certain the Soviets were up to no good at this location.

Vtorygin and Polikarpov crossed the bridge into Yorktown and ate dinner in Nick's Seafood Pavilion and then returned innocently to their motel. Polikarpov made a coded telephone call from a pay phone out-side the restaurant, which he was certain would have been without surveillance.

The next morning they rose at first light and recrossed the York River and slipped into Newport News. The surveillance vehicle, now a blue Chevy station wagon, did not appear until they were motoring down Huntington Avenue directly adjacent to the Newport Shipbuild-ing and Drydock shipyard, which they could plainly observe from the road. There on the platen area was the hull of the next aircraft carrier under construction. Vtorygin grew tense; he was amazed at how easy it was to just drive by a major naval construction facility bereft of any concealment. If they had had more time they could have stopped and eaten lunch on Huntington, observing the status of the giant carrier as she slowly grew in size and complexity. It was fascinating to see, and the two Soviet officers marveled again at how open the Americans were.

They continued through the Harbor Tunnel into Norfolk and noted again as they emerged on the raised highway out of the tunnel that they had a perfectly clear view of Norfolk Naval Base and the piers. Vtorygin was scrawling notes furiously. Polikarpov noted that there were only two carriers visible at the pier, and a third was in the main channel head-ing out to Hampton Roads and the Atlantic. They stopped at a seafood restaurant in Virginia Beach after cruising by the Naval Amphibious Base at Little Creek. Everywhere they went they noticed hustle and bustle and heavy traffic going in and out of the bases. Air traffic was heavy at the naval air station. The U.S. military was definitely on the move.

Late one evening after making repeated passes to look in and iden-tify the few ships still at the amphibious ship piers, Polikarpov, who was driving, and Vtorygin had gotten disoriented and couldn't find their way back onto the main road. The sunlight was fading, they were hun-gry, and their surveillance car remained doggedly behind them. Finally, after cruising for more than half an hour trying to get back to their motel, the surveillance car pulled out and stopped abruptly next to the Soviet officers.

"Just follow us," one FBI agent said through the open window, and Polikarpov sheepishly followed them back onto the main highway and back to their motel, whereupon the FBI car disappeared into the night. Both sides were tired of the long day in the cars and wanted to settle down for the night. They, too, were professionals doing their duty.

Vtorygin made periodic telephone calls from public phones to the Soviet attaché office, reporting in prearranged codes the status of the U.S. forces, how many and of what kind of equipment they saw loading. As Vtorygin and Polikarpov were scouting to the south, a second team of Soviet attachés slipped unnoticed out of the Belmont Street office after dark on the same day and were driven by the embassy driver to Union Station in downtown Washington, D.C. There they boarded a northbound sleeper train to Boston. They had carefully chosen a compartment on the left-hand, or western, side of the train. Their target was the closed area of New London, Connecticut, and the submarine base in Groton. Their Boston-bound train would stop during the morning hours in New London, and with the morning sun they would be able to peer into the Thames River and observe whether the submarine base had deployed many of its sleek black submarines. This was a particularly sensitive area, but without filing ahead with U.S. authorities for permission to travel to the area, they would merely get off the train in Boston and reboard a day train, taking a chance without reservations. Their northbound reservations were just as far as New York City, which they were allowed to visit. If they got caught in the New London area heading to Boston they would merely be returned to the embassy. If they made it as far as New London, they were to get off the train at Providence, Rhode Island, rent a car, and drive as close as possible to Quonset Point, where the ASW carriers of the three hunter-killer groups were based. There the men would observe the presence or absence of the carriers and then proceed to Newport and try to observe the Atlantic Fleet cruiser-destroyer headquarters and determine how many destroyers of the hunter-killer groups were moored at Piers One and Two.

If the team made it as far as Boston they were to drive all the way back to Washington. They would report along the way in the same way as Vtorygin's southern team in prearranged telephone messages to the attaché office on Belmont Street. When the group complained that they were army attachés and not as keenly appreciative of the different classes of submarines, Admiral Bekrenyev threw them a copy of a U.S. submarine recognition guide.

"Here, study and memorize this and be ready to go this evening on the seven-thirty train to New York."

While these two teams of military and naval attachés were traveling outside the capital, another team of foreign diplomats from the Soviet embassy drove down Massachusetts Avenue, turned onto Wisconsin Avenue, crossed into Rosslyn over the Key Bridge, and swung past the Pampanio Building, where they stopped briefly to count the lights shining on the ninth and tenth floors—the home of the sensitive Task Force 157, the U.S. Navy's Human Intelligence Offices. Men in these offices were responsible for the collection operations of all the navy spies around the world. After the brief stop, they drove down Highway 50 past the Pentagon. There they noted the lights ablaze, and the number of cars in the north and south parking lots—which were remarkably full for 1:00 A.M.—then returned to the Soviet embassy. An attaché never sleeps!

PART III

Russian Roulette

We knew, one mistake and we could invite disaster onto
humanity; . . . so we were careful.

> *Captain Nikolai Shumkov*
> *Commanding officer*
> *Soviet sub B-130*

If that bastard lets one fly, we'll blow him outta the water.

> *Commander Ed Kelley*
> *Commanding officer*
> *USS Blandy (DD-943)*

OCTOBER 24, 1962
USS *BLANDY*
TWO HUNDRED MILES NORTHEAST OF CAICOS PASSAGE

The antisubmarine warfare force called Hunter-Killer Group Bravo,
consisting of the Destroyer Squadron 24 Newport-based destroyers USS
Blandy, Keppler, Charles S. Sperry, and aircraft carrier *USS Essex,* was
patrolling an arc outside a barrier called the Walnut line, extending
from 27°5′ north latitude, 70° west longitude, to 20° north longitude,
65° west longitude (see chart on page 132). The Walnut line was the
name in the operation order given to the arc northeast of Cuba defining the outer limits of the quarantine, spreading in arcs five hundred
miles around Cuba. This was the line through which Soviet ships
approaching Cuba would first encounter the blockading U.S. forces.
The ASW group was steaming in formation northeast of the Bahamas,
two hundred miles northeast of Caicos Passage, two days following their
dramatic sortie from Newport. They had covered more than a thousand
miles steaming south at twenty-five knots.

131

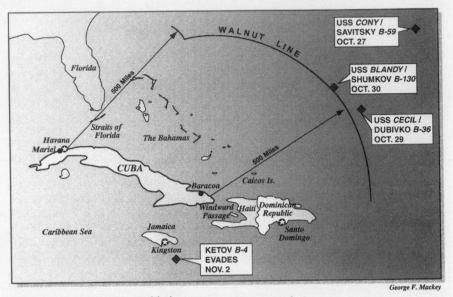

Cuban Blockade: ASW Highlights (courtesy George F. Mackey)

The atmosphere was tense, the spirits high, the future unknown. Was it war, or another exercise? No one knew for sure, but there were live torpedoes in the tubes atop the amidships deck and warshot Hedgehog antisub mortars in place on the launchers, their dull khaki paint splashed with bright yellow letters: "live high explosive."

During the four-to-eight watch, the gray dawn nudged away the black night. It was usually the most peaceful watch on the bridge, and I grew fond of the early morning routine, watching and hearing the sounds of the ship awakening from a slumber. The smell of fresh coffee drifted through the ship from the brew perking on the signal bridge, in the chiefs' quarters, in each engine room, and in the fire room. The morning routine aboard a destroyer was set in a pattern, beginning with the bosun piping Reveille over the ship's 1MC speakers to the ballet of morning sweepers. There was a certain cleanliness and purity on a ship at sea that wasn't there when the ship was in port. Somehow the sea had great purifying qualities; it seemed to clear the head and make the routine problems of life fade and become immaterial. Perhaps that had something to do with why since the beginning of time men had run away to sea for a great part of their lives. Such feelings of escape into remoteness were difficult or impossible to duplicate in the normal human life ashore. To be sure, there were those elements of life that the sailor missed, especially if he had family. There is certainly something to say for the chaste feeling the sea gives to those young and unattached with few tangible problems in life. The ship was a warm home, where they were well fed and found good camaraderie.

After screening the carrier *Essex* for several long days, we were finally given a reprieve from the tedious hours of stationkeeping in the usual eight-ship antisubmarine screen, and were abruptly ordered to plane-guard station. This new assignment provided an exciting respite from the normally dull four-hour watches spent taking bearing and range readings on the carrier and forever adjusting to be precisely on station. At all costs the aim was to avoid the dart from the screen commander, usually the staff watch officer in *Blandy*'s own combat information center, sending a curt "Station!" command on the tactical radio net, informing the entire force that one ship was off-station. On plane-guard station we would be five hundred yards astern of the carrier as she launched and recovered her AD5W Skyraiders and S2F twin-engine Tracker ASW aircraft throughout the coming nights and days. The aircraft most admired was the "Stufe with a roof," which was an early warning version of the Grumman S2 Tracker, with a huge revolving radar disk mounted on top of the fuselage, making it a pure wonder that she was able to fly at all.

"Yo!" Flanagan jumped over the combing of the door leading from the combat information center to the pilothouse where the officer of the deck, Gary Lagere, had just completed his maneuvering solution and was giving conning commands to take the ship to the new station tight under the carrier's quarter.

"Left full rudder, all ahead full, turns for twenty-two knots." The helmsman and lee helmsman repeated the commands, and the ship immediately awoke in response. The decks began to shudder with the increasing propeller turns and the ship heeled sharply, white foam churning in her wake. Tedium was transformed instantly into sharp action. The ship tore out of screening formation and headed at high speed into the plane-guard station, a spot in the ocean close in behind the port quarter of the looming carrier. The challenge was to find that magical spot and to begin a turn easing the charging destroyer into the station while slowing to match the carrier's speed. Some watch officers, such as Gary Lagere, were masters at solving the relative-motion problem mentally, while others required use of the maneuvering board to compute the exact course. Precise ship handling was an art not quickly acquired by all, and a great deal more difficult for some than for others.

The wind began to rattle the pilothouse windows. Loose papers scattered from the navigation table. Lagere picked up the sound-powered phone and dialed the captain's sea cabin, careful not to take his eyes off the huge carrier now looming larger by the second as the sleek destroyer raced at near collision course toward the hulking mass of gray steel. He dialed the phone ringer, the high-pitched *whoop*, ever so gently, not to alarm Kelley, who was a bear when he awoke. When he heard the grunt on the end of the phone line, Lagere began.

"Captain, this is the OOD on the bridge. We've been ordered to plane guard, sir. I'm coming around at twenty-two knots to station. Carrier still on course zero five zero, time to station about eight minutes."

He heard muffled coughing in the earpiece. Captain Kelley was a chain smoker and his gravel voice showed it, especially when awakening from a deep sleep. Only, Ed Kelley really never was in a deep sleep on the ship. He was a master at catnapping, and usually responded to the calls from the bridge without delay. The watch officers sometimes wondered if he really comprehended what they were reporting on the phone, but Kelley always answered.

Several nights earlier, on the long and boring midnight watch, the junior officers had argued over whether the captain really understood what they reported, or just mumbled, "Very well," rolled over, and went back to sleep. Frank Flanagan, who was on watch in the combat information center, had dared the bridge watch to ring the captain in the wee hours, and to call into the phone, "Piss call, you old son of a bitch." But Lagere was too wise to try it. He knew Kelley was full of surprises, and when he appeared to be asleep in the captain's reclining bridge chair, he never missed a trick.

"Flanagan, you're full of crap. Get one of the new watch officers to try it. I've been aboard too long."

Then, during Ensign Les Westerman's four-to-eight watch, Flanagan dared him, and the usually agreeable Westerman had taken the dare. He picked up the line, dialed the captain's sea cabin, and unknown to Flanagan, without pressing the transmit button, called so all on the bridge could hear, "Captain, sir, piss call, you old son of a bitch," and hung up the receiver. The entire bridge watch gawked at the large ensign, not believing their ears. They waited for the explosion.

Nothing happened. Flanagan caught on. "Chickenshit, you didn't press the transmit button." Westerman just grinned. Suddenly there was a roar and the bridge wing hatch exploded open with a clang and there stood Kelley in bathrobe and slippers.

"Who's got the conn, Westerman?" he yelled. "Where the hell's Westerman?" Kelley was always quick to grasp the tactical situation seconds after appearing on the bridge like this in the middle of the night. He could look out, see the loom of the carrier, and determine exactly where the ship was, and whether she was slightly off-station, or not moving smartly to the station. It was uncanny. However, during the past two days the ASW task force had been operating at complete darken ship with no running lights. The carrier was visible only from the glow of the aircraft engine nacelles on the flight deck and the dimmed red lights in her hangar bay. The task force was operating with minimal use of radar, which meant that the surface search radar was activated only when the OOD needed to reorient himself if he felt he was losing the picture, and then would activate the radar for a sweep or two only.

That night Kelley's eyes hadn't quite adjusted to the pitch dark on the bridge, and as he recovered from a fit of coughing, he grabbed the arm of the bosun mate of the watch and whispered hoarsely, "God-damnit, Westerman, you should be on station already." Then realizing he had hold of the bosun, he grumbled, groped forward in the darkened pilothouse, and suddenly grabbed hold of Westerman's arm. "Westerman, next time you want to play with the goddamn sound-powered phones, make sure you know what you're doing. I heard every word you said. Now square your watch away!"

Flanagan sniggered. Kelley spun around. "Flanagan, get back in the dark hole where you belong and stop skylarking."

But that had been during more relaxed times. On this early morning watch the bridge was silent. Captain Kelley appeared on the bridge shortly after Lagere's call and stood staring quietly out at the carrier, now ahead at five hundred yards on *Blandy*'s port bow. They were right on station. Kelley walked back to the quartermaster's navigation cubicle and studied the chart in the dim red glow. He could see that Hunter-Killer Group Bravo was now just about two hundred miles off Caicos Passage. How he longed to work a real submarine contact! One of those Russian submarines reported in the intelligence summary was there, somewhere in the dark. He could taste the excitement of the hunt.

He wanted to test his ASW team on the real thing, and he was confident they could handle any situation.

Blandy had won the Marjorie Sterett Navy League Atlantic Fleet trophy for ASW excellence two years before by holding contact on a U.S. nuclear sub for more than three hours. That was a significant feat in those years, when most escorts still had World War II sonar. *Blandy* had the SQS-23 sonar, with new high-frequency modulation, and an experimental attachment called ASPECT, for indentification and classification of underwater contacts. They had held onto that submarine contact like a bulldog, keeping out of the deadly torpedo sector, able at any moment to launch a simulated Mark 32 torpedo or lethal Hedgehog attack, an admirable feat in those years against the new and fast nuclear subs. But with his uncanny ability to foresee the next move by the sub, and with his SQS-23 sonar in only half power, Kelley had held contact on the "nuc" until the exercise was declared over. At the last moment, to prove he could have destroyed the submarine, Kelley had fired a pattern of the Hedgehog rockets armed with the training calibration rounds called SCAT, the use of which was strictly outlawed against U.S. submarines. Each of the twelve rounds in the pattern would deploy large, powerful magnets, which, as they descended through the water, struck the submarine harmlessly but would affix themselves to the steel hull. The sea flow motion around the submarine's skin caused steel hammers attached to each magnet to beat violently against the hull, increasing in intensity and rapidity as the submarine increased speed. Inside the submarine, the noise was unbearable. In this case, due to the high seas, the boat had been unable to accomplish the only remedy, which was to surface and send out swimmers to remove the magnets by hand. She had been forced to steam the ten-hour transit to Newport with the earsplitting staccato of a dozen hammers pounding her hull. It nearly drove the submariners mad; some were still suffering from ringing ears long after they moored in Newport.

During the postexercise hot washup, the attack sub skipper had been irate because Kelley had successfully deployed the banned Hedgehog SCAT rounds. He had demanded that *Blandy* be disqualified from being named the victor in the exercise. But Kelley's eloquent summary of the attack phase, in the presence of Vice Admiral "Whitey" Taylor, commander of the ASW forces in the Atlantic Fleet, had proved that had it been a combat situation, *Blandy* could have sunk the nuc. The submarine commander's protestations over the use of the banned training weapon fell on deaf ears. *Blandy* won the trophy, and the submariners vowed to get even with Kelley. Although half the submarine's crew had been temporarily deafened, the act had won *Blandy* the coveted trophy, and in the process, Kelley had secured his reputation for using unorthodox but winning tactics.

Commodore Morrison had warned Kelley afterward that such actions were poor sportsmanship and detrimental to safety. The submarine skipper had the commodore's promise that he would never let it happen again, but Ed Kelley had won the day and the trophy. And the wardroom celebrated at a beer bust at the datum officers' mess in Newport that night. That's the way Kelley was, and few could assemble the collective courage to cross him, except his own squadron commodore.

Ever since departing Newport, *Blandy*'s sailors had been anticipating contact with several Soviet submarines reported to be in the area. Intelligence reports warned of a Soviet naval oiler named *Terek*, which had been sighted by a long-range maritime patrol P2V Neptune flying out of Naval Air Station Lajes. The P2V had sighted and photographed a Soviet Zulu class diesel submarine on the surface refueling from the oiler using the astern method with the hose draped over the tanker's stern and a light cable to hold the submarine secure. United States Navy men thought this method of refueling at sea was strange. Of course, we seldom refueled submarines at sea, but often Soviet Navy destroyers were seen taking on fuel in this fashion. United States Navy standard procedure was to refuel while steaming alongside an oiler at twelve knots, using two fuel lines as explained earlier. This seemed a much more logical and more daring method than the Soviet way. *Terek* was lingering southwest of the Azores, and more submarines were anticipated in the area.

The antisubmarine warfare command headquarters procedure for keeping track of contacts gained by surface ships and aircraft at sea was a straightforward but at times confusing system. Since the goal of an ASW force is to gain and maintain contact on a submarine using some mode of detection—sonar, radar, the human eye, sonobuoy, or magnetic anomaly detector—usually there were far more contact reports submitted than there were real submarines. The compelling urge to spot a periscope or to hear a solid sonar echo often willed the senses, and sailors saw or heard precisely what they wanted to see or hear.

The Atlantic Fleet Antisubmarine Warfare Command in Norfolk designated with temporary numbers all submarine contacts reported on the ASW reporting system. If they were possible submarines, detected on the surface with radar or contacted submerged by sonar, the contacts were assigned numbers with a prefix C. When visually sighted on the surface and positively identified as submarines, they drew numbers with a prefix B. The Zulu class submarine sighted with the Soviet oiler *Terek* had been a solid visual contact, which was photographed and, therefore, designated to be a certain submarine, B28, on October 21. The many other sonar and radar contacts made during the Cuban crisis period by the eager ASW units were designated as possible submarines and numbered C1 through C26. These temporary designations were used to ensure continuity of the contacts, whether made by aircraft or surface ship. The decision to equate the reported contacts with other reports was done by analysts in the hallowed halls of the ASW Force Headquarters in Norfolk. These were usually experienced pilots, submariners, or destroyermen with significant years of experience chasing submarines. In the melee of the October 1962 weeks there were vastly more "possible" submarine contact C numbers issued than there were Soviet submarines in the area.

The reporting and evaluation system had been conceived during the dark days of the Battle of the Atlantic of World War II but had improved with new detection systems and higher-quality ships, aircraft, and submarines, with their newer equipment and advanced knowledge of the effects of seawater temperature, density, salinity, and currents on the propagation of sound. The science of ASW had grown by leaps and bounds since 1945, and the quality of training also had improved. But there still was in these days a certain lore to the science that caused some men to cross an invisible boundary from being efficient in the ASW technique to becoming an artist. Aboard *Blandy* we were blessed by having a number of ASW artists aboard, including ASW officer Brad Sherman, Sonarman First Class Larry Adcock, and several of his junior sonarmen who operated in the bowels of the ship in the frigid confines of the sonar compartment. In the brain of the ship, the combat information center, the wizards were operations officers Bob Briner and Frank Flanagan and the air controllers, radarmen Bruce Cogswell and Rudi Bump. Of course, the king of ASW artists was Captain Ed Kelley, who possessed the additional uncanny ability of either smelling a submarine or even somehow knowing what its commander was thinking.

At the time, few of us aboard knew anything about the secret new U.S. sophisticated passive underwater sound detection system called SOSUS. This vast system, consisting of large numbers of sensitive hydrophones arranged in series on the seabed at strategic locations through-out the North Atlantic, and operated from an inner sanctum called Ocean Systems Atlantic in Norfolk, enabled the tracking of noisy objects moving in the ocean. SOSUS systems later grew more sophisticated, using enhanced computers and automatic tracking; this occurred just as sound quieting on submarines also improved, making them more difficult to track.

In October 1962 the SOSUS system was still new, and the complex database required to correlate the sound levels of individual Soviet sub-marines was sparse. Soviet submarines had made relatively few deploy-ments to the broad Atlantic in the previous years. Individual long-range diesel submarines had begun patrolling the Atlantic in 1959, and their new nuclear-powered attack boats had made only intermittent incur-sions along our coast. The Soviets' newest naval threat, the Hotel class version of the SSBN, the answer to our Polaris boats, had made few patrols in the broad Atlantic, and their prototype Hotel class submarine, called *K-19*, had suffered a disastrous reactor casualty in July 1961. That unit, as described earlier, had been towed 1,200 miles back to Soviet waters, with many of the crew dying from heavy doses of radia-tion poisoning. The backbone of the Soviet ballistic missile submarine fleet at that time were the diesel-powered Type 629 (NATO name Golf class) boats, which were equipped with three R-13 ballistic missiles with a range of 350 miles. These had made few patrols out of home waters, but were capable of steaming on wartime patrols within missile range of the continental United States. So few had been tracked by U.S. sensors out into the broad Atlantic that little valuable sound fin-gerprinting, called sound pressure level data, were available to fine-tune the SOSUS system. Thus there were relatively little data on which to correlate and identify outbound Soviet submarines, including the diesel-powered Foxtrot class. So the job of making initial contact fell predominantly to the long-range maritime ASW aircraft, the P2V Nep-tunes patrolling out of Iceland, the Azores, and naval air stations along the U.S. East Coast from Brunswick, Maine, to Key West, Florida. Brit-ish forces augmented the coverage of the North Atlantic and the Iceland/Shetlands/Faeroes gap by flying their long-range ASW Nimrod and Shackelton patrol aircraft out of Rosyth in northern Scotland, while the Canadians flew their Argus submarine hunters out of Halifax, Nova Scotia, assisting the Americans flying out of Reykjavik, Iceland. The new U.S. Lockheed turboprop P3 Orions were still not widely deployed and at that time flew out of only several East Coast air stations, one of which was Naval Air Development Center Patuxent River, Maryland.

"Flanagan, here's the latest cut on the Russian force south of the Azores. Run this up to the CO and the commodore." Bob Briner, the operations officer, was a quiet officer, Annapolis class of '54. He was correct to the finest point of military decorum and calm in everything he did. No one quite understood how he could remain so totally unflinching when Ed Kelley roared at him or the mercurial XO railed against him after having caught one of Briner's officers napping after the noon meal, or one of his signalmen stealing sweet buns from the galley. Briner was unflappable, and quietly took care of his men despite the bellowing captain and skulking executive officer. Having Briner for a department head was a real godsend. He took extra time with each of his men to learn their personal problems and family situations. Most important, he shielded us from the constant wrath of the executive officer, who took no prisoners.

"And Frank," Briner said quietly, "do watch your language around the bridge area. The commodore has complained that some of our ship's company officers are too profane."

Flanagan smiled. "Too goddamn profane, sir? I can't believe why he would say that," and he quickly left the CIC and headed for the captain's chair on the starboard wing of the bridge carrying the message board.

Captain Kelley was slouched in his high, padded chair on the starboard wing of the pilothouse. He appeared to be asleep, but he was awake as usual, hunkered down like that until some unsuspecting soul on the bridge, usually the officer or junior officer of the deck, would err in some way and he would come flying out of his chair to berate the officer.

Flanagan walked up to the leather swivel chair and thrust the message board toward the captain. "Sir, the latest cut on the Russians, submarine tender, tanker, and Zulu class boat." The captain took the board silently, flipped it open, and began to read.

The officer of the deck was Gary Lagere, who was watching Flanagan out of the corner of his eye. "You're off-station, Lagere!" the captain suddenly bellowed. "Get your ass back where you belong and stay there!

"Aye, aye, sir." Lagere's face reddened as he walked out to the port bridge wing and took a bearing on the carrier *Essex*. How did Kelley know he was slightly off screening station? The carrier wasn't even visible from the captain's chair.

Lagere came back to the centerline pelorus and looked over at the captain. "Sir, the carrier bears 120, two thousand yards. We're on-station, sir."

"You mean *back* on-station, Lagere." The captain would never let a junior officer have the last word. Kelley was smiling, and Flanagan knew he was in a good mood. He generally was when the experienced Lagere was officer of the deck, and as long as the commodore was not around, Kelley could be almost pleasant.

Flanagan stood by the captain's chair as Kelley continued reading the messages. Flanagan winked at Lagere, who was still baffled that the captain had caught him a few degrees off-station. Lagere stared out over the top of the five-inch gun, Mount 51, at *Blandy*'s hurricane bow cutting though the swells. One of the best aspects about the Forrest Sherman class destroyers was the wide, gracefully spreading bow, which had improved her riding in heavy seas by cushioning the ship when pounding into heavy swells. So many new electronics had been added topside as the ship had been modernized that her center of gravity had risen to the point that in a beam sea she rolled much too slowly and heavily.

It was a beautiful Wednesday morning, October 24; the seas were moderate, and it was warm and clear, almost peaceful, as the carrier and her escorts steamed south at twenty-five knots toward Cuba. One of the bridge watch standers suddenly began to whistle softly in the bright morning sun. Flanagan, while still waiting for the captain to finish reading the message boards, was leaning on the navigation chart table. He heard the whistling and shot a look at the source across the pilot-house. It was a new deck force seaman, Richard Kloosterman, a huge Dutchman from Minnesota, who had just come aboard before the ship sailed from Newport. Kloosterman was fair-skinned, blond, 6-4, and weighed about 250 pounds. He looked just like his name, clumsy, inno-cent, rosy-cheeked, and awkward to the point where some believed he might be slightly retarded. But Kloosterman was simply slow. He was extremely polite and shy and had come from a good Dutch American farm family. He had begun to whistle probably because, like the whole watch section, he was looking forward to being relieved shortly for breakfast. However, whistling was taboo in the navy.

Before Flanagan could quietly get him to stop whistling, the first notes reached Ed Kelley's ears, and he shot up in his chair as if struck by an electric jolt. "Who the hell is whistling on my bridge?" he bellowed, turning toward the pilothouse, looking for the offender. Kloosterman, who was standing behind the helmsman—on watch under instruction—kept on whistling happily. Kelley scanned the pilothouse, scowling. Flanagan closed his eyes in anticipation of the coming explosion.

"Flanagan, find out who's whistling and get that man over here."

Flanagan knew the captain was having fun, but few others did. Kelley's rage seemed real and frightened everyone on the bridge except for the seasoned Lagere and Flanagan, who recognized the gleam in the captain's eyes.

"Kloosterman, get over here," Flanagan said loudly enough for the whole pilothouse to hear his flat Boston accent. The big baby-faced seaman lumbered toward the captain's chair, his eyes wide with fear, his fair cheeks coloring more than normal. He had never been this close to the captain, much less ever been addressed by the scowling Irishman. Flanagan stepped back to get out of the way.

Kelley glowered at the shaken Kloosterman. "Was that you whistling on my bridge?"

"Ah, no, sir, I mean, yes, sir, I think I was, sir."

"Nobody whistles here. Do you understand me, son? Only queers and bosuns whistle. Do you understand that?"

"But sir, I'm a bosun, or will be as soon as I get rated, then I'll—"

Kelley let out one of his ferocious roars. "Goddamn it, I mean bosuns whistle on their bloody bosun pipes, not through their lips."

Flanagan and Lagere were holding back chuckles. Kloosterman looked confused, "Yes, sir, I won't whistle again sir, ever." Flanagan began to snicker.

Kelley swung on him. "Mr. Flanagan, this is not funny. Get your Boston ass off my bridge." Flanagan, still smiling, took the message board and quickly walked to the aft door of the pilothouse leading to the CIC. He paused and looked around at the pilothouse watch, and saw that most wore reserved smiles, knowing that the captain was joshing. The frightened Kloosterman stood frozen next to the captain. Kelley suddenly put his arm around the big seaman's hulking shoulders and shook him. "Son, keep up the good work, and remember, never whistle on the bridge or anywhere on this ship or on any navy ship, right?"

The young giant nodded quickly, "Yes, sir, I mean, no, sir, I won't whistle again."

"Commodore on the bridge!" the quartermaster of the watch shouted. Kelley groaned and slouched down into the chair. "What the hell does he want, Lagere?" Lagere saluted as the commodore came up to the centerline and looked around.

"Anything going on, Mr. Lagere?" Commodore Charles Morrison spoke in a subdued voice. He was a short, slight man, and had a habit of walking quietly around the ship, making small talk with the crew. The custom made Ed Kelley nervous. He loathed having the staff of Destroyer Squadron 24 aboard. Since *Blandy* was built to house a staff, it was inevitable that during major operations Kelley had to give up his large and comfortable in-port cabin to the commodore, and was relegated to sleeping and working in his sea cabin on the same level of the bridge.

"Good morning, Ed." Morrison smiled at Kelley, still hunched in his chair.

"Morning, sir. What can I do for you on *my* bridge?"

"Oh, just looking around."

Kelley snorted. "Mr. Lagere, brief the commodore on our current disposition. I'll be in my sea cabin." And he slid out of his chair and walked aft to his cabin.

"Captain's off the bridge!" the quartermaster shouted. Kelley stopped, one foot through the doorway to his sea cabin. He glared at Seaman Kloosterman, who stood behind the helmsman. The seaman still looked in shock after the earlier scene.

"Remember, Bosun, no goddamn whistling." The commodore pretended he hadn't heard. Lagere suppressed a smile and continued to brief the commodore. Kelley slammed the door.

✥

After two days and nights of steaming and a series of false sonar contacts, *Blandy* was once again ordered from the screen to plane-guard station on the carrier *Essex*. This station, although entertaining for off-watch personnel who could observe the flight operations at short range, meant fast-moving work for the two officers of the deck on the bridge. During a typical four-hour plane guard watch, with the carrier steaming alternately into the wind for air operations, and abruptly downwind to regain position, the destroyers were usually on their way to, and rarely on, station. The escorts and carrier operated at darken ship, with only red flight-deck lights visible on the carrier.

Night flight operations resembled a scripted ballet dance, with tiny figures darting in and out among the Grumman S2F Trackers and AD Skyraiders that were launching and recovering on the dark stage to the accompaniment of the howling wind and the hum of aircraft piston engines. At close range, flight operations could be gripping, especially when the captain slipped quietly onto the bridge, took one quick assessing glance at the situation, and when what he found was not to his satisfaction, launched a barrage of verbal abuse at the watch officers sufficient to make a seasoned bosun blush.

The crew fell into the routine. The officers went about their watches and soon became accomplished watch standers, especially when standing a three-section watch bill (four hours on, eight off) for weeks without a break. At the time we were aware only that we were part of the cordon thrown hastily around Cuba, and we watched with apprehension as the red forms on the intelligence plot depicted an array of Soviet merchant ships approaching the cordon of U.S. surface warships. Strangely absent were any visible Soviet warship escorts.

The task group initially had no idea how many Soviet submarines might be escorting their merchant ships, and at the shipboard level we had no overall antisubmarine tactical intelligence picture. In those days tactical intelligence support for forces at sea was practically nonexistent.

We did not know at the time that Captain Agafonov's force of four Foxtrot class submarines from Polyarny was already among the U.S. naval cordon. All four submarines of the Sixty-ninth Brigade were already spread in and around the Walnut line of the blockade, and Captain Shumkov's *B-130* was no more than fifty miles from the *Essex* hunter-killer group.

October 24, 1962
Chief of Naval Operations' Flag Plot
Naval Command Center, the Pentagon
Arlington, Virginia

Meanwhile, unknown aboard the *Blandy* or the other ships in the quarantine, in the Chief of Naval Operations' Flag Plot in the Pentagon, several nervous intelligence officers and yeomen were plotting the courses of half a dozen Soviet merchants, which were approaching the quarantine's outer perimeter Walnut line. The plot showed at least a dozen red tags bearing designations of submarine contacts, many of them spurious, but all labeled with numbers from C1 through C29. The wall chart looked as if it had erupted with measles.

The deputy chief of naval operations, Vice Admiral Griffin, stood gazing at the board. Secretary of Defense Robert McNamara stood next to the admiral, his eyes locked on the plot. Both saw the encounter forming on the chart. The line of Soviet merchant ships was approaching the navy quarantine line, the first expected to reach the line the next day at about 10:00 A.M. Washington time. Soviet merchant ship traffic heading for Cuban ports had been heavy for the past two months, but since the quarantine had been announced by President Kennedy, the situation had taken a new and more deliberate form. There was a surge of merchantmen which, for some reason, had altered speed such that they were now converging on the quarantine line in an echelon rather than piecemeal. It was not known at this point whether that had been because of a command sent to all participants of Operation *Anadyr* or merely by chance. Those ships approaching the line would indeed be the test cases, the test of America's will. Leading the pack was the Soviet tanker *Bucharest*.

Looking like buckshot, red submarine contact markers were splattered all over the plot. It seemed that every ship in the fleet was reporting a suspicious sighting, sonar contact, or radar blip as possible submarines. If each reported contact had been a Soviet submarine, they would have represented nearly the entire Soviet submarine inventory. As Admiral Griffin stood scanning the wall display with the secretary of defense, he felt the question coming.

"How might our ships signal a submerged Soviet submarine to surface?" McNamara asked in his intellectual manner.

Admiral Griffin thought for a while, then launched into a long description of international signal codes and how these might be transmitted to remind ships and submarines alike of accepted international behavior in this delicate situation. As a result of that conversation on October 24, the U.S. Naval Oceanographic Office issued Notice to Mariners 45-62, Special Warning 32, "Submarine Surfacing and Identification Procedures When Contacted by Quarantine Forces in the General Vicinity of Cuba." It read:

U.S. forces coming in contact with unidentified submerged submarines will make the following signals to inform the submarine that he may surface in order to identify himself: Signals follow—Quarantine forces will drop 4 to 5 harmless explosive sound signals (hand grenades) which may be accompanied by the international code signal "IDKCA" meaning "Rise to the surface." This sonar signal is normally made on underwater communications equipment in the 8 kc. frequency range. Procedure on receipt of the signal: Submerged submarine, on hearing the signal, should surface on an easterly course.

Signal and procedures employed are harmless. NAVOCEANO, NOTAM 45-62, paragraph 5982.

The CNO Flag Plot flashed the notam to all ships and stations and placed it on the international warning lists for all countries to copy.

OCTOBER 24, 1962
SOVIET EMBASSY
MILITARY ATTACHÉ ANNEX
BELMONT CIRCLE, WASHINGTON, D.C.

That afternoon the Soviet naval attaché, Vice Admiral Bekrenyev, took the message from the communicator and grunted. He read it slowly, then a second time. It was a notice to mariners announcing that U.S. warships would be dropping explosives to signal unidentified submarines to surface and identify themselves. He turned and gave the notam message back to the radioman. "Pass this to Main Navy headquarters Moscow quickly with the recommendation that it be placed on the special fleet and submarine broadcast immediately." The admiral turned and looked at his wall map of the U.S. eastern seaboard. He glanced at the log posted on the side and smiled. Captain Lev Vtorygin and his assistant were now heading south on Interstate 95 just east of Moorhead City, North Carolina. The admiral wondered what they would observe at the Second Marine Division's loading-out piers.

OCTOBER 24, 1962
USS BLANDY
NORTH ATLANTIC

Bob Briner handed the notam to Captain Kelley, who was seated in his chair on the bridge wing. Kelley read the warning.

"Christ, next they'll want us to give him ice cream and cookies and kiss his ass. Ought to blow the son of a bitch outta the water if he doesn't come up when he knows we got him. Show this to the commodore and then make sure Brad Sherman has a copy posted in sonar. And post a copy here on the bridge on the attack director so all watch officers know it by heart. Tell Brad I want to wrap the grenades with toilet paper rolls to make them detonate deeper." Kelley had used this tactic during maneuvers with U.S. submarines, which were always deeper than the practice depth charge grenades could reach. Unaltered they would explode at about 50 feet as a safety measure. Although considered harmless, submariners detested the grenades because a near blast, small as it was, could damage some sensitive equipment on the submarine. By wrapping the grenades with a full roll of toilet paper, the handles would not spring to activate the fuse until the paper had dissolved away, letting the grenade fall deeper, where they exploded nearer 100 or even 150 feet below if enough toilet paper were used. Flanagan had dubbed these *Blandy* missiles "shit paper ash cans."

To this day I can still see the sheet of sun-yellowed paper announcing the notice to mariners stuck with masking tape on the director, flapping in the wind. I had stared at that warning for many long hours standing watches and wondered if we'd ever use it again after that unforgettable day we received it.

OCTOBER 24, 1962
CHIEF OF NAVAL OPERATIONS' FLAG PLOT
U.S. NAVY COMMAND CENTER, THE PENTAGON

The U.S. naval blockade of Cuba went into effect at 10:00 A.M. on October 24. As the tense day wore on, Secretary of Defense Robert McNamara became convinced that the navy was not informing him of everything that was going on. The chief of naval operations, Admiral George W. Anderson, seemed to indicate to the secretary of defense that the navy would take care of the details of the blockade and there was nothing for the civilian leaders to worry about. Dissatisfied with the navy's attitude, McNamara marched to Flag Plot, the navy's command center in the Pentagon. In the large center about thirty navy men and women worked silently, plotting the positions of U.S. and Soviet ships on a large wall chart. Secretary McNamara began firing questions at the duty officer just as Admiral Anderson strode into the room.

McNamara pointed to a U.S. ship plotted alone on the chart far from the quarantine line. "What's it doing there?" he asked. Admiral Anderson would not answer the secretary's question, he later admitted, because that ship was tracking one of several Soviet submarines suspected to be in the area, and there were too many people in the room to overhear that highly sensitive information.[1]

McNamara began to shoot questions rapidly at Admiral Anderson. What was the navy's plan for the initial intercept of a Soviet ship? Anderson answered that there was no need to discuss it, the operation was the navy's concern. The defense secretary began lecturing Anderson on the object of the quarantine, which was, he said, to communicate a delicate diplomatic message to Khrushchev and not to shoot anyone. What were the navy's plans if a Soviet ship failed to comply with the order to stop? Were there Russian-language speakers aboard all the blockading ships? What were Anderson's orders to the blockading ships?

The subject turned to the Soviet ship crossing into the blockade the first day, the tanker *Bucharest*. How was the navy going to challenge it?[2]

"In what language—English or Russian?" the secretary asked.

"How the hell do I know? I suppose we'll use flags," answered Anderson.

"Well, what if they don't stop?" McNamara asked.

"We'll send a shot across the bow."

"Then what if that doesn't work?" asked McNamara.

"Then we'll fire into the rudder," Anderson replied, annoyed.

"What kind of a ship is it?"

"A tanker, Mr. Secretary," said the admiral.

"You are not going to fire a single shot at a tanker without my express permission. Is that clear?" asked McNamara.

Admiral Anderson had never been cross-examined in such a manner by the civilian secretary of defense, and he grew irate. He picked up a thick copy of *U.S. Navy Regulations* and waved it at McNamara, saying that the navy had been running blockades from the days of John Paul Jones, that the details were all inside that book.

McNamara responded testily, "I don't give a damn what John Paul Jones would have done. I want to know what you are going to do now."[3]

Admiral Anderson retorted, "Now, Mr. Secretary, if you and your deputy will go back to your offices, the navy will run the blockade."

The strain of the situation was already beginning to take its toll on the leaders in Washington and Moscow, as well as on the men at sea.

OCTOBER 25, 1962
HEADQUARTERS, MAIN NAVY STAFF
GRIBAYEDOVO STREET, MOSCOW

Admiral Leonid Rybalko sat motionless in the front seat of the Volga driven by a uniformed navy driver from the Main Navy Staff headquarters. They wound through the morning sunlight of the nearly deserted Moscow Garden Ring Road, heading to the yellow navy headquarters building on Gribayedovo Street. Rybalko had just arrived on the morning train from Murmansk. He had not slept much in the double-bunked cabin, even though he had been the sole occupant. It seemed that each time he took the thirty-six-hour train ride from Murmansk to Moscow, the sleeping car seemed to have one square wheel, which made sleep impossible. The conductress had brought him the usual glass of hot tea in the metal holder, which he had drunk as he watched the train slide into the wooded northern suburbs of Moscow. It was late October, and wet, slushy snow lay in gray pools on the ground as the train pulled into Yaroslavl Station. Rybalko was worried. His four submarines were steaming into the center of a churning cauldron of naval activity in the Caribbean. Their entry into Mariel, Cuba, had been postponed, yet he could not find out what intelligence the Moscow Main Navy Staff had passed to them on the fleet broadcast. Captain Agafonov and his brigade's four commanders were operating completely in the dark. Squadron Commander Rybalko had virtually camped out for the past four days at the Severomorsk Northern Fleet headquarters command center. He had followed the deputy commander, Vice Admiral Rossokho, like a shadow. However, Rossokho was either unwilling or unable to give him any news regarding what operational information had been sent to the transiting units of Operation *Kama*.

"Leonid Rybalko, I tell you all I know for certain is that your Project 629 missile boats have been put on an indefinite hold and will remain ready to deploy on command." The seven Golf class ballistic missile submarines that made up the second submarine echelon of his Twentieth Special Squadron, founded specially for Operation *Kama*, had been scheduled to sail on October 23 for their covert transit to Mariel but had been delayed as soon as the U.S. president announced the blockade around Cuba. The surface group also was prepared to sail at a moment's notice but still remained moored in Severomorsk awaiting the final orders to depart. The growing tension in the Caribbean had caused the postponement.

Rybalko was not getting information from Moscow. So Rossokho had relented, more to get Rybalko out of his hair at the Northern Fleet headquarters than anything else, and sent him packing to Moscow to get information directly from Admiral Fokin, the head of *Kama* on the Moscow Main Navy Staff. When the Northern Fleet commander refused to give Rybalko a lift in his commander in chief's VIP-configured TU-114 aircraft, he had been forced to take the long train ride, which always left him irritable, tired, and unsure of himself. His main concern was for all the submarines and ships that he now commanded. However, his anxiety over Agafonov's brigade now sailing into the unknown gave him resolve to head to Moscow to find some answers.

The mud-splattered Volga pulled up at the front entrance to the headquarters. Two armed naval infantry sentries stood at the door. Rybalko jumped out of the car. "Park over there and don't drift too far away; we may be heading back to the train station on short notice."

"Aye, aye, Comrade Admiral." The young driver ground the gears of the black Volga and pulled it off under a tree to wait.

Rybalko mounted the steps two at a time, returned the sentries' salutes, and headed toward the basement command center. He was familiar with the building, having served a tour there earlier as a captain in the Directorate for Submarine Operations. As he wound through the narrow corridors past the flags and the bust of Admiral Makarov, hero of the Russo-Japanese War, he came to an abrupt halt at a desk where a lieutenant sat with a pistol strapped on a leather belt around his blue tunic with the red piping of a naval infantry officer. His uniform smelled of wet wool.

"Good morning, Admiral." The lieutenant rose quickly.

"Morning, Lieutenant. I'm Rybalko, Leonid Filippovich, Twentieth Special Submarine Squadron, Polyarny." He displayed his small pass.

"*Yest*, Comrade Admiral." The lieutenant opened the thick steel doors just as two more officers arrived at the desk. One wore the shoulder marks of a full admiral, the other, a captain first rank with the badge of a submarine commander.

"Greetings, Leonid Filippovich. What brings you down here? We thought you would be standing by your tender ready to sail." Admiral Fokin, the first deputy chief of staff and head of Operation *Kama*, spoke with a sour look on his face.

"I'd like to find out what's going on, Admiral." Rybalko tried to smile but had no reason to do so. The third man was Captain Vladimir Popov, who had flown with him to Severomorsk a month ago after his meeting with the minister. Popov had been his *starpom* on his last submarine command. They shook hands warmly. "Good to see you, Valodiya," Rybalko smiled for the first time that day. Popov was an excellent officer and had gone on to command his own submarine. He was in line now to take command of a new nuclear submarine now building in Severodvinsk. "How's your precommissioning assignment?" Rybalko asked.

"Haven't been able to detach from the headquarters, sir, with all this going on. I have a good *starpom* who's running the show there now. We're due for commissioning in two months; hope I'll be down there by then. It's one of the new Kit Project 627 [November class] attack boats. I can't get out of this headquarters soon enough."

Rybalko smiled again, remembering the unbridled enthusiasm of the younger officers when he was commanding his last submarine. The new nuclear-powered submarine navy was drawing the best and brightest, and the whole submarine corps was made up of enthusiastic and optimistic young officers.

The three officers entered the large command center. It was a single circular room filled with the haze of cigarette smoke. A large crescent-shaped table stood in the center, with individual stacks of shelves facing each of fifteen chairs arrayed around the table's outer perimeter. Large telephones of various colors stood in a mass of wires and ashtrays in front of each chair. The chairs were occupied by officers of various ranks, each representing one of the Main Staff directorates. In the center of the half moon was the largest chair, for the chief of staff. Plates of half-eaten cookies, empty tea glasses, and bowls of fruit were scattered around the table. A large chart of the Atlantic from a bank of charts was pulled down on the facing wall. Two young sailors were adjusting red and black markers on the board. A mass of black marks was strewn around the Caribbean and Atlantic Ocean areas south of Bermuda and all along the coast of the United States. There were not many red marks to be seen. Rybalko's eyes immediately took in the scene at the table and on the chart, and noticed that there were four red submarine silhouettes plotted near the Bahamas west of Florida.

"Tea, Admiral?" A young orderly stood with a tray with three glasses of tea and small plate of open-face sandwiches of cheese and cucumbers. Rybalko took a glass and stared at the chart.

"Comrade Admiral"—he looked at Fokin—"what information has been passed to Agafonov's boats about the current situation? Are they aware of our increased defense posture? Do they know of the deployment of the American ASW hunter-killer groups?"

Fokin cut him off. "Leonid Filippovich, the fleet commander in chief, Admiral Gorshkov himself, has prohibited us from putting anything more than the routine information on the scheduled submarine broadcasts. It is the opinion of our security department that adding too much might give away the operational facts to those who analyze our communications traffic that we in fact have a sensitive naval operation in progress." The admiral paused and picked up a glass of tea from the tray.

"The last operational signal sent to Agafonov's boats was the curtailment order on October 15, telling them to break off the transit to Mariel and to take patrol stations off the Bahamas just outside the announced American blockade line called the Walnut line. You know about that order since we copied you in Polyarny."

Rybalko nodded, listening closely. He was growing more and more incredulous. Agafonov's four boats were now in the midst of a growing number of U.S. ships, and patrolling their small areas assigned in a departure from the operation instructions. The four skippers had no knowledge of the rudimentary facts of what was going on tactically or in the larger picture.

A staff officer entered the command center from a screened-off anteroom where the communications teletypewriters clattered. A sign above the entrance warned "Entry Prohibited, Top Secret Area." He approached the two admirals.

"Sir, you need to see this."

Admiral Fokin took the piece of yellow teletype paper, read it, and handed it to Rybalko. "Read this; it's a notice to mariners. The Americans are announcing they are going to drop explosive signals to force our submarines to surface and be identified, taking a safety course of due east to acknowledge understanding."

Rybalko read the warning. "Agafonov's orders are to remain covert; they will not surface until they have to charge batteries. They need to know about this American warning. You are planning to send this warning on the broadcast?"

Fokin looked at the wall chart and then back at Rybalko. Rybalko read the warning again, then said, "We must send it so they know what's going on." He handed the warning signal back to Fokin, who gave the message back to the communications officer.

"Orders directly from Admiral Gorshkov are to send only routine traffic on the broadcast. This cannot be sent out." Fokin replied and walked over to the plot. "Leonid, Commander in Chief Gorshkov is dead set against sending extraneous material on the schedules. He believes the traffic analysis will give away our operation." The admiral looked at his watch.

"Leonid, I know you are concerned." Admiral Fokin continued, "Take a chair there, make it your home. Stay here in Moscow for a few days so you can see what's happening. Your follow-on units will not be ordered to sail before you return to Severomorsk. It looks as if this whole operation is becoming flexible, even reactive. Our biggest concern is the continuation of the Morflot transports moving the equipment and men to Cuba. So far the Americans have not taken any actions other than increasing their aerial surveillance and sending more ships to sea. We'll have to watch and wait. We can have you back in Severomorsk in several hours on the staff flight out of Vnukovo if need be. So relax, have some breakfast. You can take a room in the duty guest apartment on the second floor." Fokin hurried out of the command center.

Rybalko stood quietly surveying the situation, and watching the hum of activity continue around him. Captain Popov stood next to him in silence. Rybalko had the uncomfortable feeling that the new squadron command just given him a month earlier was turning into a shambles. He could not allow his men in the four submarines to continue to operate in a total information vacuum thousands of miles away at the enemy's front door. Too much was at stake; their lives and the mission were in danger. To let them continue without intervening was against everything he had ever believed in more than thirty years in uniform.

Rybalko suddenly sat down at the table and began to scratch out a message. He finished it and showed it to Popov, who stood behind him as he wrote.

Popov read it and looked shocked. "Sir, if you send this you're countermanding Gorshkov's order about sending traffic on the broadcast!"

"I know, Valodiya." Rybalko stood up slowly. "One thing I learned during the last war was that in combat, you owe absolute loyalty to the men under your command, just as they are loyal to follow your orders blindly." Rybalko walked over to the communications corner and called out the duty officer who had shown the two admirals the U.S. notice to mariners message.

"Yes, sir, Comrade Admiral. What do you need, sir?" The communications watch officer looked puzzled to see the admiral, who was not part of the Main Navy Command Center crisis watch.

Rybalko handed the lieutenant the message he had scrawled. "Put this on the next submarine support broadcast." He looked at the clock on the wall, "Put it on the noon and repeat it on the midnight broadcast to all units in the Atlantic."

The lieutenant took the message and looked at Rybalko. "Are you certain this should go, sir, it seems we are not allowed—"

"I am ordering you to send it, young man. Do it, and I will take full responsibility for the action. Here." Rybalko took the draft message back and scribbled his signature and time and date in the margin and handed it back. "Get it sent exactly on time."

"Aye, Comrade Admiral." The lieutenant disappeared into the curtained communications room.

Captain Popov looked at Rybalko. "Sir, I agree with sending that out. Agafonov and his boats must see that warning, but I'm afraid everyone will know it was you who gave the order to send it. That could be bad for your health, sir."

Rybalko looked at the junior captain, and smiled. "I know what I'm doing. What does an old warhorse like me have to worry about? It's absolutely the right thing to do. Wouldn't you send it, too?" The tall admiral looked directly at the young captain of whom he was so fond. "If you wouldn't send it, you are not worthy of taking command of your own men in that newfangled sub of yours."

Rybalko left the command center.

OCTOBER 26, 1962
THE WHITE HOUSE
WASHINGTON, D.C.

On October 26 President John F. Kennedy received a message from Premier Nikita S. Khrushchev in which the Soviet leader proposed that his government would withdraw the offensive missiles and destroy their launch sites in Cuba if the United States would lift the blockade and agree not to invade Cuba. The letter had been transmitted in sections via the U.S. embassy in Moscow just before 10:00 A.M., Washington time. The letter was transmitted by cable to the State Department and began to arrive at 6:00 P.M. It was 9:00 P.M. when the State Department received the section of the message in which Khrushchev called on the U.S. president to "show statesmanlike wisdom" and to offer a guarantee not to invade Cuba in exchange for a Soviet withdrawal of the missiles.[4] That message was not made known to the public for some time.

OCTOBER 26, 1962
MOSCOW

Admiral Rybalko stood looking out over the Moscow skyline from the balcony of his Moscow apartment. He could see the gold of the Kremlin cathedral domes sparkling in the evening light. His apartment on Kutuzovsky Prospekt offered him a clear view of the heart of the downtown capital. The scene of the Kremlin was peaceful and seemed solid and powerful to the admiral. The red star atop the Kremlin State House glowed in splendor. His wife, Galina, stood behind him on the balcony.

"Are you sure you have to return north tonight, Lyova?" Galina asked.

He paused and then answered, "Yes, I have to be ready for whatever happens. I'm afraid the situation is going to get worse, and I have put myself in a rather exposed position. I have to stand by my commanders; I think they're in real trouble in the Caribbean."

Galina thought she understood.

Atlantic Datum

FRIDAY MORNING
OCTOBER 26, 1962
USS *BLANDY*
TWO HUNDRED MILES NORTHEAST OF CAICOS PASSAGE

After repeated energy-sapping nights of plane guard, the fourth day out of Newport, *Blandy* was abruptly ordered away from the carrier *Essex* and the rest of the hunter-killer group at flank speed to investigate a submarine contact at some distance.

At that time aboard the hunter-killer destroyers we were under the impression that a long-range patrol aircraft, a P3 Orion or an older P2V Neptune, had luckily gained contact on a submarine too distant for *Essex*'s tactical aircraft to pursue. In fact, it had initially been detected by our SOSUS, still a closely held secret in those days. A Neptune had been sent out to intercept the submarine, but after brief contact lost it and was forced to return to base for fuel.

Late in the morning on October 26 a new P3 Orion using call sign Pinstripe 21 and piloted by Lieutenant B. W. Bartlett took off from Naval Air Station Patuxent River to take up the search for the submarine contact lost earlier. Bartlett pulled back on the yoke of the Lockheed's four-turboprop aircraft and banked to the east.

"Roger, this is Pinstripe 21, will be at angels two seven [twenty-seven thousand feet altitude] in five minutes. Heading one five zero to Adelphi [the radio call sign of the HUK group commander aboard the USS *Essex*]. Time to datum [last known position of the submarine], two point five [two and a half hours]." Lieutenant Bartlett would be guided to datum by air controllers aboard *Essex*. As soon as his P3 was within UHF radio voice range of the carrier, radarmen in the carrier's combat information center, using the call sign Adelphi of the hunter-killer task group commander, would take control of the Orion aircraft and start him on a complex submarine search pattern. Bartlett would then drop a series of passive sonobuoy patterns and monitor their signals in the effort to locate the submarine. By using the passive Jezebel sonobuoys, dropped in prescribed patterns, a P3 Orion could locate and track a submarine with great precision and had the incredible ability to remain on station for more than twelve hours with two of his four propellers feathered.

In the early afternoon of Friday, October 26, Lieutenant Bartlett's P3 approached the area, descended to twelve hundred feet, and throttled back to cruising speed. He looked out at the expanse of ocean below; it was a beautiful, clear day. The color of the ocean surface was a rich blue, with only the slightest hint of swells. For the first forty-five minutes the aircrew gained no contacts—visual, radar, or by sonobuoys. Bartlett called in to Adelphi for a confirmation of the coordinates of the last position of the datum. With the fresh coordinates he called his tactical coordinator (TACCO), Lieutenant Junior Grade George Abercrombie, on the intercom.

"George, let's put a marker buoy on the spot and drop a pattern."

"Roger, sir." The TACCO notified the operator who chose the sonobuoy frequency channels for the AN/ASA-20 recorder, which would monitor the buoys' responses. They selected the SSQ-23 passive sonobuoys and loaded the drop chutes.

Bartlett steadied the airplane on the bearing given by the TACCO, descended to a thousand feet, and approached the point. When over the point the ordnanceman pressed the switch releasing the first buoy, after which the pilot turned to the next bearing to the point of release of the second buoy. The process was repeated, and a pattern of sixteen buoys sailed to the ocean surface, hit the water with small splashes, and deployed their antennae. The TACCO then gave Bartlett another bearing to take while he monitored the buoys on the recorder. They repeated the procedure four times over the next two hours, proceeding in an expanding circle from the original position.

Two and a half hours of monitoring passed when suddenly Abercrombie's voice broke over the intercom. "Sir, we're drawing on the last pattern, possible submarine bearing zero four zero!" The call broke the boredom, and excitement began to mount.

Bartlett called in the contact to the ASW hunter-killer commander, call sign Adelphi, aboard the USS *Essex*, who immediately launched a helicopter to assist the P3 in holding the contact. At the same time Adelphi called the ASW screen commander of Destroyer Squadron 24, call sign Abigail Zulu, aboard *Blandy*, and a series of rapid commands erupted in *Blandy*'s combat information center. Within five minutes the commander of ASW forces, Atlantic Fleet, designated the contact C18, a possible Soviet Foxtrot class submarine. Then the fun began.

Blandy was quickly ordered to approach a point in the ocean computed to be on the track of the submarine and to work with the *Essex* aircraft and the P3 to locate the submerged contact and determine its depth and identity.

Captain Kelley was aflame. "This time we're going to get hold the bastard till he has to pop up."

On the same morning, U.S. surveillance aircraft were tracking two Soviet merchant ships, dry cargo freighters *Yuri Gagarin* and *Komiles*, nearing the outer quarantine line, within twenty miles of the submarine contact followed by Lieutenant Bartlett in his P3 Pinstripe 21—one merchant located to the east, the other west of the contact. As *Blandy* closed to within ten miles of the submarine contact, anticipating ASW action, we were suddenly ordered to stand off and allow the aircraft to work together with a helicopter from *Essex*. *Blandy* was ordered instead to shadow the two merchant ships.

Kelley was growing impatient and wanted to rush in and try to gain contact on the submarine with our SQS-23 sonar. "Damn bird farm'll never bring that guy to heel. They need us to lock on him like a bulldog," Kelley complained to the commodore.

"Ed, be patient, your time will come." Morrison was accustomed to pacifying the anxious Kelley.

Captain Kelley and XO Lester were huddled in the charthouse when I arrived on the bridge to relieve Dan Davidson as junior officer of the deck. We were steaming at twenty-five knots, going somewhere in a hurry. The atmosphere on the bridge was charged, and the captain was more excited than usual. I relieved the watch and was with Brad Sherman, the officer of the deck, just as Kelley came arching onto the bridge.

"Brad, come to new course three four three, stay at twenty-five knots. We're being sent to check out two Russian merchants heading into the quarantine line. I'd rather go after the sub contact that the *Essex* helos are still trying to gain. Without us they'll probably lose the son of a bitch!"

"Aye, aye, sir." Sherman made the course change. We were now steaming northwest, heading away from *Essex*, which was about ten miles now to the south, still near the contact, C18.

"We're in a meeting situation with the Russian freighter *Yuri Gagarin*; you should pick her up in about half an hour. I'll be in my sea cabin."

The captain was dead serious now; the air of joviality on the ship had given way to a feeling of seriousness and anticipation. I had always wondered if I was going to see combat during my lifetime, and now here we were about to confront two Soviet freighters heading for the quarantine line. The words of the operation order I had just decrypted the night before remained in my mind. It read: "[I]n case the Soviet merchant refuses to follow directed course and speed you will fire a round across her bow, if refusal continues you will fire a round of main battery to destroy her rudder."

Flanagan had tuned in to the radio the evening before and we had listened to the shortwave Voice of America evening news. The announcer told of the personal interview held two days earlier, on October 24, with Premier Khrushchev and William E. Knox, the U.S. industrialist president of Westinghouse International. The Soviet premier had used him as a platform to signal his serious intent to the U.S. president. Khrushchev had told Knox that if Americans would stop and search a single Soviet ship, it would be an act of piracy. He warned that if the United States did so, he would instruct his submarines to sink the U.S. ships.[5]

Frank had repeated the news item at dinner in the wardroom. "I always wanted to be a pirate. Imagine what our grandchildren will say!"

"Shut up, Flanagan, we don't need this now." The exec looked pale and glanced at Captain Kelley.

The captain didn't smile but kept eating; he looked grim and tired. The wardroom grew quiet. Suddenly Kelley slammed his fist on the table. "That's it, we're going to break out live Hedgehogs on the launcher spigots. Brad, do so right after dinner."

The rest of the meal was eaten in near silence.

FRIDAY AFTEROON
OCTOBER 26, 1962
USS *BLANDY*
NEAR CAICOS PASSAGE

That Friday we continued to steam at flank speed toward the Soviet freighters *Yuri Gagarin* and *Komiles*, which should be coming within visual range within the hour and crossing into the forbidden quarantine zone.

The XO came onto the bridge, "Brad, have the bosun mate of the watch pipe this." Brad Sherman read the piece of paper Lester handed him. He gave it to the bosun mate, Petty Officer Petit. Petit picked up the 1MC microphone. He gave the short "Attention" pipe and announced, "Now muster the boarding and search party on the 01 deck, provide."

Since I was the officer in charge of one of the two boarding parties, I left the bridge watch and headed down to pick up my gear. This was the drill for preparing to board and search a Soviet ship. I was so excited I collided with Chief Staff Officer Campbell in the pilothouse. "Sorry, sir," I stammered, and ran out of the bridge and down the signal bridge ladder onto the 01 level, then down to the ship's armory. A group of men was huddled around the armory, mostly bosun mates from the deck force and a few gunners mates and Quartermaster Emery, his tattoos showing beneath his blue chambray shirt. He grinned at me. "Looks like we're in for some action, sir." This was the kind of thrill the rambunctious Emery loved. I could just see him on a Newport barstool telling the story of this day, holding the entire bar spellbound, the single, larger-than-life eyeball tattooed on the back of his shorn head staring out at the astonished listeners.

Chief Master at Arms Caldwell issued me a regulation Colt .45 pistol and a web belt with two clips of ammunition. I ran to my stateroom, grabbed my helmet, started back out in the passageway, and ran smack into the disbursing officer, Stonewall Jackson, who had just returned to the ship via highline from the carrier during our last refueling the day before. He had been on his honeymoon and missed the sailing from

Newport. Stonewall was in his underwear and carrying a book while coming out of the head. He was not wearing his glasses, and it took a while before he recognized me.

"The hell's going on?" He sounded alarmed. As a supply officer Stonewall was not required to stand watches but had his hands full keeping the crew mess decks and the wardroom functioning and happy. There was little aboard as important to the crew as the meals they ate, and Jackson was in charge of them all. He would stay up late at night working or reading and was known to sleep during much of the day. It was not unusual to see him crawling out of his bunk in the after officers' berth area at midmorning. I smiled, feeling self-conscious with my helmet and pistol.

"Don't let them give you any shit, Duck, and while you're over there, see if you can get a couple bottles of vodka. I would sure like a martini tonight."

"Okay, Stonewall, I'll do my best."

But I felt less than jovial. In fact, I was scared. Not so much of being hurt or even killed by a bunch of Russians, but mostly because I hadn't a clue of what I was supposed to do. What did contraband look like? What was I supposed to say? How was I to deploy the troops of the boarding party? I had visions of getting lost aboard a strange ship.

I returned to the 01 level. There the rest of the two boarding parties were assembled. Les Westerman was the officer in charge of the second boarding team, and he was already there with his pistol strapped on and his helmet cinched down. Jim Bassett was there to supervise until the XO arrived. I looked at Westerman and smiled. He looked pale and pensive. He shrugged as if he, too, hadn't any idea what was going on.

Just as the exec slid down the ladder rails from the signal bridge, a loud staccato of popping rapid fire split the air, right in the middle of the assembled men. All eyes went to the huge bulk of Seaman Kloosterman, who had just inserted a magazine of .45-caliber rounds into his Thompson submachine gun and somehow ripped off half a dozen rounds into the air before he could gain control of the weapon. His wide blue eyes peered out from beneath the helmet. He blushed and then grinned. "Oops, sir, forgot to put the safety on."

"Damn it, Westerman." The XO was livid. "Get your men under control. You can't unleash this gang of thugs on any ship, let alone a Russian freighter with the whole world watching."

Then he looked at me. "Huchthausen, go below and shave. You can't go aboard a Soviet merchant ship looking like that."

"Just came off the four-to-eight bridge watch sir, haven't had—"

"Get below and clean yourself up!"

Things didn't have to make sense during moments like that. I wasn't quite sure why it was imperative to look good if I was about to be killed boarding a hostile ship. But to Lou Lester, cleanliness was everything, and I guess that if I were to die on a dirty Russian freighter I'd better look clean as I fell mortally wounded. So I went below, pistol on hip, and shaved. I was really more concerned about missing the breakfast for the late watch standers in the wardroom. I returned to my boarding party to prepare for the assault, trying to swagger a little as I neared my men, still standing in a quiet knot, just to show I wasn't as frightened as I really was.

As we approached *Yuri Gagarin,* my heart was in my mouth. I recall gazing out and seeing the large eight-thousand-ton freighter bearing down from a distance of about three miles and closing fast. Off on the horizon to the south we could just make out the helicopter from *Essex* together with an S2F Tracker still flying over the submarine contact. This was beginning to look like a special show. Two Soviet merchantmen about to cross into the quarantine zone, and the submarine contact now appearing to be placing herself between *Yuri Gagarin* and the second merchant ship, *Komiles.*

The word came out over the 1MC speaker, "Now muster the boarding parties. One and Two on the fantail, provide. This is not a drill."

I thought, Here it is! We're going to be catapulted onto the world stage. I just hoped I wouldn't do something terribly stupid like fall down the Jacob's ladder we might have to climb. Would the Russians resist? What do I do if they fire on us from the upper deck as we climb the ladder? These thoughts and others raced through my mind and I'm sure through Les Westerman's as I looked at him strapped in his kapok life vest; his pistol and helmet made him look like something out of a World War II movie.

❖

Things at sea rarely happened as anticipated. As we closed in on the freighter expecting high adventure, we were suddenly given new orders. "Turn immediately and proceed at full power to the south to intercept a Soviet tanker named *Bucharest*." For some reason the tanker had already passed through the outer Walnut line and inner Chestnut line and was now fewer than a hundred miles distant from Cuba, having declared, when passing the Dardanelles out of the Black Sea, bound for Havana. *Blandy* was ordered to proceed to intercept that ship, transmit the warning signal to her by flashing light, and prepare to board and inspect.

These orders brought a new element into the task of boarding and search. How were we to determine whether a tanker was carrying contraband? What kind of liquid load would constitute military contraband? How were we to inspect the tanker's cargo holds?

We learned later that *Bucharest* had been intercepted earlier by another destroyer, which had been guided into the intercept by a P2V Neptune surveillance aircraft as she crossed the outer five-hundred-mile Walnut line. The tanker had declared to the destroyer that she was carrying heating oil to Havana, a term we all found humorous given that the current temperature in Cuba was in the nineties.

A long delay had followed, which was not unusual. For some reason the Atlantic Fleet command had called the destroyer off, and *Bucharest* proceeded on her merry way toward Cuba at seventeen knots. There had been a change of mind in Washington, and because of the relative proximity to the transiting tanker, the *Essex* task group commander, Adelphi, had been ordered to dispatch a destroyer to intercept and escort *Bucharest* all the way to Havana. *Blandy*'s position while preparing to stop and board *Yuri Gagarin* made us the closest destroyer. Again the captain, the XO, and Commodore Morrison huddled in the chartroom behind the bridge and worked out the intercept course. Kelley burst out on the bridge with new course and speed to the tanker *Bucharest*. At this point we were all wondering if the U.S. quarantine was real. We, of course, had no knowledge of the wrenching confrontations ongoing in Washington between the secretary of defense and the senior navy admirals. These collisions of purpose and intent have in later years been explained in great detail.

❖

During those two tension-packed days of October 26 and 27, for those of us on the line off the Bahamas it was difficult to understand the confusion of orders and changes of missions. However, in the best tradition of good sailors, we continued in a highly spirited fashion to roll with the new orders and live from day to day or, in our case, from meal to meal, watch to watch, and crisis to crisis.

Late in the afternoon of Friday the twenty-sixth we picked up Soviet tanker *Bucharest*, and in a tail chase lasting several hours, overtook the low-slung tanker and took station on her starboard quarter. Adelphi ordered us to remain with the tanker and await further instructions.

That evening, as the autumn sun was setting in a magnificent twilight, the XO, Lou Lester, mustered the two boarding parties on the 01 level, and again we stood in two motley groups, Westerman heading one and I the other. This time as we mustered, the chief engineer, Bill Bangert, appeared in his oil-stained khakis with two boiler tenders in tow.

"XO, these are two qualified Oil Kings. They have their sounding gear for taking oil samples from any tank on that there big tanker."

"Who's going over if we have to board, to show them where to take the oil samples?" Lester asked. A perfectly logical question.

Bangert, a hardened veteran engineer who had come up through the ranks, looked around and then for want of a better solution replied, "Well, damn it, sir, if we're sent, I'll go, too. We can no doubt find some Russian snipe aboard to lead us around and show us. I want to take the Russian-speaker machinist mate Dubicki with us. How else can I find their sampling tubes?" Dubicki was the Russian-speaking Czech-born engineer from the Repair Division whose star would rise in the days to come when *Blandy* began stopping ships to confirm and count their missile cargoes.

The complexity of the task seemed overwhelming. The two boarding parties of U.S. sailors led by two ensigns had now been augmented with two boiler tenders and the chief engineer. We stood in the fading light, now about sixty miles outside Havana, confused but ready to do what was necessary. The two boarding teams rotated every two hours, while the off-duty team went below for rations and coffee. How it would have gone had we ever boarded we would never know. After four hours of waiting we were suddenly ordered to break off and return to our *Essex* HUK group, which was still working over the C18 possible submarine contact to the north. That evening, before the sun dipped below the horizon, I snapped a picture of the tanker *Bucharest*, which I was glad I did, for the encounter with that tanker, despite the lack of action, has been recorded in nearly every detailed account of the Cuban missile crisis.

We had passed Nassau while riding with the tanker, and now as we broke off and headed back north, we passed the island again, feeling a bit confused but relieved at not having had to board a tanker. We began to doubt whether we were really hampering the Soviet effort and wondered how effective our quarantine actually was.

To those destroyermen involved in the actual implementation of the blockade it soon became clear that the whole effort was indeed more a means of communicating a message to the Soviet leaders than stopping ships. The first foreign ship bound for Cuba to be intercepted was a Swedish ship, which ignored a signal by a U.S. destroyer to halt and identify her cargo. When the destroyer's commanding officer reported that he was ready to open fire, the National Command Authority in Washington ordered him to let the freighter pass.

On October 26 many destroyermen were witness to the administration's grand theatrics, when the first and only freighter was actually stopped and searched as a show of intent. The White House Executive Committee selected, as a test case, the U.S.-built Liberty ship named *Marucla*, which was Panamanian-owned, registered from Lebanon, and bound for Cuba under Soviet charter from the Soviet Baltic port of Riga. Several Newport-based destroyers from *Blandy*'s sister squadron, Destroyer Squadron 10, intercepted *Marucla* and were ordered to track the ship until destroyer USS *Joseph P. Kennedy*—named for the president's late brother—was called in from 150 miles away to conduct the boarding and search. *Kennedy*'s boarding party was ordered to leave all weapons in the ship's whaleboat and to board the merchant ship, offering candy bars to the crew when they climbed aboard. When *Blandy*'s Captain Kelley read *Kennedy*'s report of the boarding, he exploded. "Why, any self-respecting Russian should take those candy bars and jam them up the *Kennedy* sailors' asses rather than submit to that indignity." The event, Kelley felt, was a disgrace to the U.S. Navy efforts to form a viable blockade.

❖

Early the next morning, as we wondered what would happen next, we were startled by the bridge passing word over the 1MC speakers, "Now general quarters, general quarters, set Condition One Antisubmarine." I froze for a moment as the thought took hold—the HUK group must finally have grabbed the real sub!

That meant a reprieve. Either we had a submarine contact or were released to assist the *Essex* aircraft still gaining and losing the contact designated C18, the possible Foxtrot class submarine. We stood down from the boarding party muster, and I went back up to take my post on the bridge as the 1JS talker. I'm not sure if I was relieved or just happy that if I were going to die it would be aboard this ship and not some godforsaken, rusty Russian freighter. And in any case, I was shaved and was wearing a fresh pair of tropical khakis. The XO would be happy that whichever way I was to die, now I was looking good and clean.

I ran to the bridge, where I donned the sound-powered phones. Jim Bassett was the officer of the deck. High excitement was in the air. Finally the cloud of doubt over preparing to do something we hadn't done before, exciting as boarding a Russian merchant ship may have seemed, had gone and we were doing things we could do automatically in our sleep. In many ways it was a welcome relief. In fact, *Blandy* hadn't gained a contact but had been pulled back closer to the carrier. We were being sent out on a bearing to try to locate the contact the P3 had gained and then, we were informed, had lost.

After many hours running search patterns over the position, *Essex* had sent us we were still cold—that is, without sonar contact—and frustrated. It was around midnight when we finally heard that one of the *Essex* Tracker aircraft had gained an intermittent and unidentified radar contact fewer than five miles north of us. The task group commander ordered us to head directly for the spot.

There are many variables to the submarine search problem, the most important of which is the depth of the thermocline layer. One sonobuoy in the pattern dropped by the P3 earlier extended a temperature probe on a long line that as it sank toward the ocean bottom, transmitted the temperatures at various depths to the aircraft.

While the aircraft measured and plotted the thermocline, the Soviet submarine now on the surface ahead of us in a gently rolling sea was also calculating the depth versus temperature, so that when he charged the batteries sufficiently to submerge again, he could use the layer to hide from the probing U.S. sensors. The only difference between the U.S. aircraft plot and the Soviet submarine plot was that the latter's data read in meters versus degrees Celsius.

That moment, just as the submarine's wire probe was drifting downward and Lieutenant Bartlett's P3 sonobuoy thermometer plunged to the depths, Lieutenant Jim Bassett, officer of the deck on the bridge, decided the time was right to plot the depth of *Blandy*'s thermocline layer.

"All engines ahead one-third, turns for eight knots." Bassett depressed the 21MC squawk box transmit lever. "Sonar, this is Bassett on the bridge. Take a BT drop; we'll need the data for the rest of the watch."

"Sonar, aye," came Westerman's response.

Bassett was way ahead of most other watch standers. "Bosun mate of the watch, pass the following on the 1MC: 'The dumping of trash and garbage over the fantail is prohibited until further notice.'"

Seconds after Bosun Petit passed that word, there was a furious ring of the bridge sound-powered telephone. "Wup! Wup! Wup!"

Bassett picked it up. "Officer of the deck, sir."

"The hell did you pass that word for?" It was Bill Bangert in main engineering control.

"Because we're *not* dumping trash, Bill, we're chasing a Russian sub. That's why."

"Since when can't my men keep the holds clean and clean up the bilges just 'cause we're doing ASW?"

"Since I'm the officer of the deck! If you don't like it, Bangert, call the XO. And, by the way, if I catch one of your stinkin' Snipes topside with an oily bucket, you're going to be less one engineer. Got it?" Silence followed a long string of obscenities.

Bassett slammed the receiver down in the holder and saw that Bosun Petit had been listening to the conversation.

"Fookin' Snipes, sir, dirtiest people in the world," Petit muttered loud enough for Bassett and the whole bridge watch to hear.

"Watch your language on the bridge." Bassett smiled. "Remember what Captain Kelley said, no more profanity on the bridge, orders from the commodore."

Petit snarled softly to no one in particular. "Staff pukes."

Meanwhile, Les Westerman was on the fantail with two sonarmen lowering the bathythermograph, called the BT, from a small hand-driven crane mounted on a stanchion on the stern of the ship. He cranked a handle and the BT, which resembled a large metal dart with fins and a heavy blunt nose, streamed astern as the ship slowed to eight knots. He cranked and unwound the cable, which dropped the heavy instrument into the murky depths.

"Remember the time the OOD forgot we had a BT streaming when we were ordered to plane-guard station?"

"Do I ever!" The sonarman laughed. "He ordered twenty-five knots and the BT was broaching behind us like a fishing fly until the cable parted."

"Yeah, Captain Kelley said the OOD had to pay for it out of his own pocket. But he never did."

"The best one was when Huchthausen forgot we had a BT steaming and backed the engines down during a man-overboard drill. Backed right over the cable. We had to send a diver down to cut the cable off the screws."

"What'd the captain do to him for that?"

"Made him put on a wet suit and do the diving himself."

"Good thing he could swim."

Just then the exec appeared. "You gentlemen enjoying the evening?"

Les and the sonarmen were, in fact, enjoying the cool breeze and hadn't seen the exec approach. "Yes, sir. I mean no, sir."

"Get that damn BT reading done. Don't you know we're on our way to a hot sub contact datum? And here you two are, just having a grand old time in the sun. The captain's hoppin' mad, said if the BT is not out o' the water in three minutes he'll come back here and take it in himself." The XO spun around and disappeared as fast as he had materialized. Westerman and the sonarman cranked the handle in a hurry, and had the BT up in about sixty seconds and headed quickly back to sonar. As they passed the escape trunk hatch on the port side they saw a boiler tender fireman carrying an empty bucket still dripping black oil disappear down the ladder into the after fire room escape trunk.

"Damn good the thing the XO didn't spot that or he'd be marching Bangert to see the captain."

Some things aboard ship never changed.

SATURDAY MORNING
OCTOBER 27, 1962
WASHINGTON, D.C., AND BANES, CUBA

On Saturday morning, October 27, FBI director J. Edgar Hoover reported to President Kennedy that Soviet diplomats in New York were preparing to destroy all sensitive documents.

At 10:25 A.M. that day the White House received a report that more than twenty Soviet ships had stopped dead in the water or had turned about and were heading away from the quarantine line.

Shortly after 9:00 P.M. the same day, at a Soviet surface-to-air anti-aircraft SA-2 site three kilometers south of Banes, Cuba, the Antiaircraft Division commander, Major I. Grechenov, acknowledged a report that U.S. Air Force major Anderson, in a U-2 reconnaissance aircraft, had entered Cuban airspace at 9:10 P.M. The controllers locked on to and designated the U-2 as Target 33. Grechenov received the command to destroy the target. Sergeant Varankin, commander of the reconnaissance and targeting station at Banes, reported locked on, then read out the azimuth, range, speed, and altitude. Major Grechenov ordered, "Fire!" Seconds later, Sergeant Varankin reported Target 33 destroyed. Several more seconds later Major Rudolph Anderson was dead, the first casualty of the Cuban missile crisis.

OCTOBER 27, 1962
THE WHITE HOUSE

President John F. Kennedy said, "Isn't there some way we can avoid having our first exchange with a Russian submarine—almost anything but that?"[6]

On the same day, October 27, John Steinbeck was named the winner of the Nobel Prize for Literature. That night the play *Beyond the Fringe* opened at the John Golden Theater in New York City, starring English actors Alan Bennett, Peter Cook, Dudley Moore, and Jonathan Miller.

Carrier *Randolph* Finds Savitsky's *B-59*

OCTOBER 27, 1962
CAPTAIN VITALI SAVITSKY
B-59
NORTH ATLANTIC
380 MILES SOUTHEAST OF BERMUDA

One hundred seventy miles northeast of the *Essex* group, another hunter-killer group, called HUK Group Alfa, made up of the carrier USS *Randolph* (CVS-15) and escort destroyers USS *Bache, Beale, Cony, Eaton,* and *Murray,* picked up solid sonar contact on C19 well inside the quarantine line. The contact turned out to be Captain Savitsky in *B-59.*

After receiving orders from the Moscow Main Navy Staff to cancel the transit to Mariel, Cuba, Captain Savitsky in his *B-59* had been assigned a patrol area in the Sargasso Sea to the east of Dubivko's *B-36* and about 170 miles north of Shumkov in *B-130*. After weathering a severe storm south of Bermuda on October 25–27, *B-59*, with two captains aboard—Captain Second Rank Vitali Savitsky, the commanding officer, and Captain Vasily Arkhipov, the brigade chief of staff—continued their strained relations but worked an effective sharing of the top watch in central command.

Their first contact with U.S. antisubmarine hunter-killer groups was in mid-Atlantic after passing south of Bermuda. The USS *Randolph* carrier group, with the escorting ASW destroyers, were their first contact. The hunter-killer group held *B-59* in an iron grip, and by using combined tactics—destroyers, S2F Tracker aircraft, and Sea King helicopters with dipping sonars—they finally locked onto *B-59* and wouldn't let go. The destroyers closed in with groups of three and four and had a picnic with their sonars pinging away in active mode. Savitsky couldn't break away.

The Americans knew they held contact on a real submarine, and despite using decoys and false target cans, the Soviet submariners were unable to shake the destroyers. The USS *Cony* began to drop practice depth charges, in accordance with the U.S. notice to mariners. Savitsky had received the notice on the submarine broadcast two days earlier. To the Russians, more than a hundred meters below the surface, the grenades sounded like regular depth charges when they exploded. Savitsky was maneuvering at sixty to a hundred meters and had no isothermal layer to hide beneath. The destroyer dropped its grenades in series of five at a time, which was in accordance with the warning notice. At *B-59*'s depth the grenades exploded more than sixty meters above them. It scared the submariners, mostly because their first impression, that they were under attack, was hard to dispel, despite the warning they now held.

The first contact with the hunter-killer group was at about ten in the morning, and by four the next morning the Russians were practically suffocating and had thrown in the towel. After nearly a day of those simulated attacks, Savitsky was finally forced to surface amid his hunters to charge batteries. Savitsky surfaced slowly and carefully on the prescribed easterly course. The Russians felt defeated in a way, and Chief of Staff Arkhipov was not very pleased with Savitsky, but there was little else they could do. They were heavily outnumbered by ships and aircraft.

OCTOBER 27, 1962
USS *CONY (DDE-508)*
NORTH ATLANTIC
THREE HUNDRED MILES SOUTH OF BERMUDA

The destroyer USS *Cony* had gained solid contact at about 10:00 A.M. on October 27 and was directed to drop practice depth charges in accordance with the notice to mariners. Ensign Gary Slaughter was aboard *Cony*, and ironically was 1JS talker on the bridge at the time, the same position I was in aboard *Blandy*.

Cony chased the submarine contact for nearly twelve hours. The submarine had set his course to the northeast and was on economy electric drive at slow speed. When he finally broke the surface late on October 27, *Cony* communicated with him by flashing light. Ensign Slaughter had studied some Cyrillic transliteration tables they had aboard, and they passed the Soviet submarine a message with flashing light. *Cony*'s Signalman First Class Jessie challenged the submarine by flashing light shortly after it broke the surface.

> *Cony* signaled: "What ship?"
> Savitsky answered: "Ship X."
> *Cony:* "What is your status?"
> Savitsky: "On the surface, operating normally."
> *Cony:* "Do you need assistance?"
> Savitsky: "No, thank you."

The next morning Savitsky permitted his signalmen to ask *Cony* for bread and cigarettes. The destroyer moved in to about eighty feet alongside the submarine to set up a light line transfer. Then *Cony*'s bosun mates fired a shot line to the sail of the submarine (the shot line is fired from what appears like a sawed-off shotgun, which projects a weighted "monkeyfist," which is made up to another line, a considerable distance). When the bosun fired the line gun the Russians in the sail cockpit ducked and scampered below. They thought the Americans had opened fire on them. When the Russians realized what *Cony* was trying to do, they settled down. Apparently the Russian submariners had never seen a shot line gun—they instead used bolo lines with a good, strong arm. *Cony* steamed for hours on parallel courses on the submarine's port beam at five hundred yards. The submarine had no illusions about who was in control. Earlier as the two ships were steaming northeast together, a U.S. Navy P2V Neptune suddenly swooped out of the darkness and dropped several small incendiary devices, presumably to

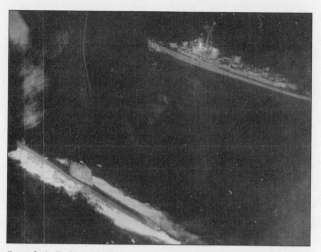

Savitsky's *B-59* under escort by destroyer USS *Waller*, which relieved USS *Cony* after it forced the submarine to surface (courtesy of Gary Slaughter)

activate its photoelectric camera lenses. The explosions stunned the bridge watches aboard both ships. The *Cony* officers looked out after regaining their night vision and saw to their horror that the submarine had wheeled toward the destroyer to unmask her forward torpedo tubes and looked about ready to launch. The *Cony*'s commanding officer immediately called the nearby task group commander aboard the carrier *Randolph* to let someone on the end of the radio line have an earful of old-fashioned navy invective, to be relayed to the pilot and squadron commander of the guilty P2V for their conduct. *Cony*'s captain then sent a flashing light message to the submarine apologizing for the pilot's conduct. According to Ensign Gary Slaughter, who was on *Cony*'s bridge at the time, it was a pretty exciting moment.

OCTOBER 27–28, 1962
CAPTAIN SAVITSKY
B-59
THREE HUNDRED MILES SOUTH OF BERMUDA

As soon as the submarine broke the surface, not knowing what to expect, they first spotted the aircraft carrier, which they thought was the USS *Lake Champlain* (another ASW carrier). It turned out to be the USS *Randolph*. According to Orlov, their recognition books were, for the most part, pretty accurate, but had some errors. Their book listed *Lake Champlain* as the ASW carrier bearing hull number 15, but in

Bridge cockpit of B-59 after surfacing, October 27, 1962 (courtesy Vadim Orlov)

fact *Randolph* was CVS 15. Orlov confirmed the identity with their recognition of the carrier radio call signs and the pilots' chatter as they launched and landed aboard. The next morning there was no mistake—they could read the carrier's name off her high stern.

According to Lieutenant Orlov, who was the radio intercept officer aboard B-59, it was quite a thrill seeing the carrier he had been listening to for more than two days. The carrier was in the process of launching and recovering aircraft when Savitsky surfaced. As soon as they surfaced, Savitsky realized they were not in a state of war. At first light, according to Orlov, the U.S. destroyers came toward them at very close range. Captain Savitsky ordered the USSR national colors flown, and instead of the normal Soviet naval ensign, they flew an oversized Soviet state flag. Orlov said they felt flying that flag was rather ridiculous, since the Americans already knew who they were.

The destroyers came in close and took pictures; according to Orlov, there was a general air of frolic aboard the U.S. ships. The crewmen waved and stood around peering at the Soviets as if they had never seen a submarine before. Eventually the crew of B-59 felt rather relaxed by the informal attitude of the U.S. sailors. It seemed, said Orlov, that the Americans were good-natured. He recalled that one destroyer had a jazz band paraded on their after torpedo deck. It appeared to the Russian submariners to be a strange accumulation of musicians; some wore blue dungarees and white T-shirts, some white trousers and white jumpers, and one was a tall black man in a white cooking outfit including a tall white baker's hat. He played the trombone and seemed like he was having the time of his life, dancing around and acting really happy. At first the Russians thought the American must be drunk; but they were told that there was no alcohol aboard U.S. Navy ships. Orlov thought that was strange.

The Russians enjoyed watching the jazz band, and as the destroyer came in close aboard, the band played "Yankee Doodle" as they passed by at about thirty meters. The submariners noticed that many of them wore short trousers and were drinking cool drinks. Orlov said later, "What a life they had in comparison with our hot submarine!" One destroyer came in close to the submarine, and with a loudspeaker in English, yelled, "Russians, go home!" The whole scene was comical, said Orlov, but their chief of staff was not laughing.

B-59 ran on one diesel and charged its batteries fully in about ten hours. Then in the middle of the next night they pulled the plug, submerged, went to economy electric drive, dove deep, and slowly withdrew as the Americans searched in vain. Orlov said he was back in the radio intercept room listening and found it hilarious to hear the excited voices of the Americans as they commenced their different search patterns to find the submarine again. The Americans named their different search patterns mostly after vegetables—plans called tomato, carrot, and celery—but the one they enjoyed hearing the most was the ASW escort screen reorientation called rum and coke. To Orlov the whole affair had an aura of a carnival.

Savitsky gave the HUK group the slip, but he had already reported the embarrassing event to Moscow, and, by the icy silence, Savitsky observed, they were not happy that he had failed to follow orders by maintaining covert. However, Savitsky had been completely outnumbered. They rested well that evening, even after they had returned to the depths and the hot, fetid air returned to the inside of the sub. Said Orlov, "We were relieved that the Americans did not appear to be on a wartime footing. We still had no knowledge of how our comrades were doing in the other boats of the brigade. Our communications with them were still nonexistent."

> Our commanding officer, Captain Savitsky, had a shadow aboard who was the brigade chief of staff, Captain Arkhipov. For the crew it was like having two commanders. But we were good, and gave the Americans the slip after being forced up only once in a month of hiding.

> *Senior Lieutenant Vadim P. Orlov*
> *Radio intercept officer*
> *Foxtrot class submarine B-59*

Wardroom in *B-59*, October 1962 (courtesy Vadim Orlov)

For me time stood still . . . can't begin to guess how long it was from first sonar contact until he surfaced. Immediately the Russian crewmen manned the conning tower—there they were! The enemy I had been trained to fear, hate, respect, and kill. They could see me!

Ensign Gary Slaughter
USS Cony (DDE-508)

Cecil vs. Dubivko in B-36

While Captain Savitsky in his *B-59* was steaming on a northeasterly course, three hundred miles southeast of Bermuda his good friend Captain Aleksei Dubivko in *B-36* was being pursued by another destroyer from an entirely different squadron, one not part of the antisubmarine hunter-killer force.

OCTOBER 28, 1962
COMMANDER CHARLES ROZIER
USS *CHARLES P. CECIL*
FOUR HUNDRED MILES NORTH OF SAN JUAN, PUERTO RICO

The USS *Charles P. Cecil* was headed south toward a radar picket station off Cuba, as part of the possible invasion task force. Their assigned station with the USS *Enterprise* task group was still some distance away on that beautiful October evening. The officer of the deck, Lieutenant John Hunter, and his JOOD, Ensign Jim Jordan, had just been relieved on the bridge for the second dog watch. (The dog watches were two 2-hour watches between 6:00 P.M. and 8:00 P.M., which were separated to allow watch standers to eat the evening meal.) *Cecil* had refueled earlier that day from the oiler USS *Kankakee* and was steaming independently in calm seas and perfect radar conditions. Commander Charles Rozier was in the wardroom, watching a Western film.

Just after 7:00 P.M. John Hunter took a routine look at the surface search radarscope. He saw a green radar contact blip about fifteen thousand yards out that looked familiar to him. It was exactly the small, irregular echo of what had been called a "snork" when he was on his last ship, which had been in the ASW Hunter-Killer Task Group Alpha. The bridge watch quickly compared notes with the combat information center watch, which also had picked up the contact. In the CIC it had been sharp-eyed Radarman Third Class Russ Napier who first noticed the radar contact.

Hunter quickly called the captain. In his calm manner Rozier told Hunter to continue on course and speed and keep him informed. When the ship was about seven thousand yards from the radar contact, Hunter called the captain again and asked if he could pursue the contact. Commander Rozier gave him permission.

By that time the two officers on the bridge were convinced they had a living, breathing Soviet submarine, and they charged ahead like two boys on a rabbit hunt. Hunter then made a bad call: he ordered the sonar put in standby, so they were not actively transmitting. He thought they might fool the submarine by racing toward him at twenty-two knots without active sonar. They set the ASW attack team Condition One AS.

With *Cecil* kicking up a rooster tail of white foam at twenty-two knots, their radar blip quite naturally disappeared. As soon as Hunter activated their sonar again and made several transmissions, they immediately gained contact—then bloowie! The sonar went out of commission. In the midst of all the excitement they had gone acoustically blind. Hunter felt as if he had lost his first chance at a big coup. Nevertheless, the *Cecil* sonarmen were good, and a technician quickly replaced a fuse with a screwdriver.

OCTOBER 29, 1962
CAPTAIN ALEKSEI DUBIVKO
B-36
FOUR HUNDRED MILES NORTH OF SAN JUAN, PUERTO RICO

Captain Dubivko watched his navigator, Captain Lieutenant Sergei Naumov, plot the hydroacoustic conditions—which were excellent, for the hunters. There was near constant temperature to depths of a hundred meters, making it extremely difficult for a submarine to hide under an isothermal layer. All the advantages were on the side of the hunters, yet Dubivko's quick reactions and alert officers had kept them away from detection until late on October 29.

Dubivko's crew, like the other Soviet submariners, were suffering terribly from the heat. The temperature on board hovered around 65 degrees Centigrade, and sometimes hotter in the engine room. The crew had all lost about 30 percent of their body weight. They looked like they had just been freed from Auschwitz or Buchenwald. When they had surfaced at night to charge, Dubivko rotated the men on the bridge for fresh air, which he hoped would strengthen their morale and physical stamina.

Early on the evening of October 29, after Dubivko had heard on the U.S. radio news that all the Soviet merchant ships had been ordered to reverse course outside the blockade perimeters and head home, B-36 was running at snorkel depth, charging batteries. Dubivko had carefully adjusted their depth so they ran with the sail just two meters above the smooth surface, and had as many men as could fit on the open bridge cockpit for air. While on the surface he had ordered very low engine revolutions while charging, so they were barely moving. It normally took them eight to ten hours to fully charge with one diesel, and Dubivko had about half a knot ordered just to keep their bows into the seas while charging. It was a pleasant night, calm and slightly cooler for a change. Dubivko managed to cycle a good number of the crew into the bridge cockpit to get fresh air. The men looked pitifully pale standing in the light glow of the moon. They were emaciated, yet none complained. Dubivko gazed off into the distance and wondered just how the U.S. sailors in the area felt. Were they aware of what was going on? Were they better informed than his crewmen? It was incredible, he mused, that the current situation had developed without their knowledge. What had triggered the U.S. response? he wondered. He recalled that ever since their transit south through the North Atlantic, the U.S. antisubmarine forces had acted as if they not only expected them but also seemed to know their track. Of course, on second thought, there wasn't a great deal of variation of track coming out of the Barents down to the Caribbean. If Soviet submarine forces were to deploy, the Americans would know approximately what their track would be. But the American timing had been uncanny.

Dubivko knew a little about the U.S. underwater passive hydrophones, called the Caesar System. But he didn't know they had been as accurate as apparently they were. Many times the long-range antisubmarine aircraft came right over their track and dropped sonobuoy patterns almost directly ahead. He felt they must be using other information, yet he had been careful not to radiate their radar, except in low power and only for single sweeps when visibility dictated and safety was an overriding issue. Dubivko radiated his radar only when there was real danger of collision. During the entire transit Dubivko had gone active on his search radar fewer than half a dozen times, and then only for short sweeps, which were nearly impossible to detect unless the hunting aircraft had a great deal of luck.

As Dubivko stood in the bridge cockpit thinking of all these things he was interrupted by the sharp report by Lieutenant Zhukov of the contact. Captain Dubivko's world was transformed in an instant to the tactical situation. It would not ease in intensity for the next three days.

Dubivko heard Zhukov shout, "Hydrophone effects, starboard bow bearing zero four five, probable surface ship, high speed, closing!"

Dubivko quickly ordered the bridge cleared and "Emergency dive!" Just before leaving the bridge he peered out into the dark horizon and saw a form heading at him, no lights. The ship was close. He dove down the trunk, and a seaman slammed the hatch.

As soon as Dubivko was down in central command, Zhukov shouted again, "Contact splitting, now two contacts same bearing. Up Doppler! Range estimated two thousand meters." He knew instantly it had to be a torpedo.

So this is how it's going to end, Dubivko thought. Why hadn't we been told there was a war under way?

All kinds of things raced through his mind. He thought of all these poor men, down to bare skeletons now, no complaints, all doing their duty; then to be surprised—ambushed, almost. It would all be over soon. He went through the automatic functions of giving orders, changing bow plane settings, and trimming the tanks, but knowing it was already too late.

Dubivko ordered all engines ahead full, turned the boat to the bearing of the double contacts, and watched the depth gauge slowly creep downward. Much too slowly!

The contact had emerged from nowhere, just suddenly materialized. No advance warning from Zhukov's intercept operators. Dubivko was not activating the surface search radar for fear of detection. It was a trade-off: use no radar, possibly get surprised, but don't give a free hint to the enemy by blasting the radar all over the horizon.

The depth gauge was just passing eight meters when Dubivko heard the sound of the screws of a high-speed surface ship; he knew it was a destroyer. What was the second contact? Dubivko realized then that if it were a torpedo, it would have hit them already, but still he heard the sounds of propellers closing. Then suddenly he thought the one contact might have been Shumkov in *B-130*. Dubivko thought that *B-130* was patrolling the area to his west. But no, this contact was still bearing down. Maybe the second contact was Shumkov getting a bead on the destroyer to shoot before the American could drop whatever weapon he had on them!

OCTOBER 29, 1962
COMMANDER ROZIER
USS *CHARLES P. CECIL*
FOUR HUNDRED MILES NORTH OF SAN JUAN, PUERTO RICO

Commander Rozier appeared on the bridge, relieved John Hunter of the conn, and ordered the old ASW Operation Tomato search procedure after losing sonar contact. In spite of the submarine's evasion tactics, which usually consisted of heading into the destroyer's wake or diving deep, *Cecil* regained and held sonar contact. The sonar conditions were unusual and nearly perfect, with the isothermal layer below about three hundred feet, too deep for a submarine to hide beneath. With the excellent conditions and Commander Rozier's good seamanship, *Cecil* held the contact.

The Russian tried new tactics. The most effective was his effort to lose himself in *Cecil's* wake. He seemed particularly adept at this tactic.

"Sir, contact is dead in the water," sonar was reporting, based on *Cecil's* active sonar. The submarine stayed this way for long periods. It sat for about thirty minutes completely still at what Commander Rozier computed was about 250 feet. Rozier circled on the edge of an arc about 2,000 yards from the contact. Suddenly the submarine came alive.

"Sir, contact surging to three knots, now five, coming directly at us." Rozier continued circling, and when the range reduced to about 500 yards he kicked the engines ahead, ran at about fifteen knots, and then spun toward the contact to keep him out of the destroyer's baffles, which were the blind spot for their sonar directly astern in a cone that spread out in an acute angle of about fifteen degrees. The submarine had tried this before, but Rozier managed to keep his stern away. The submarine released several false target cans and one long, loud noise-maker, which *Cecil's* sonarmen were able to identify and which did not deter them from keeping contact.

The admiral commanding the carrier screen *Cecil* had been ordered to join was getting nervous that Commander Rozier stuck with the sonar contact and was not proceeding to his assigned station. Yet Rozier still had no confirmation that their contact was a submarine, other than on his own antiquated sonar. About an hour after gaining contact, John Hunter heard two aircraft talking over the fleet ASW net. Using his own initiative, Hunter called them and, as good luck would have it, they were long-range P2V Neptune ASW patrol aircraft from Patrol Squadron 56 flying out of Naval Air Station Jacksonville, Florida. One of the P2Vs, with the call sign Pollyboy 5, was relieving the other on a search station. The new Neptune on station answered Hunter's call and came flying down a bearing *Cecil* provided to their contact. The aircraft arrived overhead in short order.

Since John Hunter was a trained ASW air controller, Commander Rozier set up a radio headset for him on a circuit to talk to and hear the pilot in one ear, and on the other ear he wore a sound-powered headset to talk to the combat information center. After a few "no joy" vectors, when the Neptune flew over the submarine with no contact, the controllers finally got their lead angles right. With these angles corrected for turning the aircraft accurately, they sent the Neptune on a line of bearing over the contact and inbound toward the ship, not the reverse, as they did when working with carrier-based S2F Tracker aircraft. How wonderful it was when the pilot suddenly reported "Madman!

Madman!" as his instruments read out the fluctuation in the earth's magnetic field caused by the twenty-five-hundred-ton steel hull of the submarine. They gained the confirmation they needed: It was certain they held a submarine.

Cecil continued this routine throughout the night, with another P2V Neptune from the same squadron relieving on station. In the morning more Neptunes arrived in force, and two together dropped active sound charges and passive sonobuoys, working the patterns and obtaining excellent sound pressure level readings. *Cecil*'s contact was classified a Soviet Foxtrot class, long-range, diesel attack submarine C20.

Later in the morning *Cecil*'s bridge watch saw a new construction Adams class guided missile destroyer *(DDG-11)* heading to station, and Commander Rozier invited him over to ping with his modern sonar a while on the target. Meanwhile, Jim Donicht, the *Cecil* communicator, took a turn after quickly learning to control Neptunes doing MAD vectors—the term for directing the aircraft over the submarine using the ship's plot of the target. The two officers now could relieve each other to stay fresh.

Commander Rozier stayed on the bridge but let the watch officers take the conn while carefully maintaining continuous sonar contact on the submarine. The captain remained calm and soft-spoken, as he was in any situation.

OCTOBER 30, 1962
CAPTAIN DUBIVKO
B-36
FOUR HUNDRED MILES NORTH OF SAN JUAN, PUERTO RICO

Reluctantly, over the next hour Dubivko crept up slowly to periscope depth. The destroyer continued to transmit her sonar on low power, and held *B-36* in an iron grip. The airplane working with the destroyer made periodic passes directly overhead. The destroyer was staying out on a circle at about two thousand meters from the submarine contact.

As Dubivko continued remaining as close to the thermocline as possible, the sonar operator reported a new contact: "Comrade Commander, new hydrophone effects bearing"—he hesitated—"right off our port baffles, sir. A weak signal."

Dubivko was curious. They had solid contact on each of the U.S. destroyers, yet here was another signal behind them.

"Sir, new contact appears to be at a depth of approximately twenty meters, matching our course and speed."

Dubivko wondered what it was. Could it be a U.S. submarine? The navigator, Naumov, approached the captain holding the plot of their assigned patrol areas.

"Sir, I believe that the new contact may be Shumkov in *B-130*. Their patrol area is directly to the west of us, and if they are on the easterly edge of their area and we were near the extreme west of ours, it could very well be *B-130*."

Dubivko pondered this for a while. At the time he knew nothing of Shumkov's encounter with the U.S. ASW forces. The Main Navy Staff continued to include all four submarines as collective addressees on the assigned patrol areas and on all communications. This new contact could well be their own *B-130*—or, on the other hand, a U.S. hunter-killer submarine. That added a new and very uncomfortable element to the tactical picture for Dubivko. He was relieved that they were not engaged in hostile action, but how would he know if that contact was a Soviet submarine or an American, which at any moment might launch a torpedo right up *B-36*'s baffles?[7]

"Sir, the new contact is remaining in the same relative position."

Dubivko began to feel more uncomfortable the longer this situation continued. He was not operating with a full deck of information, and he didn't like it; plus it was unbearably hot. Navigator Naumov stared at him as if he were losing control of his mind.

Dubivko knew it was beginning to get dark out but still about an hour until complete nightfall. He was uncertain of the overall strategic situation, but he suspected now that since the destroyers had not attacked, they were still at a standoff and war had not begun. He felt relieved but confused.

B-36 reached periscope depth, and Dubivko scurried up the trunk to the navigation platform in the sail. He stood in the dripping space, which was somewhat cooler than the CCP below, grabbed the commander's periscope, and swung it around quickly in a 360-degree sweep. There on the surface were three destroyers running without lights. He peered longer, then saw the blinking lights of another contact, but too high up for a surface ship. That was a helicopter low over the water. Dubivko could just barely make out that the helicopter had a sonar on a cable, a dipping sonar, and was just on his side of the nearest destroyer. The weather was clear; no rain squalls to hide in. Seas were calm. He marveled at the peaceful sight, of the gentle, rolling seas, the last of a sunset still casting red and golden rays from the west. The destroyers were circling about a mile out around the helicopter; they were holding contact on B-36 but were slightly off the center of their circle.

Dubivko called the chief mechanic up to the navigation bridge. He kept the submarine's sail just below the surface. "How much time left?" he asked his chief.

The engineer looked grim. He had just checked the batteries. "Sir, there's hardly any power left; the electrolyte is practically pure water. We'll have to charge and vent within a quarter hour."

"Can't we snorkel, since they're swarming all over us? Perhaps they'll make a mistake and miss us; it's happened before." But he realized to do that was to risk a disastrous collision.

Dubivko asked, "Sonar, do you still hold the contact astern of us?"

"Yes, sir, now on our starboard quarter, still at about twenty meters depth, holding at the same range."

It was spooky, and Dubivko was not sure of what it was. Then, to aggravate the situation, the navigator approached again: "Sir, one of the destroyers is towing a variable-depth sonar!" That turned out to be the destroyer USS Zellers. Navigator Naumov looked up the destroyer's call sign picked up by the radio intercept team back in compartment four. They knew Zellers was operating in the vicinity, but this was their first indication that the destroyer was also with them. On the stern of Zeller's fantail was a large reel on which fathoms of black cable were wound, attached to a sonar transducer resembling a giant teardrop-shaped fish. This transducer could be towed at various depths of choice to get an acoustic look beneath the thermocline layer. Although the towed transducer provided a significant increase in detection possibilities for the hunters, to B-36 it also presented a serious collision threat. If they weren't careful and maneuvered too radically, they could end up striking the heavy, towed transducer and getting more than a hundred meters of cable wound around their screws. Dubivko didn't need this added threat. He was beginning to believe the cards were stacked against them.

"What's the layer now?" he asked Naumov.

"Sir, still eighty meters."

Dubivko calculated; that was certainly shallow enough for Zellers to lower the sonar below and gain a clear look. Again he thought of the sonar and hydrophone contacts, which seemed to be following astern of him. Could that be the variable-depth sonar on the end of a tether streaming behind *Zellers?*

"Right five degrees rudder," Dubivko ordered. He would soon see if that contact would turn with one of the destroyer contacts, which was a difficult problem in three-dimensional relative motion. "Which surface contact is *Zellers?*" he asked.

"Not sure, sir; I can't tell. They're too closely bunched to tell which correlates to the radio intercepts."

Dubivko knew there wasn't much hope of evading three U.S. destroyers that were supported by several airplanes and a helicopter with a dipping sonar. But he'd try.

Dubivko ordered control to come to the safety course, which was due east, according to the U.S. warning signal. That had been one message that had been broadcast repeatedly over their communications schedule periods, and Dubivko and his men knew it practically by heart. Whoever was sending it was certainly eager for them to receive it, Dubivko thought. They had no idea it was their squadron commander, Kontr Admiral Leonid Rybalko in Moscow, who was behind the repeated transmission of that key warning message from the Americans.

B-36 came to a heading of zero nine zero degrees. The captain then gave the order to surface slowly and to stand by to start port outboard diesel for charging as soon as their main induction was opened. Dubivko waited, nearly breathless. He had a sort of guilty feeling that he was surrendering, but knew there was no other option.

Dubivko stood in the navigation bridge waiting for the sail to break the surface. He watched until it was time to climb to the upper cockpit, then stood back while the lookout opened the hatch. Water poured down, and the sweet smell of the late evening air filled the bridge. Dubivko climbed up the ladder and looked around quickly. There were three surface contacts, but only one was close. The other two for some reason were fading, and seemed to be leaving at high speed.

The scene was magnificent. Dubivko felt that he should have been afraid, but for some reason he began to get his courage back, certain they were no longer in danger of being attacked. He stared at the destroyer, wondering what its commanding officer was thinking at that moment. Was he excited? Did they hold us yet on radar? Did they know we had come to the safety course? He watched a while longer.

There was a slight moon rising, and the stars were now winking above: his favorite time of day at home. Dubivko saw that the helicopter must have spotted them, and it began to retrieve its sonar. It reminded him of a fisherman hauling in his line; on the end of it was a round ball. It then began to approach the submarine. The destroyer turned and began to circle cautiously, keeping the submarine at about half a mile distance. The helicopter approached at a very low altitude, and suddenly a blinding light burst above Dubivko. He cursed and closed his eyes.

The powerful light ruined his night vision even after closing his eyes. When he could see again, he realized something was wrong on the bridge, something was out of place. It is strange that you can feel something is askew without seeing it. When you spend as much time in one spot on a ship, and something changes, you can feel it without knowing what has changed. He glanced around. There! Their radio loop antenna was sheered off and dangling by wires outside the edge of the cockpit. Dubivko studied the mount and saw it had been cut off cleanly. That had been the loud sound when they had crash-dived thirty-two hours earlier. Something had probably hit their antenna as the destroyer passed overhead while they were submerging more than a day and a half earlier. He couldn't believe his eyes. Had the destroyer tried to ram them, or had he just misread his sonar range and come too close too quickly? Dubivko had no idea.

5:53 A.M., OCTOBER 31, 1962
COMMANDER ROZIER
USS CHARLES P. CECIL
FOUR HUNDRED MILES NORTH OF SAN JUAN, PUERTO RICO

Lieutenant John Hunter heard the words over the 1MC loudspeakers: "Russian submarine on the surface! Russian submarine on the surface!" "It was beautiful," he said. The submarine was wearing white tactical numerals painted on her sail, reading 911 on the starboard side and 011 to port.

OCTOBER 31, 1962
CAPTAIN DUBIVKO
B-36
FOUR HUNDRED MILES NORTH OF SAN JUAN, PUERTO RICO

After standing a few moments on the bridge cockpit watching the destroyer, Captain Dubivko remembered that they had been ordered to

Dubivko's *B-36*, forced to surface by USS *Charles P. Cecil* (courtesy © 1998. Jasper Communications Pty Ltd. Sydney, Australia)

display the Soviet national flag instead of their naval ensign. He wasn't sure of the reason other than that they apparently were part of a larger operation and were to ensure that they were identified correctly and quickly. He thought that that was another silly order—after all, the Americans surely knew the Soviet naval ensign, and frankly he preferred to fly that.

"Lay below and get the national colors," he ordered to the assistant navigator, who scampered below. After a few moments he returned with the flag but without a staff. "Find the staff," Dubivko said. The young officer disappeared again and later, after a long delay, returned to the bridge without the flag staff.

"Can't find it, sir." So Dubivko had the officer tie the flag to one of their antennas that was still standing.

Dubivko studied the destroyer *Cecil*, which was flying a flag hoist signal that caused the Russians some difficulty to comprehend. At first they couldn't find the international flag codebook. Lieutenant Zhukov, looking sheepish, finally emerged with the book. Suddenly the destroyer turned on his running lights and began to signal them with a large signal lamp.

The American sent a long signal that Zhukov read aloud as it came across the gentle waves. Zhukov was a wonderful communicator and knew English very well.

"Sir, they're asking, 'Do . . . you . . . need . . . assistance?'"

Dubivko was dumbfounded. Why would they ask such a question? If they were going to attack us, would they ask that question first and

USS *Charles P. Cecil* after forcing Dubivko in *B-36* to surface on
October 31, 1962 (courtesy Jim Jordan)

then blow us out of the water? He was tempted to turn into them and
to unmask their forward torpedo tubes. They might get a shot off before
the destroyer did. But then Dubivko realized they had their gun
mounts manned, and surely could have shot the submarine's bridge out
before his torpedo could clear the tube. Dubivko waited.

The ship identified herself then in deliberate flashing light: ". . .
U.S. Warship *Cecil.*"

Dubivko thought that was very nice, to introduce himself. Zhukov
already knew by his sonar parameters that *Cecil* was an old World War
II destroyer with SQS-4 sonar and that he was a Gearing class. Now
they could call the destroyer by her true name. How polite! he thought.

The Russian submariners watched as *Cecil* came to a parallel course
and dropped back slightly on their port quarter. In that position the
destroyer was invulnerable. Dubivko would have to turn to unmask a
torpedo tube from astern or a bow tube to launch. Whoever the destroyer
commanding officer was, he was clever and very polite.

Dubivko ordered Zhukov to answer the destroyer, "No assistance
required." Then they started one diesel and began to charge batteries.
While charging they selected their own course, the most comfortable,
slightly off the direction the seas were running, which, Dubivko recalled,
was southeast. He was anxious to choose a course off the U.S.-dictated
safety course to see their reaction.

Cecil took station about twenty to fifty meters on their quarter. He was close, but he ceased his constant pinging, just hitting the submarine every ten or fifteen minutes with a reduced-strength sonar pulse, as if to say, "I am watching you, don't try anything stupid!" Dubivko could see that the destroyer was disciplined, maintained a steady course and speed, and never crossed his bow or interfered with his operations.

October 31, 1962
Commander Rozier
USS *Charles P. Cecil*
Four hundred miles north of San Juan, Puerto Rico

Commander Rozier was quick to do the right thing. He remained clear of the submarine, at fifteen hundred yards, and hoisted the international signal "Can I be of assistance?" He then had the signalmen send the message by flashing light. The *Cecil* crewmen consulted a Russian tourist guide, which someone came up with, that had phrases they joked about sending but did not. For example: "I will be your guide on this trip."

The submarine stayed on the surface heading east for two days, watched *Cecil* refuel from a passing replenishment group at night, and when sonar conditions suited him, gently slid beneath the waves with fully charged batteries, which he obviously had not had when *Cecil* surfaced him. It was still dark; he had been on the surface for more than forty-eight hours.

When the submarine submerged, *Cecil* left the scene and proceeded to the rendezvous with a carrier group. They took aboard an officer who spoke Russian, and then, over the next weeks, participated with other destroyers counting the Soviet missiles aboard freighters heading away from Cuba.

> At one time, while chasing that sub, we were ordered to turn over the submarine contact to a more qualified ASW destroyer; but Captain Charles Rozier refused to do so, saying that we had found this submarine and we were going to finish the job. He was quite a man; the crew would have done anything for him.
>
> *Clarence Alford*
> *Radarman*
> USS Charles P. Cecil (DDR-835)

When we encountered this submarine, I was not aware that in the international eyeball-to-eyeball face-off, "the other fellow had already blinked" a few days before. I saw my duty as twofold: to stay with the submarine as long as we could, and to ensure that we did nothing that might start World War III.

> *Charles Rozier*
> *Commanding officer*
> USS Charles P. Cecil (DDR-835)

OCTOBER 31, 1962
CAPTAIN DUBIVKO
B-36
FOUR HUNDRED MILES NORTH OF SAN JUAN, PUERTO RICO

After submerging and escaping from *Cecil* at night, Captain Dubivko took B-36 back to resume their patrol. When the navigator reckoned they were right in the center of their area, they came up for a look, and there, smack in the center of their area, was the carrier USS *Randolph* and her hunter-killer destroyers. Dubivko was astounded that they were not detected. He quickly descended below the thermocline layer depth and drifted off with barely any headway, and was not discovered. B-36 headed toward the northeasternmost part of their assigned circular patrol area until they were about 120 miles distant from *Randolph*.

After nearly a week on patrol it was November 7, the Soviet national holiday for the observance of the October Revolution. Dubivko surfaced in the late evening twilight; there were no contacts, and seas were flat calm. The B-36 electronic support measure operators detected no aircraft, so Dubivko decided finally to go topside for a wash in the shower within the sail. He had been cycling the other crewmen to the showers over the past week but had not taken the time out of the central command to do so himself. He was sure his presence was becoming a foul menace to the others standing watch in that confined space, so he put the exec in charge and scurried up the trunk into the sail for an overdue shower.

While Dubivko was enjoying himself in the luxury of the saltwater shower, the exec momentarily forgot that both outboard diesels were on the line and failed to purge their air intakes. An immediate hydraulic shock occurred when water was ingested into the engines; both were quickly put out of commission. That left B-36 with only one working diesel.

Dubivko returned from his refreshing shower only to learn of the misfortune just as Lieutenant Zhukov, the communicator, handed him the message, which had just come in on the evening broadcast, ordering *B-36* to return home. The engineers immediately began to disassemble the two outboard diesels and to cannibalize parts from one into the port engine, which was the lesser damaged. They would work for the next two weeks rebuilding the one with usable parts from the other. They finally got the port diesel back in commission when the submarine was due west of the United Kingdom heading into the Norwegian Sea. It would take *B-36* twenty more days to make it to home waters, and the ship would encounter still more problems en route.

> As we surfaced we had the very real fear that the American destroyer might try to ram us. We still were not sure if we were at war.
>
> *Lieutenant Yuri Zhukov*
> *Communications officer*, B-36

> When we surfaced, the U.S. destroyer *Cecil* was there. He signaled to us, "Do you need assistance?" I knew then that he would probably not attack us.
>
> *Captain Aleksei Dubivko*
> *Commanding officer*, B-36

Blandy vs. Shumkov in *B-130*

LATE MONDAY NIGHT
OCTOBER 29, 1962
CAPTAIN NIKOLAI SHUMKOV
B-130
ON THE SURFACE, CHARGING BATTERIES
THREE HUNDRED MILES NORTHEAST OF CAICOS PASSAGE
FIFTEEN MILES NORTHWEST OF *BLANDY*'S POSITION

Shumkov leaned against the forward railing of the cockpit atop the sail, feet braced, locking himself in position in the swell. A light rain fell. He reached over and shouted down the voice tube to central command, "Get the chief mechanic up here on the bridge!"

"Aye, Comrade Commander," the answer came back immediately. Shumkov was pleased with the reactions of his men. The conditions aboard the boat were worsening. The temperature was approaching sixty-five degrees Centigrade in the diesel engine compartment. Life aboard was becoming more and more unbearable. Seventy-eight men, three toilets, two saltwater showers. Deteriorating personal hygiene aboard was becoming oppressive. Diesel fumes had made nearly everyone who stood watch in the engine room ill, and it was only slightly better in the rest of the compartments. Most of the crew now had a painful rash over much of their bodies. Shumkov's feet had grown extremely painful, especially after long hours standing on the bridge. He peered at the strobe lights of the U.S. P3 that was circling at about two thousand meters altitude some distance away. He wondered why the aircraft had not made a pass directly over them, as they usually did. Perhaps his radar was malfunctioning; maybe he didn't see them at all.

It was pitch dark, overcast, and the submarine had been in and out of rain squalls the past few hours while trying painfully to charge batteries. The process was excruciatingly slow and nerve-racking, but they had to risk detection. They had no reserve power, and only one diesel working at less than half capacity.

"*Yest*," Comrade Commander." Chief Parshin arrived beside Shumkov in the dark. He was breathing heavily, and he smelled of diesel fuel, lube oil, and sweat.

"God, you stink, Chief!"

"Sir, is that why I came all the way up here, so you could tell me I stink?" The engineer was tired; he had not slept in the past two days. Two main diesels were now out of commission due to cracked main gears, which drove the auxiliary fuel and cooling water pumps; the third was now charging batteries, but at only 30 percent capacity. Diesel number three had suffered a still-undiagnosed problem, and Parshin was becoming more and more frustrated trying to fix it without taking it fully off the line.

"How're the batteries now, Chief?"

"Sir, we're still less than 30 percent of full charge. Sorry it's taking so long, but I can't get any more power out of number three, and you know the other two are dead now. The electrolyte is so hot it takes twice the normal time to charge."

"Understand." Shumkov really did not fully understand, but was patient and sympathetic with the engineer. "We'll keep on charging; that aircraft still doesn't know we're here, so we'll continue, but be ready to secure from charging quickly if we have to submerge."

"Sir, if we have to submerge at this state we'll be limited to fewer than two knots, and we'll just have to resurface in a few hours. We're just flat out of power, sir, and you know the batteries are not holding their charges, electrolyte is at a dangerous temperature, 120 degrees last look. That's pretty scary."

"Understand. Go back below, Chief, do the best you can. We may be out of this in a few hours." Worried about his engineer's mental state, Shumkov was trying to make him relax a little.

The boat continued wallowing slowly in the swell at fewer than two knots as the sole working diesel wheezed out the meager charge on the massive banks of 448 two-volt batteries weighing a total of 1,430 pounds and producing 224 volts. Shumkov could smell the faint aroma of chlorine all the way up in the open bridge, thinking that it must be dreadful below. The ballast was adjusted so that only the sail was out of the water, not really surfaced, but more exposed than snorting with just the snorkel mast aloft. In this way they were able to purge the boat of its foul air while charging. In this fashion they also made the smallest radar signature, which hopefully the Americans would not notice in the choppy seas.

The wind was picking up from the southeast, blowing more squalls toward them, but it was still warm and humid, even in the open cockpit. Below, the air was foul. Shumkov thought of the men standing watch in the electric motor compartment: Why not take advantage of the overcast and bring more men to the fresh air? They could always clear the bridge quickly. It would do wonders for morale and overall health. The system of keeping track of the men on the open navigation bridges had been carefully thought out. They had a system of metal tags beside the main trunk ladder in the central command. Each time a crewman, whether on watch or not, ascended the ladder and passed through the outer watertight hatch, he was required to take a numbered tag with him. When he returned, he placed the tag back on the hook. In that way there was a running count of how many men were aloft so that in case of an emergency dive the officer of the watch knew precisely how many men to clear from the bridge before securing the hatch. Although this practice seemed redundant, in hours of darkness it was often impossible to see or hear much in the din of the rolling waves breaking against the hull. It was too easy to make mistakes. It had happened before that a crewman who had gone aloft to sneak a quick smoke in the sail without taking a tag had been left topside during a

crash dive—an unpleasant situation not only for the man left alone outside the pressure hull but also for the captain faced with the decision of
whether to surface again to retrieve and save the man or, in a life-and-
death situation, to leave him caught inside the flooded sail or on the
sea surface to feed the sharks.

Just as Shumkov was contemplating rotating more men to the
bridge for fresh air and a chance to get some sweet rainwater on their
burning skin, the aircraft on the horizon suddenly descended and
began a direct approach toward them. Within seconds a sudden flash of
light exploded on the water as the plane flew over.

"He's got us!" Shumkov grabbed the lookout by the arm roughly,
"Get below, we're going down!" He leaned into the voice tube. "Emergency dive! Emergency dive! Clear the bridge!"

1:30 A.M. TUESDAY
OCTOBER 30, 1962
USS BLANDY
THREE HUNDRED MILES NORTHEAST OF CAICOS PASSAGE

After returning to the USS *Essex* group on Sunday, October 28, *Blandy*
had spent two days with the other HUK units trying to regain contact
on C18. Then, early Tuesday morning, Lieutenant Bartlett's P3 gained
radar and visual contact about fifteen miles northwest of *Blandy*. We
steamed at twenty-five knots toward the contact, relieved to be back in
the ASW game we knew so well.

In the combat information center, radarmen Bruce Cogswell and
Rudi Bump stood on the dead-reckoning trace, a glass-covered plot on
which they inscribed marks on tracing paper for the positions called in
by Lieutenant Bartlett's P3 visual contact. The "own ship's" position was
shown by a white dot, which moved automatically in sync with *Blandy*'s
course and speed. Cogswell was north, Bump was south plotter. With a
cigar in the corner of his mouth, Frank Flanagan stood next to Cogswell.

"Cogswell, take the phones over on the air search repeater. The
captain's trying to get Adelphi to pass us control of the P3. You're our
best controller."

"Sir, Sarella's better."

"Get over there, damn it, I know what I'm doing." Flanagan turned
to the status board and checked the aircraft call sign. "He's Pinstripe
21. Get those phones on, quick." Just then Commander Campbell, the
chief staff officer, approached Flanagan.

"Frank, the commodore wants our staff controller to take the P3."

"Damn it, you know Cogswell's way better'n your guy. He's the best in the fleet."

"Frank, I'm not here to argue. Give us his headset and position."

Captain Kelley suddenly emerged like a phantom. "What the hell are you two arguing about? Where's the P3?"

"Sir, he's still under the carrier's control—"

Kelley cut off the chief staff officer, "We're taking the aircraft over from Adelphi, your boss just told me."

"Sir, he meant we, the staff, should take over the aircraft."

"Bullshit. He said we, that means us, the ship. Frank, who's taking him?"

Flanagan pointed to Cogswell, who was sitting ready at the scope with headset on. "Radarman Cogswell, sir, he's our—"

"Goddamn it, Frank, I know he's the best, he's the best in the fleet, we trained him. Now get hold of the P3 and put him in an expanding spiral search. We'll commence a rectangular search, from here." Kelley pointed to the plot.

So, in typical *Blandy* fashion, Ed Kelley and Frank Flanagan took over the operation from a hesitant and subdued staff. Commander Campbell—our Fatty Arbuckle—quietly disappeared into the flag mess.

After about two hours of guiding the Pinstripe 21 P3 in his search pattern, the air was still tense, but we were feeling good to be back in our normal groove. We did not really expect anything more than the usual hours of alert boredom. The hours ticked by. The wind was freshening from the southeast, the seas were increasing with chop, I was mesmerized by the flashing aircraft light ahead, and was awakened suddenly from my thoughts.

"All stations, this is combat. We have an intermittent radar contact bearing 350 about seven miles." The contact was extremely small and only painted on the scope every two or three sweeps; but it was enough to spur Kelley into action.

"This is the captain. I have the conn! Come right to three five zero, turns for fifteen knots." Kelley looked serious but calm as I adjusted the straps on my sound-powered phones. It was still extremely dark and overcast, and visibility was poor due to several rain squalls ahead. We all strained our eyes looking on the bearing of the radar contact.

We could make out the P3's lights orbiting four miles ahead but could see no surface contact. It had to be small. The temptation was to increase speed, to get to the point before it submerged, if indeed it was a submarine. But Kelley was wiser; he knew that increasing speed could tip off the contact that he had been detected, and at the same time, the higher speed would render our sonar less accurate due to the increase in turbulence. Kelley had actually slowed, from twenty-two knots to fifteen. Most others would have increased speed out of sheer anticipation.

3:00 A.M. TUESDAY
OCTOBER 30, 1962
CAPTAIN SHUMKOV
B-130
THREE HUNDRED MILES NORTHEAST OF CAICOS PASSAGE

"Emergency dive! Clear the bridge!" Shumkov barked. The crew in central command reacted quickly to his command to submerge.

"Aye, sir, emergency dive, the board is clear. Stand by to secure the main trunk and induction, flood main tanks forward, bow planes down ten degrees, all ahead one-third. Dive, dive." Exec Frolov's voice was tense as he issued the orders crisply from central command." Then came the clincher from their sonar operator.

"Central command, hydrophone effects broad on the starboard beam, surface contact—probable destroyer!"

Shumkov quickly swung down the ladder on the heels of the lookout. A *michman* was hanging on the ladder ready to secure the main trunk hatch after the captain slid clear into the CCP below. "Sonar, give me a classification, quick." The smell inside the hull was foul.

"Aye, sir. Contact has twin screws, making medium speed, definite destroyer."

"Shit." Shumkov spat out the word through his teeth, realizing the situation would not improve, as he told his chief. The stench inside the hull was overpowering. He had been in the fresh, sweet air for more than four hours, and returning to the fetid interior was like entering a stinking sauna.

"Sir, diesel secured, main induction closed."

"Very well. Take her down to 150 meters, ahead slow, make turns for two knots. Engage economy electric motor. Rig for quiet! New course two seven zero." Shumkov suddenly had the thought that they might as well head for the U.S. coast, because the Americans would assume that they would run northeast, for home.

The engineers repeated the engine order, and Frolov sang out the depth: "Five meters, seven meters."

"It's too slow, get us down!" Shumkov gripped the overhead handle behind the planesman. "Down, down!"

The planesman felt the pressure of the captain's eyes on his back and forced the bow planes farther than the command Shumkov had given. Too steep an angle could throw the stern up too high and just complicate the situation. They needed depth fast!

All the men in the command center could already hear the thrashing screws above. The destroyer had emerged from nowhere, was closing fast, and appeared to be aiming to hit them amidships. Shumkov's mind was racing. Hadn't they seen them on radar? Maybe the conditions were too bad. Right—the aircraft hadn't seen them either, for more than two hours. Must be the conditions—"atmospheric polarization." He thought back to his years as a communicator. Whenever radio or radar transmissions failed for some reason or other, his mentor taught him to use that term as an excuse for all occasions of poor radio frequency transmission performance.

Shumkov's mind reeled in the close heat. The sweat ran down his back, his crotch itched, sweat dripped off his nose. For a while he felt like vomiting but didn't have anything to throw up—he hadn't eaten since sometime before they had surfaced. He had lost track of the time. He wished he had a better handle on the situation. Were they at war? It was unfair; they had to know whether to shoot in self-defense or to pretend that they were still in the Cold War. Why hadn't there been any low-frequency transmissions with news on the fleet broadcast? It was failing; something was going terribly wrong.

"Sir, he's going to hit; we're not deep enough. Should I sound the collision alarm?" The exec was always one step ahead of everyone else.

"No! Just hang on. Bow planes down twenty degrees." Again Shumkov had to force himself to act calmly. The submarine hardly slanted downward; they were barely making headway. The sound of the thrashing screws grew louder. He froze.

"Passing eight meters, sir."

The screws were nearly overhead. The destroyer had either not seen them or was deliberately trying to ram the submarine. Shumkov then decided to accept their fate. He had given the correct orders, they had been carried out perfectly. If they were struck, well, it was the fault of having to operate in an information vacuum. That was the stuff of the system. Keep information close. Tell them only what they needed to be told. Yet for combat submariners to operate in a condition of total ignorance was wrong, terribly wrong.

The submarine swayed slightly as the wake of the churning screws passed directly overhead. Shumkov quickly glanced around the command center: all were standing still, involuntarily looking upward. Time stood still. He thought of the quiet mornings when he used to fish on the Volga. Sun rising in the early morning—he loved the sweet smell of the marsh grass in the backwaters near the family dacha in Yaroslavl. He wished he were there now.

The thrashing screws began to fade.

"Sir, contact has passed over us."

"I can figure that out!" He immediately regretted losing his cool, thinking that he never showed panic.

"Sir, their sonar dome missed us by a few meters." The exec was still staring at the depth gauge as he whispered, "Passing twelve meters, fifteen meters. . . ."

Shumkov knew the destroyer probably had a draft of about ten meters at the sonar dome. They had been extremely lucky. He quickly glanced around the command center. His eyes caught a small card placed above the helmsman's position. He had not seen it before. It was a Russian Orthodox postcard of a picture of St. Nicholas, patron saint of sailors. The words below the image were neatly handprinted: "Submarine life is not a service but a religion."

He wondered why the political officer had not confiscated the card. Open religious expression was strictly prohibited in the Soviet armed forces. He stared at the card, secretly hoping it would remain there. He pretended not to see it. The card remained there for the entire deployment. Shumkov wondered how many other crewmen found its presence pleasing, yet pretended not to notice it.

The hydrophone effects continued away on a straight-line bearing for at least half an hour. "Sir, they didn't turn, they didn't see us, or had just a bearing and no accurate range. Or—they tried to ram us!"

"They wouldn't try to ram unless we are at war, unless . . ." Shumkov stopped in midsentence. Maybe they were at war and didn't know it! Just because they had not received any broadcasts or special communications didn't mean there was no change in the larger situation. He began to think deeply. He was a loyal officer and tried to follow the spirit of the rules. However, they were now in a situation where he felt completely ill prepared. He lacked information; they were without the basic understanding of the strategic situation or, for that matter, the full tactical picture. Without amplifying instructions from Moscow or fleet or brigade commanders, the submarine was completely in the dark. Shumkov would have to take the initiative. Despite the strong emphasis in Soviet military training on following the rules to the letter, initiative still was an option. Initiative was not considered by the rules of Marxism-Leninism to be high on the list of options open to commanders, because in theory the Party organization and central planning and command were not supposed to err. In this case, however, in view of the total lack of information, he felt there was no other course.

"Frolov," he whispered, "go down to the radio intercept shack and have the communications officer get the voice intercept files. You and Cheprakov sit down, read them, and tell me what the Americans have been saying in their tactical communications over the past forty-eight hours. Are they sounding any different? Do they appear to be on an increased level of alert? Read them all, study them, and come back and report to me."

"Aye, Comrade Commander." Frolov quickly left the central command heading aft, folded himself through the hatch, and closed it gently. The boat grew silent again. Only the humming of electrical equipment and the sound of the steersman and the planesman adjusting their controls could be heard. The long minutes ticked by, and Shumkov began to feel a new pressure. Suddenly the silence was shattered by the high pitch of a sonar ping.

"Command, sonar. The destroyer's gone active and is doubling back. They still haven't got us."

"Hold our depth at 120 meters. All stop! Total silence!" Shumkov began breathing heavily. He listened. His men listened.

They drifted for hours, then inched ahead to hold their heading—generally west, toward the U.S. coast. The destroyer was circling about two miles away but had obviously not gained solid sonar contact. Their high-pitched active sonar ping repeated every twenty seconds.

"Voronov, where's the layer now?" He recalled that his last look at the navigator's plot of the thermocline layer had indicated it was at about 75 meters. That meant that at 150 meters they would be well below the line where sound waves were refracted differently, rendering them only partially visible or, with any luck, invisible to the destroyer's SQS-23 sonar, now actively scouring the depths for them.

"Still around the one-hundred-meter line, sir."

"Very well, we'll hold this depth."

And they waited and watched and sweated for hours.

3:00 a.m. Tuesday
October 30, 1962
USS Blandy
Three hundred miles northeast of Caicos Passage

Blandy's SQS-23 sonar was working well in those waters, and even the classification system ASPECT, which never seemed to work earlier, was on the line and functioning perfectly. Brad Sherman classified the contact after a few minutes of tracking as a probable Soviet Foxtrot class, long-range diesel submarine, by correlating its acoustic signature with one held in a database on the sonar.

The tension was heightened when we were informed by the task group commander that Soviet merchant transport *Yuri Gagarin* was five miles east of the submarine contact, and *Komiles* was five miles to the west.

The bridge erupted in bedlam. Calls were coming in for the commodore, whose call sign was Abigail Zulu. Then came calls directly to *Blandy*, whose call was Exclamation, first from the task group commander in *Essex*, who was Adelphi, and then from Atlantic Fleet, whose sacred call sign was the lofty Top Hand.

"Exclamation, this is Top Hand *himself.*" I heard the dreaded call sign for the commander in chief, Atlantic Fleet, boom over the open bridge radio speaker. My knees weakened. I looked around and observed that Captain Kelley, the commodore, and the chief staff officer were huddled on the outer wing of the bridge, deep in discussion. No one heard the call. I picked up the radio handset. This was the high command voice net; it was supposed to be monitored by the staff alone. And here they were calling our *Blandy* call sign, Exclamation! I looked out at the gaggle of senior officers. They still didn't hear what was going on. I knew I had to take action.

I gingerly took the handset. Why was everyone out on the wing of the bridge?

"Exclamation roger, over." I was answering God Himself.

There was a pause, then someone on the other end spoke: "Wait one." I could visualize the crowded command center at Atlantic Fleet headquarters. I had once visited the center for orientation during a course I was attending in Norfolk on nuclear weapons. In my mind's eye I could see the crowd of senior officers bedecked in dark navy blue with gold braid glistening. The navy had a way of instilling in its junior officers a great awe of seniors, so much so that it bred an innate apprehension of high rank. I recalled meeting the commander in chief of the Atlantic Fleet at a reception following completion of the course of instruction. Admiral Robert Denison had addressed our class on the importance of the course we had just taken, then stood in a receiving line during the reception. As I neared the admiral I had been nearly overcome with dread. He towered in his blue uniform bedecked with ribbons and edged with so many gold stripes I was unable to count them. He looked straight at me and waited for me to introduce myself; I was frozen, unable to speak. That was my first encounter with a senior admiral, and the memory flashed through my mind anew as I stood on *Blandy*'s bridge holding the radio handset as if it were a loaded weapon. This was an operational emergency and certainly I could handle it, I thought, as I mustered my courage.

A new voice boomed over the net: "This is Top Hand actual. With whom am I speaking? Over." The voice was deep and dripped with authority. I opened my mouth to answer when suddenly Captain Kelley appeared at my side. He had just then rushed into the pilothouse. He looked at me and smiled uncharacteristically, apparently sensing my hesitation.

"I'll take it," he said gently, and to my relief he took the pilothouse handset and continued the call. "This is Exclamation actual. Go ahead, Top Hand."

I could hardly breathe. I watched as the scene in the pilothouse erupted in near bedlam. The chief staff officer was conferring with the commodore; Kelley was speaking in loud tones, giving the Atlantic Fleet commander in chief his estimate of the situation; and suddenly in my sound-powered phone headset I heard the call:

"Bridge, sonar. We have sonar contact, bearing three four five! Up Doppler. Bridge, do you roger?"

Everything seemed to stop. A feeling of excitement pulsed through my body. We were at our best, doing what we could do better than any other fleet destroyer. We had him! I suddenly realized that I was expected to reply.

"Roger, sonar." And at the top of my lungs I shrieked, "Sonar contact bearing three four five, classification possible submarine." All eyes on the bridge swung to me. I felt as if I were standing naked, uncovered alone on the bridge.

The captain was suddenly next to me again, his hand gripping my shoulder and staring at the hallowed ASW attack director. I felt relief surge through me.

"Tell sonar I want an evaluation now!" Kelley barked.

The whole world was suddenly focused on the USS *Essex* and our hunter-killer group. According to the operation order, we were to signal the submarine to surface and identify herself.

The mood on the bridge grew even more tense. Commodore Morrison was now talking over the single-sideband, high-command voice radio net with Atlantic Fleet headquarters, Top Hand. I heard Morrison speaking nervously into the handset from the bridge. "Top Hand, Top Hand, this is Abigail Zulu. . . . Exclamation is holding sonar contact on a possible Soviet submarine. Classification possible Foxtrot class."

The report had gone out earlier to Adelphi, the task group commander, but due to the sensitivity, for some reason the Atlantic Fleet command center had called *Blandy* directly, and Commodore Morrison was speaking in the clear, without encoding their conversation, directly to a voice we all presumed to be that of Admiral Dennison, the Atlantic Fleet commander in chief himself. After all our secure communication training I was surprised that the voices were used in the clear on the high command net for all to listen who possessed a radio receiver tuned on that frequency.

"Officer of the deck," whispered Kelley in an uncharacteristically subdued voice, "get Gary Lagere up here to spell you, and then, Bassett, you got the contact, you can work her—go down, get a cup of coffee, have a quick pee, and come back. I want you up here in ten minutes." He was dead earnest and in total control.

I'll never forget hearing the clang of the bell and the sounds of the crew running to stations, "forward and up to starboard, back and down to port." We all knew the drill by heart. When the sounds of running feet broke the silence of the early morning watch, I was still the 1JS sound-powered phone talker on the bridge. My job was to be the continuous communicator linking the vital sonar with the bridge, combat information center, and the main battery plot, where the weapons officer was stationed, able to control the firing of all weapons, both ASW— Hedgehog, torpedoes, depth charges—and the main five-inch and secondary three-inch guns.

The torpedomen loaded the Hedgehog ASW rocket launchers with fused war shots; live torpedoes had replaced the exercise Mark 32s amidships. We all donned battle gear at general quarters stations. Looking down from the open bridge, I could see the Hedgehog launchers on the torpedo deck below the bridge and could just make out the olive-drab projectiles with the yellow stenciling "high explosive—war shot" and the blunt-nosed, notched fuses glistening in the salt spray. That was the first time most of us had ever laid eyes on a live Hedgehog round— other than on the training posters in the ASW simulator in Newport.

Gary Lagere arrived on the bridge out of breath and relieved Jim Bassett of the deck and the conn. Jim then went below, first to his main battery plot; as the weapons officer he would have live high-explosive rounds brought up the ammunition hoists to the ready service trays in mounts fifty-one and fifty-two. He went to the wardroom, got a cup of coffee, and returned to the bridge. As he reached the top of the ladder he stopped suddenly, turned, and went down again. He had forgotten to stop off at the head. Later he was glad he had done so.

4:00 A.M. TUESDAY
OCTOBER 30, 1962
CAPTAIN SHUMKOV
B-130
350 FEET BELOW
THREE HUNDRED MILES NORTHEAST OF CAICOS PASSAGE

Shumkov stood rigidly in central command, his eyes boring through the depth gauge. Chief Engineer Viktor Parshin was standing next to him.

"How much left on the batteries, Chief?"

"Not more than half an hour, Comrade Commander." They both heard the commotion of noise being painted above by the passive sonar piped to the command center.

"They've got a P3 Orion, plus Tracker and a Sea King helicopter with a dipping sonar working against us with the damn destroyers." Shumkov pushed a button on a squawk box: "RTS, give me an identification of those destroyers working with the aircraft. They must belong to the Essex group."

"Aye, Comrade Commander, they are Blandy and Sperry from Destroyer Squadron 24, part of HUK Group Bravo, with aircraft carrier Essex. Blandy has the squadron commander aboard. There's a third destroyer, USS *Borie*, but she's from the blockade line, not part of the hunter-killer group.

"Very well," Shumkov acknowledged, then strangely began to wonder what they looked like. Who were their commanding officers? Did they have children? He began to think ridiculous thoughts.

"Continue on economy electric drive. All quiet! We'll try to lose them. We have to surface to charge in half an hour." Shumkov was covered with sweat, which poured into the rash under his arms and in his crotch, but the burning sensation cleared his head. The ulcers on his legs had caused them to swell, so he sat on the small leather-covered seat behind the planesman and rested his legs on the navigation scope. The only thing that relieved the pain in his throbbing legs was to raise them slightly. The temperature was 65 degrees Centigrade.

EARLY TUESDAY AFTERNOON
OCTOBER 30, 1962
USS BLANDY
THREE HUNDRED MILES NORTHEAST OF CAICOS PASSAGE

The U.S. destroyers were still maintaining contact. Captain Ed Kelley stood transfixed before the attack director while Jim Bassett gave short, quiet commands to the helm and lee helmsman, who drove the thirty-eight-hundred-ton destroyer in an easy circle four thousand yards from the submarine contact. Every fifteen minutes the S2F Tracker from *Essex* would make a slow, droning pass over the contact, confirming each time with the excited call on the net, "Madman! Madman!" that her magnetic anomaly detector read the aberration in the earth's magnetic field caused by the twenty-five hundred tons of the steel Soviet submarine.

LATE TUESDAY AFTERNOON
OCTOBER 30, 1962
CAPTAIN SHUMKOV
B-130

Shumkov stood in the central command post, sweat running down his back, darkening his blue working uniform. He tried to look nonchalant, but had come to realize the stakes involved in this game. One hundred meters above them were the twin screws of the U.S. destroyer; he had just looked at the identification book with the navigator and noted their hunter was a Forrest Sherman class destroyer called *Blandy* wearing the bow number 943—ironic, he thought, just two digits away from his own tactical number 945 painted on both sides of his sail in white lettering. It was ridiculous to think, but the lower number should be his and not the American's, since they were below. His mind was racing madly, and he was suffering again from the long hours with no more than a few catnaps. How long would it continue?

For a while Shumkov felt as if his entire central command watch were looking at him at once, staring, glaring, trying to force a solution from him. How were they to follow orders, avoid detection, and be ready to strike the carrier? What nonsense! He had no idea where in hell the carrier *Essex* was now, with *Blandy* and that persistent Tracker airplane keeping them in a state of continuous flight.

Shumkov glanced at the depth gauge and saw that the planesman was wavering again. "Damn it, Panin, watch your depth! Steady at 150 meters, and stop vacillating!" He immediately regretted shouting; it was poor leadership. How was this all to end? His mind raced, looking for a solution.

"Right five degrees rudder, slow to one knot, keep the bow up. Panin, keep the bubble up! Sonar, give me a bearing to the contact."

"Sir, he's off our port beam at four thousand meters, circling on the fence."

The helmsman glanced anxiously at the captain, anticipating another course command but getting none. He repeated, "Sir, the rudder is five degrees right. Engineering answers turns for one knot."

A sudden clang echoed through the center. It brought up the hair on the back of Shumkov's neck and he spun around automatically, eyes sweeping the gauges as he turned toward the damage control officer. "The hell's that?"

"Sir, that's number two main shaft bearing again, this time something—" The damage control officer broke off in midsentence, listening to a report on his headphones. "Engine room reports flooding beneath number two main shaft, salt water coming in from somewhere."

Shumkov swung around, holding onto the handle above his usual position. "Get me the chief mechanic on the line," he said, trying to keep his voice steady.

"Sir, forward torpedo room requests permission to arm numbers one and two torpedoes to run prefiring check."

"Permission not granted. We're not at war, we're still just tracking! Get the torpedo officer. Have him pick up the sound-powered phone."

"Sir, chief mechanic on the line, channel three."

Shumkov reached up for the mike swinging from the overhead cord.

Shumkov blinked to clear his eyes. All he could see in the back of his mind were the "special" torpedoes being hoisted aboard in Sayda Bay, already more than three weeks ago, by the small crane and being carefully slipped down the tilted loading hatch into the forward torpedo room. The sight had seemed slightly obscene to him at the time, as if his boat were getting "hosed," as the crew often said during torpedo loading. It definitely had been a Freudian scene, their submarines accepting the 533mm steel shafts with special paint on their noses, differentiating that they were special weapons. Only the captain and the weapons officer were supposed to know the color code; all others were supposed to believe they were just conventional warheads from a different batch.

He knew they each carried warheads of supposedly fifteen kilotons, enough power underwater to kill everything within a radius of ten miles, if they were really rated as claimed. Shumkov began to wonder how exact the physicists were, how they knew each warhead was fifteen kilotons and not fifty, and whether he and his crew stood a chance to escape the blast if they fired one into the underbelly of a U.S. destroyer.

Shumkov pushed those thoughts from his mind; he certainly never expected to have to use the special fish, yet the orders he logged from Admiral Rossokho the night they sailed had been explicit: "first, in the event you are attacked with depth bombs and your pressure hull is ruptured; second, if you surface and are taken under fire and hit; and third, upon orders from Moscow." They couldn't have been more clear!

Shumkov was certain he had heard the telltale sound of depth charges hitting the water, then reminded himself that Blandy had the ahead-thrown Hedgehog ASW rockets and Mark 32 torpedoes. Why then did the American keep turning in and passing over them as if he was about to drop charges? That was a tactic of the last war. Either this guy was trying to intimidate him, by going through old-fashioned acts, gambling he would know and interpret the maneuver as a warning before a real attack, or he was just playing with them.

"Shift your rudder," he said, his voice gaining confidence again. The sweat was running down his nose, then dripping onto the plotting chart. It was hot. The water injection temperature in this part of the Caribbean was almost 30 degrees Centigrade. The sores under his arms itched, and the skin under his leather belt around his waist burned with pain of the last three weeks without washing.

"Comrade Captain, chief mechanic on channel three."

Shumkov switched the sound-powered phone dial to three, then spoke into the mike again, trying his best to calm his voice.

The voice of the chief mechanic suddenly boomed loudly over the speakers: "Sir, Comrade Commander, we've disassembled number two main diesel, the main gear is cracked through and not driving the cooling pumps, it's not going to get enough cooling; when we're on the surface it will overheat. Request permission to take it out of commission. I have to, sir, or when we light off again we'll burn her bearings and freeze up."

"Very well, Chief, we'll continue to drift." Suits the situation anyway, he thought.

"Stop engine," he whispered to set the tone. "Rig for quiet. Chief Mechanic, shut down main electric drive, engage economy drive motor, rig for quiet. Sonar, give me a bearing."

"Bearing 120, range four thousand meters. Sir, the American's turning in again, and increasing speed. Sir, she's going to run over the top." They knew *Blandy* had depth charges, but if they were going to attack, why not use the standoff weapons? Why the old depth charges? Suddenly three loud explosions ripped through the submarine. *Click-boom, click-boom, click-boom.* Dust flew from the overhead. A slight mist formed in the air.

The men standing near Shumkov showed eyes wide with fright. He realized they needed a calm leader, and that thought suddenly cleared his head. "Rig for depth charges."

Shumkov couldn't believe they had actually dropped explosives in this situation. They were under attack!

"Steady, stand by. Sonar, any indication of where the Tracker aircraft is?"

The exec, who had been through mock depth charge attacks before, suddenly shouted, "Sir, these are not depth charges, they're reduced charges, hand grenades! That's a signal, sir, not an attack!"

"Bullshit, Frolov, those are depth bombs! They're too loud at this depth for grenades."

"No, sir, they're not! If they were, we'd be going down; there, one just bounced off the bow planes forward. They're loud and scary but not terribly deadly."

"Any sign of the aircraft?" Shumkov asked the sonarman.

"No, sir . . . well, yes, sir, I can still pick up the pings from the last active sonobuoy pattern but no low-frequency drone. Sir!" The sonarman suddenly sat up stiffly. "Sir, contact is speeding up, and . . . he's turning right toward us, sharply, sir. He's going balls to the wall, sir."

"Understand. Helm, steady as she goes. He'll come flying over again and we'll just sit tight," Shumkov whispered to no one in particular. The sounds of the destroyer's screws were now audible to all in the submarine. "Range?"

"Two thousand meters, sir." Shumkov gripped the plot table, certain the American wouldn't attack, at least not unless he had a solid reason to think they had launched something first. Did they perceive that they were generating a fire control solution to fire?

The sound of the screws swished overhead. Shumkov blinked, then imagined they began to fade. The American had dropped more of those charges. The charges exploded one by one. Shumkov involuntarily closed his eyes each time, trying not to blink, but he couldn't stop himself.

"Contact opening again, sir. He's heading out to the fence again. I'm not sure now." There was a long pause.

"Comrade Captain, he's opening, he's at three thousand and turning again. He's circling clockwise at four thousand meters."

Shumkov relaxed, sweat was pouring down his back. It was dreadfully hot now. The leading sonarman was showing signs of fatigue. Shumkov beckoned to his *starpom*, Frolov. He approached the captain, and Shumkov realized for the first time that the body of the exec was covered with ulcers and a horrible red rash.

"Why the hell do you look so bad?"

"Sir, it's the diesel vapor fumes and the battery acid fumes together. Can't do anything about it unless you can rig a swim call. We could all jump into the sea and wash. Can't do it in the shitty shower the engineers can't even make work."

The second in command came over, looking concerned. Shumkov took him by the arm and led him into the curtained-off navigation cubicle. "Sonarman Kutov is beginning to lose his edge; put on the port section man. He suddenly couldn't remember the name he knew so well. He was their second-best sonar operator, but his mind drew a blank.

Frolov caught on immediately, sensing his captain's fatigue. "Senior Petty Officer Pronin, sir."

"Yes, of course, get him immediately. Have him spell Kutov. He's doing a good job but he's beginning to lose it. I need someone fresh. This is too tight."

The *starpom* nodded. "Yes, sir, right away. I'll get Pronin." And he left quickly, folding his tall frame through the hatch going aft, out of the command post, and shut the hatch softly and dogged it.

Shumkov turned his gaze back to the corner of the steaming command center. "Damage control officer, take a survey of oxygen level in all compartments, log them on the plot. Show me when you have them."

"Aye, sir." The young officer began to talk rapidly but quietly over his headset mike, dialing the different compartments for the readings. After a few seconds of rapid writing he looked up anxiously at the captain. "Sir, it's been almost seventeen hours—"

Shumkov cut him off: "I'm aware of that." Then, immediately regretting his harshness, he said, "Go ahead. What are they?"

"Sir, looking bad." The officer looked up at the captain, his eyes red with fatigue but wide open with concern. "Sir, worst is in the engineering spaces, below minimum for submerged operations. After machinery space reading nearly as low. Central command post is below normal, but above minimum. Forward torpedo room, below normal."

Shumkov knew that they frequently operated below standard healthy oxygen levels; it was a fact of life in the old diesel boats. But he had never operated submerged with oxygen levels this low and carbon dioxide this high—after almost seventeen hours submerged, and at the varying speeds. "Very well; update that plot every half hour."

Shumkov knew they could barely last another half hour submerged without replenishing air from the emergency banks, and that was for emergencies only. It was the carbon dioxide that worried him the most. Carbon dioxide scrubbers couldn't keep up with the load, and they were already overheating, making them an additional fire hazard. The oxygen generators took carbon dioxide from the surroundings and scrubbed it to produce oxygen, but they were in poor shape and inefficient. Plus, the slightest amount of oil touching them or near them could cause a serious explosion and fire.

Well, this isn't an emergency, we're not at war, he thought. But if they couldn't surface they'd have to use the emergency bank, but later. We'll hold on, he thought.

"Sir"—the navigator suddenly appeared in the front of him—"we're getting an unscheduled low-frequency broadcast. Our schedule is not due for two more hours. Sir, it's an operational signal telling us to avoid contact."

Thanks a lot, fleet commander, Shumkov thought. How the hell can we avoid contact with an American holding us down for almost seventeen hours, one thrust bearing gone, and running out of air? We've got to surface to recharge and to vent. But how the hell can we, with a full-time Orion and destroyer following like a hound on a hare?

"Sir"—the navigator continued reading the low-frequency message— "they're sending us a U.S. notice to mariners about using harmless grenades to signal submarines to surface. . . . Then we're supposed to surface on an easterly heading to show we understand—"

Shumkov cut him off: "We're not surfacing till we have to. Here, let me read it."

Shumkov took the signal, a piece of teletype paper that was already limp from the humidity, and read it through slowly. So this was being repeated by Moscow, but with only the cryptic remark by Admiral Rybalko to follow these instructions when deemed necessary. That was not much guidance at all. Shumkov had not heard from the brigade commander, Agafonov, for more than a week. They were supposed to be in periodic contact, with the VLF station in Moscow rebroadcasting orders from the brigade. They were prohibited from using HF unless in emergency. Shumkov wondered if being attacked was considered an emergency.

"Frolov"—he handed the message to the exec—"draft up a message giving our coordinates and the situation. Give the status of our diesels; we'll transmit that when we're back at periscope depth."

"Aye, sir." Frolov took the U.S. notice to mariners, read it, then disappeared into the communications cubicle. Later they tried sending their situation report a total of forty-two times before receiving acknowledgment from Moscow—five days later.

"Igor"—Shumkov turned to the damage control officer—"give me a reading. How long can I maintain this depth—minimal speed, say— turns for one and a half knots without snorkeling?"

The young officer paused, made some calculations, then reported, "Comrade Commander, at the rate the ventilation is working, we have about half an hour; then we'll have to cut in emergency breathing banks in all but the forward torpedo room. They can last another ninety minutes."

Shumkov stared at the younger officer and wondered how he could be so quick. "Very well."

"Comrade Commander," the sonarman shouted, "they're coming in again, from the outer fence, straight in from the north, high speed!"

"Rig for quiet." He meant rig for depth charges. His mind racing, he couldn't find the words anymore.

"Range two thousand meters, sir." The scene in the CCP suddenly froze as all hands stared at the sonar operator. He tore his earphones off and stood up, looking terrified. "Sir, something's in the water, dropping. Sounds like a depth charge."

Shumkov grabbed the mike and shouted, "Hold tight, rig for depth charges. Prepare to flood numbers one, two, three, and four torpedo tubes!" The navigator looked at the captain.

"Sir, number two has the special warhead!"

Shumkov was dumbfounded. How did the navigator know? Maybe all the crew knew; they probably did. Things like that can never be kept from the crew. "Don't you think I know that?" Then, softer: "I know. I watched them load them." And again Shumkov thought back to the ominous steel torpedo sliding into the hatch in Sayda Bay. He suddenly shivered, as if someone had walked over his grave. If only he were back in Yaroslavl, where it was beautiful, green, and quiet!

"Sir, the special weapon security officer in the forward torpedo room wants to talk to you on channel four." Frolov held the receiver in his hand.

"The hell does he want? I've hardly seen that fellow since he came aboard. Guess we woke him up!" Shumkov took the receiver.

"This is the captain. What do you want?"

The voice the other end of the line was shaky and weak. "Speak up, man, we're rather busy here. What's wrong?"

"Sir, we can't arm that torpedo without specific instructions from the Special Weapons Directorate of the Main Navy Staff, sir—"

Shumkov cut him off with a foul oath. "Why the hell don't you dial the headquarters on your little telephone and ask them? Or doesn't it work a hundred meters below the sea?" Shumkov was beginning to believe the whole special weapon issue was just a bluff to scare the Americans, who probably knew by now, too. Yet the stern words of Admiral Rossokho rang in his ears.

Shumkov said, "For God's sake, the torpedo's in the tube, right? Be realistic, son." Then Shumkov paused, thinking of the man—he must be frightened. "Have you ever been aboard a submarine before, young man?" Then he regretted shouting that into the phone. "Look, just do as you're told, and I'll handle the permission." He gave the line back to the exec. Frolov continued the conversation for a few seconds, then put the receiver back in the cradle.

"What do you think?" Shumkov asked the exec.

"The security officer just passed out after you finished talking to him. That was Voronov on the line; he said the guy just pitched forward on his face. He's been sick off and on for days. I sent the medical officer up to look at him."

Shumkov smiled. "He's just scared." Shumkov wiped his face with a rag and automatically scanned the gauges on the status board. Then he pulled Frolov by the arm out of earshot from the others and whispered, "I have no intention of arming or shooting that weapon. We'd go up with it if we did. That conversation was for his ears," and he nodded over at the *zampolit*, who was looking at the depth gauge. "Regardless of what happens I know he'll report what I was or wasn't prepared to do."

Frolov stared at the captain for a moment, then slowly nodded in full understanding. The skipper was covering his ass by appearing ready to fire the special torpedo, but in fact had no intention of firing anything. The *zampolit* would report it all, if they survived.

The CCP was deathly quiet. The sound of the destroyer's propellers was suddenly apparent, coming closer.

"Up Doppler. Hydrophones coming closer, sir. He'll be on top in thirty seconds, sir."

"Very well." Shumkov hesitated briefly; then, with new conviction, he said, "Stand by; make turns for two knots, right full rudder, prepare to launch a decoy noisemaker aft."

The decoy tubes were in the forward end of the after torpedo room on either side. The small tubes were like miniature torpedo tubes, to be flooded and then to discharge a can that emitted a chemical-induced bubbling whir to draw off the opposing sonar and mask a sudden turn or change in the submarine's depth or heading. In reality it sounded to the untrained and unaccustomed ear like a small torpedo.

"Hope this guy knows what he's doing," Shumkov said softly to no one in particular.

"Sir," the torpedo officer chimed in, excited, "they'll think it's a torpedo, sir. They may open fire based on that!"

Shumkov turned and looked at him coldly. "I'll take that chance. Now, stand by, all hands hold tightly, bow planes down ten degrees, increase speed to three knots, make depth 350 meters." They could barely make three knots for a few minutes on the electric drive.

"Sir." The *starpom*, Frolov, was in the compartment and standing uncomfortably close to Shumkov. He smelled like a goat and had terrible breath. Frolov whispered, "Sir, our max safe depth is 325 meters."

The boat began to shudder as the single electric motor whined and thumped up to speed and the bow dropped noticeably.

"Release decoy can, port side, now!"

"Sir, the American is coming straight in."

"Good. Maybe she'll go for the decoy and lose us in the knuckle." Shumkov was smiling carefully. "Bow planes level, hold 250 meters, steady on zero nine zero. In twenty seconds stop engine, ultraquiet."

They waited. The sound decoy shot out of the port launch tube from the after torpedo room and began its hissing, bubbling transit toward the surface.

Shumkov stepped over to the sonarscope and watched closely. The U.S. destroyer was still heading for the center of the circle they had been circumnavigating. But then his boat was no longer in the center but a good half mile to the north, and the noisemaker was heading straight for the center. The turbulent water, called a knuckle, stirred up by their last maneuver might successfully mask the American's sonar. The seconds ticked by. Then several minutes. Again Shumkov felt the trickles of perspiration running down his back and into his shoes. The pains in his legs were excruciating. He longed to sit and raise his feet again, but he knew that he had to be stoic.

The command center was suddenly stung by a high-pitched ping: the U.S. destroyer had gone active, full power on his sonar. The sound of a full-power SQS-23 active sonar transmission at close range was excruciating on the Russians' ears; some crewmen held their hands over their ears to protect themselves from the high squeal. Shumkov watched the depth gauge, then turned to the exec, about to say something, but then stopped himself. He held up one arm as if getting ready to give a signal. Shumkov was thinking. Was the American going to fire Hedge-hogs into the center of the previous circle, or had her skipper figured out their maneuver?

The entire watch stared at the second hand swinging around the face of the chronometer: forty, thirty, twenty seconds. Then zero. "Engine stopped, sir."

"Roger. We'll now begin to make for the surface. Bow plane up ten degrees! Be ready," Shumkov whispered to Frolov. "Tell Torpedo Offi-cer Voronov to be ready to fire if I give the signal."

"*Yest.* Bow planes up ten degrees." Several seconds passed. "Sir, only one bow plane's working. The starboard plane was jammed by that last explosion."

"Very well, keep on trying. Chief, stand by to cut in numbers two and three diesels when main induction's open." It was an automatic command. Shumkov gave it without thinking, although he knew they were both out of commission.

There was a pause. Then the chief's voice came over the squawk box. "Sir, all three diesels are still down. We'll have to drive to the sur-face on the economy electric drive."

"I know; I hoped one might be back. That's not nearly enough power." Shumkov looked at the depth gauge: they were still diving. He had actually given the order by accident, routine force of habit.

"*Bozhe moi!* [My God!]" Shumkov swore. They were still descend-ing; they lacked sufficient power to drive to the surface and had only enough battery charge left to drive with the economy motor. It wasn't nearly enough.

"Blow the forward ballast group, quick. Main Engine Control, give it all you can with the minidrive; it's all we have left." They all stared at the depth gauge. Could it really come to this? Shumkov thought. They had to surface, yet they didn't know if they were at war. If they surfaced, would those U.S. destroyers *Blandy, Borie,* and *Sperry* blow them out of the water with their main battery guns? Would the aircraft open fire? He thought back to the illegal intercepting of the U.S. radio programs the night before when near the surface; he, the *zampolit,* and the comm officer had heard all about the U.S. blockade of Cuba. Per-haps by now they were in a shooting war. What difference would it make if he couldn't get his *B-130* to the surface, anyway? They would just disappear into the depths. Was it more than two miles down?

Shumkov suddenly began to get his breath. So this was how it was at the end. He stared at the depth gauge; he thought it might be slowing down, but they were still descending, 265 meters, 270. Shumkov suddenly relaxed. He wondered whether this was the way it was when you knew you were going to die. It would be certain death if they kept going down. But if they managed to surface, what would happen?

6:00 P.M. TUESDAY
OCTOBER 30, 1962
USS BLANDY
THREE HUNDRED MILES NORTHEAST OF CAICOS PASSAGE

The entire bridge, combat information center, and sonar general quarters crew had acquired a gripping personal involvement in the hunt. I relieved Dan Davidson again as the 1JS talker on the open bridge at the captain's side, connected via a sound-powered phone circuit with sonar, CIC, and the weapons control officer, to relay all communications among the three stations.

After the first few hours, the tracking evolution became automatic, although brief maneuvers by the Russian submarine would shatter the calm and require resuming a search pattern before regaining contact, a hair-raising action that started the adrenaline flowing. The crew ate battle rations in place and rotated positions only to go to the head.

Halfway through the seventeenth hour, the contact slowed, came dead in the water for about ten minutes, and then began a rapid series of hard turns.

Following the third hard turn, Westerman suddenly called over the phone, his voice showing strain. "Bridge, sonar; hydrophone effects bearing zero five zero; sounds like a torpedo!" I repeated the report from sonar and felt my knees weaken.

Captain Kelley spun around, grabbed the front of my khaki shirt, lifted me, and slammed me against the forward bulkhead of the pilothouse. My helmet clanged and fell over my eyes.

"Goddamn it, tell sonar to say again."

Trembling, I repeated, "Say again, sonar."

"Wait one, bridge," Westerman replied.

"Wait, shit!" the captain shouted, dropping me from his grip and running to the starboard bridge wing. "Right full rudder, all ahead flank, prepare to fire port and starboard Hedgehogs! Combat, give me a range and bearing to the contact. Sonar, give me a firing solution for the Hedgehogs. Train out the starboard torpedo launchers."

I ran after the captain as the ship heeled sharply to starboard and lurched forward as the shaft revolutions surged and we turned into the contact.

Feeling totally lost, I quickly reached the end of the headset wire and was snapped to an abrupt stop, nearly breaking my neck as the sound-powered phone piece jerked against my chin, knocking my steel helmet to the deck with a clatter.

The captain grabbed the radio handset of the high command voice net in one hand and my shirt in the other. "For Chris'sake, sonar, what's going on?"

I expected the world to end in an ever-increasing ball of fire. Time stood still as the evening sun transformed into a glorious sunset. Then came Rug's excited voice on the earpiece: "Jeez, Cap'n, it's not a torpedo, it's a false-target can; they're trying to lose us again." A tremendous wave of relief settled over the bridge as I repeated Rug's words to the captain and to CIC. The situation was still dangerous as we ran directly at the submarine at flank speed. At least now we all understood more or less what had occurred.

Blandy continued at flank speed past the bearing of the contact to emphasize to the submarine that we were turning away. The submarine skipper might still misinterpret our maneuver as the breakaway after firing a weapon. Did he know we were still too far to fire the Hedgehogs? Did he know we had not launched a torpedo? Would he not have heard it hit the water? A string of questions begged for answers as we opened the contact to a mile and a half and then turned to parallel the submarine's course and speed. Thankfully, the submarine skipper either knew he had triggered our reaction with his false-target can, or he was very trustful that the U.S. destroyer commander was smart enough to discern the difference between the can and a real torpedo. Shortly following the episode, I went below for a needed head call; Dan Davidson took the phones for me then. *Blandy* steamed calmly at about eight knots, rolling slightly in the evening swell, with the sun's rays illuminating the twilight seas.

As I began to climb the starboard ladder from the main deck to the torpedo deck level, feeling doubly relieved, I glanced out onto the water. There, like a dragon emerging from the depths, a black submarine sail broke the waves and slowly surfaced.

For a moment everyone aboard gaped in awe. Suddenly, without any apparent order given, *Blandy*'s forward five-inch gun mount slewed out to starboard and aimed directly at the black submarine sail, which was still cutting the surface at a slow speed.

On the starboard wing of the bridge Captain Kelley exploded, "Get that goddamn mount back to centerline! Bassett, get control of your guns. Who the hell ordered that gun out there? If that bastard sees that, he's got every right to launch one at us!"

The gun mount immediately trained around to the centerline position. Weapons Officer Jim Bassett, standing on the bridge wing with the captain, was there in case the order had come to open fire. He was talking rapidly into the phone when I returned to the bridge to relieve Dan Davidson. Seeing the commotion, I stepped back to wait before relieving Dan.

What apparently happened was that as the submarine was coming to the surface, the staff watch officer in CIC had said something like "Looks like the ship should prepare for surface action starboard." That term "surface action starboard" was somehow overheard over the gunnery circuit, and the nervous gun captain in mount fifty-one switched his mount into manual control, virtually taking control of the five-inch gun from the weapons officer, on the bridge, and trained it momentarily onto the submarine before the bridge rectified the mistake. That brief incident showed just how close we were to a human error that could have ignited the entire situation into an uncontrolled catastrophe.

6:30 P.M. TUESDAY
OCTOBER 30, 1962
CAPTAIN SHUMKOV
B-130
ON THE SURFACE
THREE HUNDRED MILES NORTHEAST OF CAICOS PASSAGE

Shumkov stood in the central command waiting for the depth to register fifteen meters. As it passed twenty, dropping slowly as the submarine inched toward the surface, he bolted up the ladder, and with the help of a *michman*, twisted the wheel on the main trunk hatch. Together they turned as seawater began to pour in around the gasket. The hatch sprang open and Shumkov shot through, followed by two officers. Frolov remained in the CCP. The water reduced to a dribble when Shumkov grabbed the periscope and powered it up. They were just passing ten meters when he slewed the periscope around, focusing the optics by turning the knurled knob. The air of the navigation platform inside the sail was wet and steamy, but it no longer smelled like the inside of a sewer. Shumkov took a deep breath of the clean air as the image of a sleek gray destroyer formed in the eyepiece. He watched, mesmerized as the boat continued to surface. The *michman* who had followed the captain up the ladder opened the hatch leading up to the open bridge cockpit. More water drained down, but clear sky showed through the hatch. Shumkov left the periscope and raced up the ladder to the cockpit. In a moment of brilliant color and light he blinked his eyes at the glowing sunset.

The scene was surreal. Shumkov stared for a moment as the bridge watch organized itself. Suddenly he spotted the forward gun mount on the destroyer train out in his direction so that he was looking directly into the end of the five-inch muzzle fewer than a thousand meters away. Shumkov's submarine was heading exactly east, course zero nine zero. Although their slow speed caused them to swing slightly in the medium seas, there was no question that his B-130 was on the safety course prescribed by the U.S. notice to mariners they had received via the broadcast less than two hours earlier.

Shumkov shouted, "Left full rudder! Open the outer doors on numbers three and four! Frolov, tell Voronov to stand by with a firing solution. The bastards have a gun trained on us. They're about to shoot!"

Frolov in the CCP hadn't the chance of seeing the threatening muzzle. "Sir, we're on their safety course; they won't shoot."

"The hell you say; report when ready to launch!"

Shumkov watched the destroyer, now through his binoculars, which were wet from the water going through the hatch, but nonetheless enhanced the image. He could see khaki-clad figures on the wing of the destroyer's bridge, all wearing steel helmets. Shumkov felt his bowels relax involuntarily; happily he hadn't eaten in days and was spared the ordeal of fouling himself in front of his men.

Suddenly, as the bow of the submarine began to slowly swing onto the destroyer's bearing, Shumkov observed the large-caliber-gun mount swing away from his submarine and come to a stop, pointing forward on the destroyer and away from him. "Shift your rudder," Shumkov called below.

Shumkov's *B-130* shortly after surfacing on October 30, 1962 (U.S. Navy photo)

"Shift rudder, aye, sir, the rudder is right full, passing, zero four zero," the helmsman answered.

"Steady on course zero nine zero," Shumkov ordered, gaining his composure.

Within ten seconds the helmsman replied, "Sir, steady on new course zero nine zero."

"Very well." Shumkov watched the destroyer, which was matching his slow speed now and was dropping back so he was abeam at about a thousand meters on a parallel heading. A flashing light suddenly began to wink from the destroyer's signal bridge area. "Get the comm officer up here quickly; they're sending us a signal by lamp," Shumkov said. He was feeling relieved for the first time. The fresh air was making him giddy.

Cheprakov suddenly emerged beside him, reading the flashing light and paging though an international codebook. "Sir, they're asking us, 'Do you need assistance?'"

"Do we need assistance?" Shumkov laughed almost hysterically, "Sure. How about a couple diesel engines, a ton of freshwater, and some green vegetables?" he muttered. "Don't send that. Don't answer the light until I think for a few moments. Get the national flag up here."

A sailor brought up a flag and began to fix it on the small folding flagstaff. "No, I said the national flag, not the naval ensign. Our orders are to fly the national flag, for some reason. I'd prefer the navy flag. Hurry, put it up, and get the chief mechanic up here quickly." Shumkov felt elated. He relaxed. For the first time he realized they might not be at war, at least not yet. The Americans seemed to be acting correctly; nevertheless, he would not lower his guard.

USS *Blandy* escorts Shumkov in *B-130* on October 30, 1962
(courtesy Dan Davidson)

Shumkov, standing now with his chief next to him, gazed out at the escort. The destroyer had impressive lines, looking as though it were leaning forward as it sliced through the gentle swell. The skin of the gray ship glistened in the early evening sunset. The sleek destroyer seemed to show pride in the recent encounter as he took station a thousand meters off the submarine's port quarter. The Americans had indeed been professional and businesslike. There were no trivial signals, no embarrassing maneuvers—that is, except for the brief gun mount incident, which Shumkov was putting in his report to Moscow.

Blandy came in to about thirty meters distance to take photos. The destroyer was correct, did the job, and then resumed station on the submarine's quarter. Shumkov wondered who the commanding officer was. What was his name? He wondered about the condition of the crew aboard the destroyer.

Shumkov had not received a single message from Brigade Commander Agafonov for more than a week, ever since the twentieth, when they had finally received their new patrol orders curtailing their transit to Mariel, five days after the other three boats had received the order. Shumkov had a fair idea now what had transpired based on the study of the U.S. communications and what the comm officer had briefed him on from the U.S. news radio stations. *B-130* had steamed right into a hornet's nest. There must have been more than two hundred U.S. Navy ships buzzing around the area now. Shumkov and his communicator were still trying to send their message report out to Northern Fleet headquarters and Moscow containing the details of the incident. They had tried more than twenty times already, with no response.

Shumkov wondered about the fate of his good friend Aleksei Dubivko, commander of sister sub *B-36*, and of the other submarines of the brigade. He found out what happened only after they returned to Polyarny.

6:30 P.M. TUESDAY
OCTOBER 30, 1962
USS *BLANDY*
THREE HUNDRED MILES NORTHEAST OF CAICOS PASSAGE

We watched the submarine on whose sail was painted, ironically, the tactical pendant number 945 in white numerals, two digits higher than *Blandy*'s hull number, 943. Cheering broke out throughout the ship.

The U.S. destroyermen did not know at the time that when the submarine surfaced fully she had casualties to all three diesel engines and could not submerge again. However, as far as we were concerned, we had caused her to surface by holding her down for almost seventeen hours, and no one could convince us otherwise.

PART IV

Hide-and-Seek

Soviet Shell Game

WEDNESDAY MORNING
OCTOBER 31, 1962
CAPTAIN NIKOLAI SHUMKOV
B-130
480 MILES SOUTHWEST OF BERMUDA

After steaming in company with *Blandy* for a while, Captain Shumkov began to feel comfortably aware that whoever the commander of the destroyer was, he seemed correct in all actions, cautious of safety matters, and yet dogged in his pursuit. Now that they were on the surface and limited by their casualties to one diesel with reduced power on the line and with speed down to one and a half knots, there was little left to do as far as evading the U.S. forces.

Blandy seemed able to get aircraft support on short notice. Several times when the seas deteriorated, *Blandy* opened the distance to about two thousand meters and stationed on *B-130*'s port quarter. Shumkov was certain this was to keep them in a clear radar window when visibility deteriorated in squalls. The Americans were certainly aware by now that the submarine had suffered a mechanical failure, but Shumkov was sure they had no way of knowing the full seriousness of their situation. He had been extremely careful not to radiate any communications that might be exploited as far as divulging the extent of their diesel casualties. Shumkov's communicator had transmitted the encrypted message reporting their situation on high frequency now a total of forty-two times before receiving confirmation from Moscow.

At first there was no more than confirmation of receipt, no further instructions. Then, after forty-eight hours, during which they steamed northeast at one and a half knots, *B-130* received instructions to conduct a rendezvous with the rescue tug *SS-20*, called *Pamir*. They learned later that the Main Navy Staff continued to include assignments to *B-130* in all the operational messages to the remainder of the brigade, thus keeping them in the dark concerning their true location and condition. Indeed, Shumkov's friend Dubivko aboard *B-36* actually thought *B-130* was operating in close proximity to his assigned patrol area. This was unfortunate, since at times when he held passive sonar contact he believed he was holding them. Shumkov learned later that this nearly cost Dubivko dearly when he was first detected on the surface snorkeling by the U.S. destroyer *Charles P. Cecil*.

Shumkov never fully understood Moscow's reasons for keeping the rest of the force in the dark, except perhaps for security reasons. Certainly they knew where they were, and the only reason to keep them in the plan with the brigade may have been to make the Americans believe there were more submarines in the area than there were. For a full twenty-four hours following their surfacing *Blandy* had remained with *B-130* alone, except with the occasional help of a long-range patrol aircraft, generally a P2V out of Naval Air Station Jacksonville, Florida.

Then, on the morning of the second day, the Soviet submarine had more company.

"Sir, hydrophone effects bearing one eight zero," the sonar operator sang out. Shumkov was on the navigation bridge and was allowing three crewmen at a time up in the cockpit to enjoy the fresh air and hopefully to gain the benefit of a sudden warm rain squall.

"Roger. Report Doppler."

Within a few seconds the report came back, "Up Doppler. Contact twin screw and closing at twenty knots."

Shumkov waited patiently until finally, within a few minutes, came the report for the radio intercept watch: "Sir, contact is calling *Blandy* on the tactical ASW net. Her identity is USS *Keppler*, also from the Twenty-fourth Destroyer Squadron."

THURSDAY MORNING
NOVEMBER 1, 1962
USS *BLANDY*
480 MILES SOUTHWEST OF BERMUDA

"Bassett, have we got communications yet with *Keppler?*" Ed Kelley sat in the commanding officer's chair on the starboard wing of the pilothouse.

"Not yet, sir. Combat is watching for her to check in on ASW Common."

Bill Morgan was the combat information center watch officer. He was sitting at the corner of the DRT with radarman Cogswell. "Cogswell, call quick down to radio and have them bring ASW Common up on the GRC 27 as a backup." The GRC, nicknamed the "Greek," was a reliable transceiver that Morgan, as the radio officer, liked to reserve as a spare. Communications had been spotty, and Morgan liked to back up an important frequency with a second radio. Just as he finished bringing up the new radio, the speakers in combat boomed, "Exclamation, this is Rear Guard [USS *Keppler*], reporting in."

Kelley jumped out of his chair just in time to see the chief staff officer, Commander Campbell, stepping over the hatch coaming from the CIC. "*Keppler* should be reporting directly to us, not relaying through Exclamation." He was his usual fussy self.

"Maybe he's been calling you, and you didn't answer," Kelley responded, a suppressed grin forming slowly. Commander Campbell stewed visibly, his face reddening.

Kelley quickly went into the CIC and grabbed Morgan by the arm. "Has *Keppler* called in to the staff yet?"

Morgan had a twinkle in his eye. "Sir, Cogswell and I have been guarding ASW Common and have heard nothing addressed to Abigail Zulu, the squadron commander's call sign. But we just heard her call in to us using Exclamation."

"How can that be?" Kelley caught on immediately. "Bob Summers [commanding officer of *Keppler*] knows the procedure. Why would he intimidate the commodore by addressing *Blandy* instead of the staff?"

Just then Commodore Morrison entered Combat. "Good morning, Ed. Understand *Keppler*'s arriving to relieve you."

The chief staff officer joined the group of officers around the DRT. He had already told the commodore that *Keppler* was calling in by radio to Exclamation, *Blandy*'s call sign, instead of to Abigail Zulu, the commodore's call sign—a serious breach of etiquette.

"Doesn't Summers know who the squadron commander is? He should be reporting in to me, not you, Ed." Morrison looked genuinely confused.

Kelley looked at Morgan, who quickly looked at radarman Cogswell. "Sir, Cogswell and I have been guarding this frequency all morning and have only heard our call sign, Exclamation, used. But then again, communications have been pretty poor, and *Keppler* is still quite a ways off; must be atmospheric polarization."

"Right." Kelley caught on. "Yes, indeed, we've been having those problems, absolutely, atmospheric polarization."

Finally they all heard *Keppler* call in again: "Exclamation, this is Rear Guard ready to relieve you as ordered."

Morgan quickly answered over the voice net, "Rear Guard, this is Exclamation. I will relay to Abigail Zulu that you are reporting as ordered. Out."

Kelley grinned and left Combat. He pulled Morgan with him by the arm as he went for the door. "Morgan," he said quietly, "good show, but do refrain from trying to embarrass the staff, it's not nice," and he smiled broadly and returned to his chair on the bridge. Morgan was grinning and Chief Staff Officer Campbell was glowering as he and Commodore Morrison drafted an operational signal for *Keppler* to relieve *Blandy* and continue trailing the Foxtrot.

After a few minutes Frank Flanagan arrived on the bridge with the message board.

"Captain, latest cut on the Soviet tug SS-20, *Pamir*. She's about forty miles north of Bermuda, heading this way. We figure she's going to meet up with this 945 to give her assistance and probably a tow. The tug was sighted by a P3 out of Norfolk heading south."

"Thanks, Frank." Kelley was still smiling. "I'm afraid we're going to miss the fun. We're being vectored off to start counting missiles heading out of Cuba. That should prove to be much more action."

Bob Briner had arrived on the bridge and was standing next to Flanagan.

"Bob, alert Jim Bassett to get his boarding teams ready again; this time maybe we'll have to use them, although we shouldn't have to. Apparently the Russians have agreed to allow us to inspect and photograph the missiles as they withdraw them. We'll have to be prepared in any case."

Just then the exec came flying onto the bridge, breathing heavily after climbing the ladder on the double. He had been below, inspecting Westerman's boarding party. This time they seemed ready.

The commodore came out on the bridge. "Commodore on the bridge, sir," the watch called out.

"Crap." Kelley barely concealed his irritation. He liked to plan on his own without the intercession of the staff.

"Ed, you're going to pick up a combat cameraman from *Essex* when we get within helo range. That should be tomorrow morning."

"The hell do we need a combat cameraman for, sir? We have our own cameras."

"Ed, the task group commander is sending him over; it should be a great help, since he'll have a good camera. He'll be a photo mate trained in intelligence photography. You can set him up on the signal bridge to get good coverage."

Kelley thought for a few moments, then walked out on the wing of the bridge and looked up. "The higher the better." He pulled the exec with him, then pointed up the mast. "See the air search radar platform?"

The exec craned his neck looking up. Eighty feet above the bridge level was the SPS-6 air search radar platform. Steel ladder rungs were welded to the mast all the way from the 04 level above the Mark 56 Director up to the platform, which had a sliding steel plate to enable a man access onto the platform for repairs.

"We'll send the cameraman up there and shoot from the platform. Get the EMO, Huchthausen, to go up there with him, he knows the drill, he goes up there a lot with his men to work on the SPS-6. Put safety belts on them and a sound-powered phone so he can adjust the ship for the best angle." Kelley paused. "Oh, and Lester, make sure Huchthausen secures the radar before he goes up there or we'll have fried EMO for lunch." He grinned, pleased with himself for having another unorthodox idea.

The exec sprang into action, and the newest shipboard bill was born, titled the photo aloft bill. It was soon on paper and drilled, and lacked only the arrival of the photo mate.

I was expecting a professional with a lot of technical equipment. Since I was going to have to escort the man aloft, I was preparing in advance for the drill. But no matter how carefully one plans ahead in the navy, something always renders the plans moot.

❖

After escorting Captain Shumkov's *B-130* for the night and into the daylight hours, we passed the contact to USS *Keppler* and departed at twenty-five knots to check one of the first merchants departing Cuba under the conditions of the new agreement with the Soviet Union. We had been ordered to join the forces assigned to intercept and track Soviet merchant ships departing Cuba as part of the agreed compromise. That last Sunday morning, October 28, the Soviet government had announced on the air that they would withdraw their missiles from Cuba.

Blandy became one of dozens of U.S. destroyers sent to intercept designated Soviet merchantmen removing military equipment and personnel from Cuba. The mission called for the destroyers to come close enough to the merchant ship to be in good camera range and photograph the deck cargo; the most immediately important were the medium- and intermediate-range ballistic missiles. Given the sudden exposure of the Soviet treachery in covertly inserting the equipment and forces into Cuba, an openly announced agreement to remove the mischief was quite naturally suspect by the West. The air of the presence of the Soviet troops and equipment on the ground in Cuba was so blatantly underhanded, the military had been required to wear civilian clothing, which they did, ironically with the traditional blue-and-white-striped, long-sleeved jersey under their tropical shirts. But it certainly wasn't difficult to tell the Russians or the Ukrainians, with their high cheekbones and ski jump noses, from the swarthy Cubans.

The first merchant ship we intercepted was the Soviet-flagged dry-cargo ship *Dvinogorsk*, a ten-thousand-ton freighter from Odessa with a deckload apparently of the SS-4 missiles. A helicopter from the carrier *Essex* delivered a photographer's mate to us from the Combat Camera Detachment at Atlantic Fleet headquarters. The photo mate, a young third-class petty officer barely nineteen years old, arrived on the fantail looking pale and frightened with a sophisticated camera and a huge telephoto lens to ensure that we obtained top-quality photos.

With a fresh mission in hand our XO, Lieutenant Commander Lou Lester, was catapulted into action, briskly organizing a special action bill for the new assignment. In the navy the shipboard bill is used as the organizational basis for life itself. All activity is keyed to a written chart, called a bill, which assigns every man a place and a function for every

activity. The custom is a vestige from the old sailing navy, when common seamen were often conscripted from the dregs of humanity, and
although mostly brave and robust, were not noted for their mental acu-
men. But it soon became evident that bills were the key to prevent the
simplest evolution aboard ship from becoming confused—which could
happen with remarkable regularity.

Aboard *Blandy* there was a watch quarter and station bill, ASW
action bill, replenishment bill, abandon ship bill, boarding party bill,
dress-ship bill, and cheer-ship bill, plus now a count-the-missiles bill.
The executive officer designed the special bill, and the division officers
adjusted it for execution by their men. The resulting evolution became
a happy blend of the junior officers' recent training and college theory
spiced with the wisdom of the chiefs, the practical experience of the
petty officers, and the faithful action and dedication of the seamen and
the firemen.

Anything was possible and no task too complex for this system,
which had evolved over many centuries of plodding naval tradition.
How then, one wonders, could things in the fleet get so uncommonly
fouled up?

During preparations for this mission, not more than a few hundred
miles northeast of Havana, at the height of an international crisis, the
XO's tireless efforts unearthed a Russian-speaker aboard. The linguist
was a naturalized U.S. citizen named Walter Dubicki, originally from
Czechoslovakia, who spoke native Czech and some Ukrainian in addition to some Russian. Dubicki was the classic sailor, a second-class
petty officer, machinist's mate from the repair division who had been
on destroyers in Newport for decades. He was well known within the
squadron and in Newport as a legendary bluejacket who, although
somewhat older than most of his peers, was always immaculate in his
uniform. On liberty in home port he hung out with Quartermaster
Emery. Each would don a gold earring in one ear, and sometimes they
would carry a parakeet on their shoulders. Both were excellent petty
officers, never in serious trouble but always walking the narrow line
between good order and Captain's Mast. Dubicki had achieved the
grade of first-class petty officer several times but had never been able to
keep his stripes. He was arrested with Emery once for riding a pogo
stick down the center of Thames Street in Newport while intoxicated,
and again for "borrowing" a taxi to bring a sick friend back to the ship.
Dubicki wasn't covered quite so completely with tattoos as Emery, who

had them over a good portion of his visible body, including the eye on the center of the back of his head. When closely shorn, as he always was, and sitting on a barstool, as he frequently was, the eye could be seen peering out from the back of his head. The two were classic salts.

As assistant communications officer working under instruction with Bill Morgan, I was responsible for preparing signals to send by flashing light to the Russian ships, directing them to a specific course and speed. I worked with Petty Officer Dubicki to get the signals right in simple English so he could put them into phonetic Russian. The process seemed to work well, but in the end there were always many more words needed by Dubicki to put the message into what he claimed was good, understandable Russian. I began to grow suspicious when Dubicki was unable to translate each of the words, explaining that the filler words were needed in Russian for "emphasis." In later years, when I studied Russian, I learned that generally fewer words are needed to impart a thought in Russian than the less exact English language. Nevertheless, I trusted Dubicki, and the XO was in a hurry. Years later, when reviewing a copy of the signals, which I had saved, I discovered that Dubicki had used the most foulmouthed profanities imaginable in Russian (which is rich in obcenities) when giving the Soviet ships instructions during our Cuban operations.

As we steamed toward the first missile-carrying merchant ship we rehearsed the new bill. Since the exec had suddenly designated me as the ship's collateral duty intelligence officer, I was put in charge of getting the new photo mate eighty feet up the mast to perch with me on the air search radar antenna platform, to take photos when alongside the Soviet merchant ship. We planned to photograph each of the missiles as it was uncovered and then forward the film and the accompanying intelligence report by helicopter to the carrier for forwarding onward to Atlantic Fleet headquarters as quickly as possible.

Blandy moved in close to the merchant ship *Dvinogorsk* from astern after a long, six-hour chase and signaled her by flashing light in international Morse, in English and Russian, the required phrases from the new operation order: "Please steer course zero six zero degrees true, at twelve knots, and begin uncovering your missiles for inspection, in accordance with the agreement between our two countries."

The newly designated intelligence photo team, consisting of the frightened photo mate and me, climbed up the solid steel rungs welded permanently to the mast. I improvised a knapsack to carry the large box camera, lenses, film, and sound-powered phone set. A slight sea was running, with two-to-three-foot waves. Eighty feet up the mast, however, these were magnified in intensity so that it took all my strength and concentration to haul the camera gear and to coax the reluctant photo mate while holding on for dear life. We secured ourselves to the mast with safety straps, and I donned the sound-powered phones and watched. Happily, the weather was fair, since we were within a hundred miles of Havana, and the wind, although at that height strong, blew warmly.

Dvinogorsk complied with the flashing light signal and came slowly to the required heading and speed. There was a long delay as our signalmen sent and resent the directions to uncover the forward missile port side. Four canvas-covered missiles were arrayed on the ship's main weather deck. There were also about five hundred Soviet soldiers in khaki uniforms lounging at the rails on several levels, peering at us as we inched ever closer. The Russians began slowly to comply and, while sitting quietly high up the mast, I noticed, to my dismay, that the photo mate was apparently suffering terribly from vertigo and beginning to turn green. He motioned to me suddenly that he was going to be sick; and while unable to do anything to help him because of the violent pitching and rolling, I hung on and watched helplessly as he literally blew his breakfast to the winds. As the poor sailor retched repeatedly, I worried that if events did not move more quickly he would be too weak to hold the large camera.

Slowly the topside Soviet soldiers on the merchant ship went below-decks, and a working party of five deckhands and a large bosun mate set about uncovering the first missile. I helped position the ship by adding and reducing revolutions by phone to the bridge watch and got the photographer's mate ready. With the application of some soda crackers and an orange, which I had brought from the wardroom, the photo mate was able to stop heaving. Later, on a second run of this same evolution, I passed him some seasick pills, but these, too, also left him after a short stay. Nonetheless, we repeated this routine until we had obtained detailed photos of each missile uncovered and, with the photographer's mate in a much weakened state, descended the mast during a long break to clear up some problem we were having with the Russians.

During the long period alongside *Dvinogorsk*, Commodore Morrison had been in constant conversation with the task group commander

Author atop *Blandy*'s
mast, November 1962
(author)

aboard *Essex*. While I was up on the mast with the photo mate, I wondered about the long delays between times when the Russian crew
uncovered one of the four missiles on deck and before we were told to
take the photos. The issue arose over the presence of the inside rubber
casing that wrapped each missile tightly. The missiles were encased in
this rubber shielding presumably to protect them from the weather. As
Blandy flashed over to the freighter, in Dubicki's foul Russian phrases,
to uncover the missiles, the Russian deck force team would proceed to
the missile and take off the outer canvas wrap and stand back so we
could observe and shoot a photo. But that wasn't good enough for Captain Kelley.

"How the hell do we know there are missiles under those casings
and not some gigantic sausage, Commodore?"

"Ed, we were told to direct them only to uncover their missiles.
What do you think is inside?"

"I think we should send Westerman and his team over to open the
entire casing and have the combat cameraman shoot the damn things
close up," Kelley roared. "How the hell else can we be certain?"

Captain Kelley's insistence had caused great furor aboard the carrier; the admiral kept repeating the question, "Can you verify that those are missiles?"

"Of course I can't verify those are missiles, Commodore, until I have Westerman go aboard and touch them." Kelley's response merely exacerbated the situation.

Eventually Commodore Morrison sent the same answer back to the task group commander in *Essex* in a long flashing-light message. Then came an inordinately long delay. I remained on the mast with the seasick photo mate. The commodore called for a meeting of his staff to discuss the issue, the OOD drove the ship out to a safer distance of about a hundred feet from *Dvinogorsk,* and the XO huddled with Stonewall Jackson, planning how to feed the crew while standing extended hours at special sea detail for refueling. But we weren't refueling, and there was no such drill in the books, and Jackson was adamant that we wait until we finished and then he would serve everyone at the regular mess. But the exec insisted; he was obsessed with the tradition of looking out for the welfare of the crew at all costs, and we had already been alongside the stubborn Russian for two hours. And it looked as if we were to remain alongside until the issue was solved.

Apparently the issue went all the way to Atlantic Fleet commander in chief in Norfolk and to the defense secretary and the White House. At question was whether the Russians were complying with the recent agreement to submit to inspection by U.S. ships to ensure that they were removing their missiles from Cuba. Ed Kelley's stubbornness in insisting that the Russians open the inner seals was sticking in the craw of the agreement. Although other U.S. destroyers were alongside Soviet merchant ships inspecting and taking photos of the missiles in their rubber casings, only Ed Kelley demanded that the Russians fully expose the weapons.

Finally Captain Kelley drafted a message describing the issue succinctly. It has since been quoted in records of the Cuban missile crisis as one of the issues that went unresolved. Kelley described the missiles when we were alongside *Dvinogorsk:*

About sixty feet long and four feet in diameter. Apparently missiles without nose cone attached. Appears to check with unclassified photos MRBM [medium-range ballistic missile]. Small tarp removed. Skin-tight canvas tailored to fit not removed. Four stubby canard stabilizing fins noted. Bulge of wiring conduit visible . . . although outer cover removed, and outline of objects appeared to correspond with MRBM, fact that objects remain covered with tailored cloth makes positive identification of objects as missile problematical.

Commander ASW Group Bravo (CTG 136.2) message 09134Z November 62.

This message was sent to the commander in chief of the Atlantic Fleet from the ASW group commander in USS *Essex*, although originally drafted by Captain Ed Kelley.

The problem was finally addressed in the Pentagon when Deputy Secretary of Defense Roswell Gilpatrick announced to the press on November 11: "The Soviets said there were forty-two [missiles] and we have counted forty-two going out. . . . Until we have so-called on-site inspection of the island of Cuba, we could never be sure that forty-two was the maximum number the Soviets brought into Cuba."[1]

Meanwhile, I remained atop the mast, and Steve Jackson had been ordered to conduct battle messing, which meant feeding the crew on extended sea detail stations. We all ate baloney sandwiches on station with coffee—that is, all who weren't aloft on the mast. I was finally called down and handed two sandwiches by Stonewall, and happily was able to eat both, eighty feet up on the SPS-6 air search radar platform, since it was doubtful the seasick photo mate could hold down anything more than the few saltines and orange he had already consumed.

That was the first in a series of *Blandy*'s encounters with Soviet merchant ships, and probably one of the most exciting. We were sent to check a second, called *Fizik Kurchatov*. This time we thought we had the procedure down, but things never go the way they are planned. I was standing the eight-to-twelve watch on the bridge with Gary Lagere. It was initially a quiet watch following a day that had been tense and full of surprises.

We sighted *Fizik Kurchatov* and found her steaming northeast at twenty knots. That put us in a long stern chase, but we finally pulled alongside at first light the next morning. We repeated our signal, "Your government has agreed to uncover missiles. Please do so beginning on the starboard side, number one missile."

Again we repeated the drill. This time the seas were running from the north, and a good wind was blowing. As we went alongside at refueling distance, I stood poised on the 04 level above the pilothouse on the

Translator Petty Officer Walter Dubicki on *Blandy*'s bridge alongside Soviet merchant ship *Dvinogorsk* hauling missiles from Cuba, November 1962 (courtesy Steve Jackson)

Mark 56 Director deck waiting for the signal to go aloft. As I stood there watching the Soviet ship as we made our approach at about fifty feet, I noticed that the main deck of the Soviet merchant was full of troops who wore khaki trousers and blue-and-white T-shirts. They were standing observing us just as our crew were, at least those not busy on a sea detail station. We sent over the distance line, which they understood and handled as if they had done the drill before. As we were jockeying for position and transmitting the signals to uncover the missiles, a hatch on the side of the *Kurchatov* superstructure burst open and a female emerged, who took one step over the hatch coaming. Apparently surprised to see a U.S. warship at such close range, she poised, startled. As she stood there, a gust of wind suddenly blew her yellow skirt up, which enshrouded her head and revealed a comely pair of legs and finely turned ankles. A loud roar and applause erupted on the inboard side of *Blandy* as the poor lady struggled to pull her skirt down to cover herself. The Russians, too, when seeing the American reaction, applauded loudly. At that moment I wondered what we were really doing here, and all fear of the other side seemed to vanish. They were pretty much like we were.

Ketov Evades in *B-4*

NOVEMBER 2, 1962
CAPTAIN RYURIK KETOV
B-4
ONE HUNDRED MILES SOUTH OF KINGSTON, JAMAICA

Once Captain Ryurik Ketov crossed the twenty-degree-latitude meridian in submarine *B-4* and passed through the Windward Passage, the weather improved. The seas quieted significantly and became like glass. When the submarine surfaced to charge at night the sea was beautiful. Ketov's engineers were able to improve the seal on the leaking weather hatch so they could submerge down to eighty or ninety meters, which gave them a significant advantage against the still-prowling U.S. ASW aircraft.

B-4 had passed through the Windward Passage on October 20 and, to Ketov's great relief, they were less than a day's sailing out of Mariel when they received the message to curtail the transit. Ketov had been clearly disappointed, as were all the crew. As it turned out, they had made the best time of all the four in the brigade. They were snorting and had an antenna up to copy the scheduled broadcast that afternoon. With a downcast look in his eyes, Pronin came to Ketov in the central control post. Pronin had a piece of teletype paper in his hands. "Sir, you won't believe this." He handed the message to the captain, who quickly read it.

The message read: "Abort transit to destination, repeat, abort transit, take station at [coordinates were given]. Assume combat patrol. Maintain covert presence."

"Sir, what's going on that we don't know about?"

Ketov looked at Pronin and was genuinely sorry he couldn't answer. Here they were, in the enemy's backyard and had no information about what was going on. "I don't know any more than you. I assume something has caused the temporary halt to Operation *Kama*."

Pronin looked at the captain and then had the sudden urge to confess that he had been monitoring the forbidden radio waves. There was a serious confrontation in progress around them, and they only knew what they managed to purloin from the ether. Although *B-4* had not missed a single scheduled fleet broadcast, they still knew precious little about the tactical situation in the Caribbean. It was criminal, Ketov felt, that they continued south into what they would later learn had become a churning cauldron of naval activity. Moscow normally transmitted twice a day on the broadcast, but the only real information offered was the domestic news, how well the harvest was going in the USSR, and that the Party was solving all international problems. Like the other submarine commanders of the brigade, Ketov had given authorization to his radio operators to tune in to American radio broadcasts, where they had learned of the U.S. blockade on October 22.

Ketov altered their track when he realized the surface was crawling with U.S. warships. He and the brigade commander, Captain Agafonov, decided to head south and around the southeastern point of Cuba to avoid contact with the swarming hordes above. When they thought they were clear, they headed north to B-4's assigned patrol station. Since they were still required to remain covert, they took their time getting to the patrol station by passing quietly through Turks Island Passage, which, although narrow, was a choice that probably would not be anticipated by the Americans. B-4 crept around the coast of Cuba, and at night, while snorkeling, actually observed lights from the Cuban coastline. They proceeded at slow speed with the sail awash, venting the boat and charging. Ketov watched the lights ashore and smelled the aroma of charcoal and the sweet scent of sugarcane fields burning. It was tantalizing to be that close to their goal but then to be turned back at the last moment. They had so looked forward to being stationed in this wonderful tropical land. Ketov felt as if they had been offered a sumptuous prize, only to have it snatched away at the last moment.

"Aircraft three points off the starboard bow, closing fast!" the lookout whispered hoarsely.

"Emergency dive! Clear the bridge!" Ketov gave one last fleeting glimpse to the shoreline and scampered below, slamming the hatch behind him. Thus began a two-day period of protracted hide-and-seek from which Ketov reckons he never really recovered his nerve.

On November 2 an S2F Tracker aircraft from the carrier USS *Independence* picked up a brief radar contact on the snorkel of Captain Ketov in B-4. The carrier was part of Task Force 135, the invasion attack carrier force, south of Cuba and just east of Jamaica. The Americans designated their radar contact C21, and then gained solid radar contact by helicopter, with a Tracker confirming the contact with their magnetic anomaly detector. The task group commander prudently took his forces into shallower waters, where it was difficult for the submarine to evade.

It was a clear day, but what Ketov's monitors heard over the U.S. news was so bad that they thought, clear weather or not, they had better copy the broadcast, and so they went shallow. This was when Captain Ketov had a serious run-in with the brigade commander, Captain Second Rank Agafonov, who was aboard.

It was clear to Ketov that from communications there was certainly an ASW patrol aircraft overhead. Agafonov was growing anxious to receive new orders from Moscow. They were at twenty meters depth. It was nearing the time for their next broadcast. At this point, obtaining orders was vital. During their previous attempts to copy, they had failed. Their antenna was not completely free of short circuits, and consequently they had received nothing. Agafonov wanted to surface immediately with the sail awash and the antenna fully extended to try to receive the broadcast using high frequency to back up the ultra-low-frequency transmissions that were not always reliable in those latitudes. Ketov recommended against surfacing. The last thing he thought they needed was to be detected outright by the P2V Neptune, which he was certain was nearby. Earlier they had heard his sonobuoys, which were activated by the Julie explosions trying to triangulate their position. Ketov was certain that they had not gained solid contact or they would have called in a surface ship, one of the numerous destroyers that were working with the carrier *Independence*. However, Ketov could see that Agafonov was getting more and more nervous. Agafonov seemed certain that there would be vital new instructions for them on the broadcast. Ketov was less hopeful. They had come all that way in more than three weeks and had received minimal instructions other than the short directive canceling their track to Mariel and assigning them a small, twenty-five-mile-radius circle in which to patrol. It would be difficult to stay within the boundaries of the new patrol area, and they were curious why they were relegated to such a tight area.

Naturally, as Brigade Commander Agafonov was senior, Ketov was obliged to follow his orders unless the submarine commanding officer was certain they would hazard his command. Agafonov was relatively new aboard, at least in comparison with the time Ketov and most of his officers had served. They had commissioned the boat and knew her idiosyncrasies thoroughly. Agafonov decided that they should surface to copy the schedule. Ketov opposed strongly.

"Surface," Agafonov ordered.

"Brigade Commander, I believe we have an aircraft nearby. He will lock onto us for certain if we surface." Ketov was not going to stand by and watch them get trapped.

"I'll check personally," Agafonov responded, and scrambled up the ladder to the navigation bridge, where the attack and commander's periscopes were located. Ketov watched the brigade commander scurry up the ladder into the main trunk while a petty officer opened the inner hatch. Water cascaded down into the command center as always when first opening that hatch. Ketov watched and got an uneasy feeling in his stomach. Granted they had been at close quarters, into each other's knickers for weeks, and naturally both felt a little compressed by the situation. However, Ketov knew Agafonov was not as certain of the situation as he was.

Ketov went to the navigation periscope, near the after bulkhead of the command center. He knew it had a better capability to observe zenith for navigation purposes; he often used it to spot aircraft. Ketov looked through the scope, saw nothing then, and waited for Agafonov's response.

"I see no contacts; the horizon and skies are clear," Agafonov called down on the sound-powered phones.

"Sir, I am certain there is an aircraft there—I observed it a few minutes ago. No, I don't see it now either, but it's likely still in the vicinity."

"If there were an aircraft there I'd see it," Agafonov said. "Surface— that's an order!"

That was enough for Ketov. "Comrade Agafonov, relieve me of command of this submarine and I will make an entry to that effect in the ship's log. Navigator, bring me the log." Ketov took the log from the navigator and made the entry "Brigade Commander Captain Second Rank Vitali Naumovich Agafonov relieved Captain Ryurik A. Ketov of command of submarine *B-4*."

Ketov announced over the ship's speaker system that Captain Agafonov had relieved him of command, and then went to his cabin. Agafonov did not realize that by standing on the navigation level inside the sail, the commanding officer's periscope was limited to a narrow cone of visibility of about seven degrees either side of center. Ketov was certain the Neptune would begin dropping depth bombs or grenades, whatever they were using, depending on whether they were in a state of hostilities or not, and they frankly did not know.

As soon as *B-4* broke the surface, the lookouts spotted the Neptune aircraft about three miles ahead, but it was too late, and the aircraft flew toward them and began dropping grenades. The first explosive landed very close to the hull. The lights aboard went out and the engineer switched to emergency electric power while *B-4* crash-dived to a hundred meters with lighting restored. Agafonov took charge and tried to evade. Ketov was sick at heart, but as a matter of principle, remained in his cabin.

Initially Agafonov did not succeed, and the U.S. aircraft stuck right with them. They could hear his sonobuoys splashing in the water, and then the occasional explosion of the grenade to register their location on the passive buoys. Ketov remained in his cabin for most of an hour, until it was too much for him to remain absent. He returned to the central control to observe and after a few moments realized Agafonov was doing the best he could. The brigade commander waved him away, so he retired again to his cabin, certain that they were going to be forced to surface eventually, probably into the teeth of a gaggle of destroyers.

For three hours Agafonov evaded the aircraft, but he failed, and each time he thought they had achieved an advantage of a few extra miles from the pursuing aircraft it would swoop down again for an update on their position. After three hours of futile maneuvering passed, Agafonov called Ketov back to the central command post.

"Captain Ketov, take command again."

Ketov resumed command, elated that he had won the dispute. Ketov recalls that the confrontation was not as serious as it first sounds; such arguments happen often when senior unit commanders are embarked aboard ships. They normally can handle it, but the stress was enormous. Ketov considered the crisis past, and could now concentrate on losing the Americans. He began to hatch a scheme to evade.

If the Americans had been ordered to force them away from their coast he would assist them, and he turned east to course zero nine zero at four knots. They steamed quietly eastward, but on a gently zigzag course. Ketov knew that the aircraft would have to be relieved soon, since he had been on station now for more than four hours. The P2V Neptunes did not possess the staying power of the newer P3 Orions.

One hour passed and they heard nothing more. Ketov was certain the aircraft had left, but may have been relieved by another aircraft on station or by one that would soon arrive. Suddenly they heard the new aircraft on their passive sonar. He swooped low, laid a pattern of buoys, and then began to release explosives every five minutes to determine *B-4*'s track. Ketov was now at sixty meters depth, and when he read the navigator's hydroacoustic plot realized that they were just below the thermocline layer. They had been extremely lucky with the thermocline shallow, located just above sixty meters and giving them some acoustic protection. The local seas had developed a number of currents—"acoustic soft spots," as the Russians called them—that Ketov decided to use to their advantage. The time between explosives increased from five to fifteen minutes. Ketov could hear several surface ships close to their position attempting to locate them. Then the times between explosions increased to twenty minutes. Ketov was relieved and exclaimed that they had had enough of this and were now going to slip away.

"Chief engineer, how much longer on the batteries?"

"Enough power for ninety minutes at medium speed, Comrade Commander."

"Navigator, how long until sundown?" Ketov asked.

"Sir," he answered, "one hour and forty minutes until sunset."

Ketov waited until the aircraft dropped the next series of buoys and then listened for the following explosions. He turned east again and increased speed to ten knots. By the time the aircraft dropped the next series of buoys he had lost *B-4*. By that time it was dark. After dark the aircraft was unable to fly as low to confirm with his magnetic anomaly detector. Ketov could hear the aircraft to the south of them dropping more buoys and trying to find them, but he was already way off. He surfaced slowly in the dark and charged batteries with only the snorkel awash. The aircraft did not detect them again, either on radar or with his Jezebel buoy patterns. Ketov's sonarmen heard the hydrophone effects of numerous surface ships south of them trying to locate them with the aircraft; they gradually opened the distance from them and escaped into the tropical night.

The next day Ketov received the broadcast message from Moscow confirming that they should curtail the transit to Mariel and to resume the patrol in the small area of twenty-five-mile radius. To do this, Ketov used his newly installed RG-10 passive sonar for the first time. *B-4* had it installed just before they left, but until now it had not worked. One of Ketov's superb electronics technicians had finally gotten it to work after fiddling with it for more than three weeks. They never understood why it hadn't functioned prior to this, and Ketov wondered if it had been sensitive to the cold. In any case it was working now, and it enabled them to detect the Americans at ranges greater than their normal acoustic systems were capable. *B-4* was the only submarine in the group with this new equipment. From then on they were able on numerous occasions to detect the Americans early and to scoot away before they could be detected. Whenever an American came close, Ketov would descend to 120 meters to ensure that he was beneath the layer. Over time the Americans eventually lost all contact, thus giving Ketov and *B-4* the honor of being the sole submarine of the brigade not forced to surface in the teeth of surface ships.

Ketov finally departed their patrol area after a month and began making their way northward. They still had not received the order to return to base but kept getting assigned new patrol areas 100 to 120 miles farther and farther north. Finally, on November 20, *B-4* received orders to return to its home port, Polyarny. It was curious that shortly following their receipt of the orders to return home, Ketov's radio intercept operators intercepted a message from the U.S. Atlantic Command broadcast in the clear, thanking the Soviet submarines in the area for the opportunity for the mutual operations. That was indeed a surprise and confirmed in Ketov's mind that the Americans knew exactly what their mission and orders were the whole time. They just did not have the tactical capability to force all of the Soviet submarines to the surface. As far as Ketov and his men aboard *B-4* were concerned, they had evaded and had not suffered the embarrassment of having to surface in the teeth of the numerically superior Americans.

PART V

Endgame

Kola Homecoming

NOVEMBER 8, 1962
CAPTAIN NIKOLAI SHUMKOV
B-130
NORTH ATLANTIC

B-130 continued northeasterly through heavy seas now, with USS *Keppler* escorting them. On the surface with two diesels out of commission and the third operating at reduced power, they could do only one and a half knots on the electric drive. It was monotonous, and the seas were getting very rough. The number one diesel, the only one Chief Mechanic Parshin could get on the line, had power enough only to continue charging the batteries.

They were expecting to contact the rescue tug *Pamir* at any moment. She was last heard heading southwest at ten knots. Voronov was the watch officer. Shumkov was preoccupied by their retreat from the action. They had finally received a response regarding their diesel casualties. Northern Fleet Submarine Command had informed them that replacement drive gears for the diesels had been placed aboard *Pamir*. Shumkov called the chief mechanic to the bridge.

"Aye, sir," Parshin sputtered in the rain, which had again engulfed the navigation cockpit. It was a glorious feeling to stand in the fresh water, even though it somewhat hampered conversation with his captain. After the weeks of rank heat and foul air it was good just to stand in the fresh air and purge the lungs.

"Chief, we just heard that *Pamir* is carrying parts for our two diesels with cracked main gears. What do you make of that?"

The chief looked over the cockpit railing at *Keppler*, riding shotgun on the starboard quarter at about two thousand meters. He shook his head.

"Sir, we told them that the repairs could be done only in the shipyard; we can't possibly replace those gears. We need to be dry-docked."

"Why not, Chief?" Shumkov was normally perceptive of engineering questions but suddenly realized they had not discussed the details of replacing the gears. They had known the cracks had existed since their commissioning, but the fact that they had completely sheared through seemed to him a job that merely required replacements.

"I can't believe the engineers at the flotilla and Northern Fleet haven't realized that it can't be done at sea." The chief shook his head in disbelief.

"Why not, Chief?" Shumkov asked again, feeling a little foolish for not discussing the question earlier.

"It's, simple sir. We can remove the broken gears because they come out in two pieces, but to install replacements we need to cut out a plate in the hull with minimum dimensions of two meters by one and a half meters. I have the welding equipment to do the job but we can't do that at sea in this weather; we'd go down like a rock. Even in port it would be unwise to try unless on the blocks in a dry dock!"

Shumkov was dumbfounded. He hadn't thought of the size of the gears, or that they might be far too large to get down the main trunk accesses or the torpedo loading hatches. He gazed out at the gray swells and the equally gray sky, hardly able to discern the horizon where the two met. The two men stood silently together, watching ahead for the tug to emerge in the distance.

When they finally sighted the rescue tug, Shumkov was relieved, but not for long. Their initial radio contact with *Pamir* had given them new hope that they might indeed be able to effect temporary repairs and head back to the brigade to help them in the seemingly never-ending battle with U.S. ASW forces. However, their hopes were soon dashed.

"That leaves no other solution, Chief; *Pamir* has to take us under tow." Undesirable as that seemed, it was far better to return under tow than wallow for another month at one and a half knots to get home. Their orders were to rendezvous with *Pamir* and make repairs as necessary before returning south to support the other three boats from the brigade. It was out of the question now. Shumkov understood exactly why they couldn't replace the gears under way. It all seemed hilarious to him suddenly, and he was tempted to burst out laughing. He restrained himself before his chief mechanic.

"Surface contact dead ahead." The call came from the ESM operator below in the central command. That was surely *Pamir*.

"Roger, contact. Sonar, any hydrophone effects?"

"Not yet, sir; heavy swells are masking our passive reception, but we should pick him up shortly."

Shumkov waited, straining his eyes against the spray and the rain. He felt depressed after all the action, and the close calls, the nearness of the enemy, and now they were out of it, done! They had only the long trip home ahead of them. Within ten minutes the lookout reported a visual contact dead ahead. It was beginning to grow darker, although it was still only midafternoon.

"Sir, airborne radar contact to the west, approaching. An American Neptune heading toward us."

"Roger," Shumkov replied. What did it matter now? They were out of the game, useless in any form, and not a threat to anything.

"Sir, the American destroyer is chatting with the aircraft on their ASW common net. Sir, they expected us to meet the tug."

"Very well." Now they'll have a free show if they can see anything at all in this weather, Shumkov thought. No point in maintaining voice radio silence. "Tell Cheprakov to make radio contact with *Pamir* and let me speak to the commander."

"Aye, sir," Voronov responded. Within a few minutes he called back. "Comrade Commander, captain of *Pamir* on the line, channel six."

"Very well." Shumkov picked up the handset and turned the salt-encrusted dial to channel six. He could see *Pamir* now as the visibility improved somewhat. She was swinging around to take station on their port quarter. Now, he thought, we have two escorts, one of ours and one of theirs, plus an aircraft. We certainly are well looked after.

Shumkov began shouting into the handset; the radio contact was poor and the voice on the other end hardly audible. Shumkov managed to explain the matter to the tug's skipper and then passed the line to the chief, who had returned to the cockpit. They began discussing the length and the size of the towing cable to be used. Shumkov seriously doubted that they could successfully tow the submarine on a short-haul cable in that weather; they would have to rig an extremely long cable to preclude the seas from snapping the towline. It would be a long and tedious trip home.

After much chatter and cursing the chief and the tug skipper agreed to wait until the weather improved. The three ships continued in their little formation on the same course and speed until the next day when, after two failed attempts during which the towline parted, they successfully rigged a three-hundred-meter towline, which seemed to work. They surged homeward at the amazing speed of five knots. When the tug began the towing they were three hundred miles from the U.S. East Coast; it took *B-130* three weeks to make it back to Polyarny. They made landfall at North Cape on December 3.

After rounding North Cape their spirits began to soar. It was already Arctic night, and they rarely saw the sun again. The prospects of arriving in home port were sufficient to keep their spirits buoyed. It took them another two days to the point where they turned and headed south, toward the Kola Peninsula. The tug had arranged for two harbor tugs to meet them at the sea buoy, but Shumkov was against it. They had been able to fully charge their batteries by a clever electrical jury rig the chief had thought up, using the one remaining diesel at low power and some help from *Pamir*. His idea was to drop the towline when they passed the sea buoy and head in under their own electrical power. At first Shumkov had some trouble with the Polyarny flotilla staff, who assumed he had no power left and insisted the submarine should be towed in by the two harbor tugs while *Pamir* would follow, since she had the two big gears aboard to transfer for the eventual repairs. When the flotilla staff continued to insist, Shumkov merely turned the volume down on his radio receiver and said he was unable to copy their last due to atmospherics and that they intended to enter port under their own power. That was the last said.

Shumkov dropped the tow at the buoy and began to make his way into the channel. It was pitch dark but considerably better visibility than when they had departed that dark night more than two months earlier. Shumkov had been ordered first to tie up in Sayda Bay and to offload the special weapon. He headed *B-130* in without difficulty and moored to the same pier they left on October 1.

After they finally completed mooring, Shumkov looked over at the pier and saw a single black Volga sedan standing under the pier lights, its engine running. Inside were several figures he could not make out.

He knew there would be no arrival ceremony, since they had come in late, following the orders they had received via *Pamir*. The shroud of secrecy was still over them, and Shumkov wasn't sure why. It is customary when returning from patrol for a Soviet submarine commander to report to his next in command; in this case it would have been Agafonov, the brigade commander, but he was aboard Ketov's *B-4* and still somewhere—God knew where—in the vast Atlantic. During normal daytime arrivals the commander would go ashore and officially report "mission complete" to his senior and would be presented a roast piglet signifying the successful accomplishment of the task. This would unfold with great pomp—a small band made up of local base musicians with dented brass horns and a big drum, and the crew of the submarine paraded in ranks on the boat's weather deck. Shumkov always enjoyed these arrivals after a long patrol. This time, however, it was not the same, since they had been, and apparently were still, considered a covert mission—that is, except to the Americans, who knew exactly where they had been and, probably, where they were now. Some things just didn't make sense, Shumkov thought.

Although it was late, Shumkov watched carefully to see who was in the sedan, just in case some senior officer appeared for him to report to. He felt a little deflated that there was no one else on the pier except the three sailors who came from the port captain's office in the shed at the foot of the pier. They stood huddled together in the light snow. When *B-130*'s lines snaked over the side, the three sailors looped them over the large steel cleats on the floating pier. Shumkov ordered the engines, such as they were, shut down. After a short delay they received an electrical hookup so they had power and could shut down their auxiliary generators.

Shumkov stared out into the night, thinking how much of an anticlimax it was after the weeks of strenuous activity, sleepless days and nights on end, only to return to the Motherland, where only constant darkness and snow flurries greeted them. Granted, there had been no battle, and no lives were lost. The only casualties they had sustained had been the navigator's broken ribs during the rough weather. They had all lost weight, something that, no doubt, would delight their wives. Somehow he felt empty, drained of energy. He should have been pleased that he was returning with the same number of men as he started with. The men aboard had all aged because of the encounters; they had been close to a shooting war and had lived to sail away from it.

Shumkov observed a dark hulk in navy greatcoat emerge from the front seat of the Volga next to the driver. He could make out the gold shoulder boards with the single star of a kontr admiral and a senior officer's karakul fur *mushanka* cap. Shumkov quickly slid down the ladder from the cockpit to the main deck and approached the brow, which the line handlers were pulling up and over the side. The light snow on the piers and the main weather deck made the job much easier than normal. As Shumkov began to cross over to the pier, the admiral, as he grew closer, raised his hand and motioned him to remain aboard.

"I'll come aboard," the admiral called out.

Shumkov thought that was very strange, as admirals did not casually walk aboard ships or submarines, especially before the commander had reported the mission complete. Shumkov stood at the inboard end of the brow and returned the salute of Kontr Admiral Leonid Rybalko as he walked briskly aboard.

"*Ztorovye zhelau* [to your health], Comrade Admiral," he began. "Captain Nikolai Shumkov, commander submarine *B-130*, reporting mission complete."

Rybalko returned the salute and stepped forward and grasped Shumkov's hand with both of his. He shook the captain's hand heartily and, at first, seemed to grope for words. Finally they came.

"Nikolai, I'm glad you returned safely. How are your men?"

That was the first time in Shumkov's long career that he had ever had a senior officer inquire about the welfare of his crew, and it impressed him greatly. "Sir, they are all fine, a little thin, tired, and with some minor medical problems, rashes and skin ulcers; nothing that a little rest and fresh air won't cure." Rybalko gripped his hand solidly and shook it again. He seemed genuinely moved by the crew's return.

"We are, or rather, I am, terribly disappointed in the way things turned out; it should not have occurred," the admiral continued. He seemed desperately overwrought and anxious to get some words off his chest.

Shumkov assumed Rybalko was referring to their casualty and having been forced to surface in the teeth of the U.S. hunter-killer force. He was ready to continue his verbal report, but the admiral countered thoughtfully, "There was no excuse for sending you into that melee without informing you all along the way about what was going on. I know you probably figured it out some other way, but it was criminal to have sent you in blind. I have protested to the fleet commander in chief, who himself also was concerned. So far we have had no assistance or cooperation from the Main Navy Staff. Ever since mid-October they have been frozen in silence and indecision." The admiral's speech was extraordinary; it sounded like a confession being made by a terribly wounded man.

Rybalko continued, "I am obliged to pass on orders to you that because of your operational exposure to the Americans, against the requirement of the operation to remain covert, you and your crew will be restricted to the confines of your boat until a full investigation is completed."

Shumkov stared at the admiral. Rybalko was visibly shaken, and Shumkov believed somewhat embarrassed to have to impart that message. Nevertheless, the captain was still stunned by the impact of those words. He, too, had expected some recriminations, but not so soon or so sharply as to see the entire crew, including officers, restricted to the confines of the submarine.

"The rationale is," continued Rybalko, "that the whole operation is still secret, and of course, the results even more so. Earlier the secrecy was imposed to protect Operation *Kama*, but now it is to protect the navy and the government from embarrassment. This effort to shroud everything to do with *Anadyr* with a cloak of secrecy still permeates Moscow and is present among all the combat services. Rumors are flying all around. I am being candid, Nikolai. I know how you must feel."

"Admiral," Shumkov responded, "come below and have some tea." He thought it better that they go below rather than standing on the weather deck in the wet snow.

"Thank you, Nikolai; I appreciate your kindness but actually I must go back to Polyarny. I should not have been here, but I couldn't stand the thought that you had made it all the way home from this debacle without someone greeting you and your men. Your wife and family, by the way, are fine. I called Irina this morning and told her you were due in tonight. She promised to keep the word to herself. She has indeed been worried, as we all have been. That you made it back despite your mechanical casualties is certainly a great credit to you and your whole crew."

As they were speaking, a large truck ground its gears and drove noisily down the pier, stopping just by the brow. Rybalko began to move toward the brow, then pointed at the pier. "We've brought you and your men some refreshments to help you celebrate your safe arrival. I assume you have very little left aboard in the form of fresh provisions."

"We have none, sir; any we didn't consume were spoiled in the heat." Shumkov regretted admitting that they were suffering from lack of provisions. He wanted to avoid sounding as if he was complaining. "Freshwater is our greatest need, sir, but I understand we'll be receiving a water barge alongside soon."

Two orderlies crossed the brow carrying two large boxes. They returned to the pier and took two more large, sealed containers from the open-bed truck. "These are fresh stores for you now," Rybalko added. "More will arrive when the others come in. Please be discreet about these, as I had to arrange for them myself. The base commander was ordered not to replenish you until later, but I had a feeling you would appreciate a little relief from your ordeal."

Rybalko shook the captain's hand again, then looked at Shumkov closely. "The investigation will begin as soon as Brigade Commander Agafonov arrives with Ketov in B-4. We have a report that they have made it to North Cape and should be here within forty-eight hours if they are in full operating order."

"And the others, sir?" Shumkov was especially concerned about his close friend Aleksei Dubivko. He had seen partial reports of his confrontation with the Americans and saw one signal that the U.S. destroyer *Cecil* was attempting to communicate with B-36. Dubivko had requested instructions regarding whether to respond.

"We last heard from Dubivko two days ago, when he was located just west of the Lofoten Islands," Rybalko said. "He appears to be all right, but we're not certain of his arrival date." He smiled briefly and then added, "I'm sorry for all this, I truly am."

Rybalko turned, saluted the officer of the watch, who had just set up the duty stand on the main deck, crossed the brow, and walked back to the sedan. Shumkov watched the admiral quietly in the dark, barely able to believe what had transpired and of the strange circumstances that seemed to prevail there and in Moscow. With very little information at hand he could ascertain that the whole operation had been compromised and that it had been a grave and humiliating defeat for the country. He was still shocked to see an admiral, their squadron commander, out by himself in the middle of the night, with no staff, on his own to meet them and tell them that they were, in essence, under house arrest on board their own submarine. This was unbeliev-able, especially after having escaped death and avoided a shooting war. Suddenly Shumkov was tired, very tired.

He turned to go below and saw his *starpom*, Frolov, standing by the hatch. "Comrade Commander, come below to the officers' mess—we have something to show you." Shumkov was surprised to learn that Frolov had been standing there for some time. Frolov walked closely behind the captain as the two went below into central command.

"I heard what the admiral said," Frolov began, "and, well, sir, I don't understand either, but we should take this one day at a time." Frolov was a mature officer, and Shumkov could see that the whole experience of the past two months had mellowed him even more. They walked aft silently through the submarine toward the officers' mess.

Frolov ushered the captain into the confined space and there, in the small cabin, all the *B-130* officers and *michmen* had gathered around the small table. Shumkov thought of how over the past two months they had barely scratched by on the limited rations in the overwhelm-ing heat and humidity. The officers' wardroom had always been close and crowded, but now, in the cool of the North, the space seemed larger, even though it was crowded with the officers. Shumkov suddenly noticed the table, which was covered with plates of fresh *zakuski*—green salads, sardines, pickled herring, and sliced beef tongue. There were bottles of chilled vodka and champagne standing along the sideboard. He looked at Frolov.

"Sir, I know what you are going to say, yes, the crew, but they are sitting down to a similar spread, courtesy of Admiral Rybalko and his wife," he said thoughtfully.

Shumkov looked at the officers crowded around the space. They were a pathetic-looking lot. Eyes red, some totally unshaven, others with trimmed beards. Many had sores on their faces and arms. Most were now wearing their full blue coveralls with the blue-and-white navy jerseys underneath. Although it was hovering near freezing outside, the temperature inside the submarine was still warm, the atmosphere close and stuffy.

"Wait just a moment," Shumkov said. "I'll be back in a few min-utes." The exec and he walked aft together to the crew's mess. As they passed through the hatch into the confines of compartment six and were stepping into the after torpedo room, which served as the crew's mess in port, there was an audible shuffle and the sound of many men in the small space. Almost the entire crew was jammed inside. In the middle of the deck, on two temporary tables, was a spread similar to the one he had just seen in the officers' wardroom.

"Captain on deck!" someone shouted. They all rose.

It was a moving sight. The men looked rather shabby. Most of them looked tired, red eyes, matted hair, and dirty hands. They were very thin; some looked as if they hadn't eaten in weeks. Shumkov gazed around the space, trying to look at each of them separately. He saw that they expected him to address them. He looked around at the space and noted that the special weapon security officer was there, too, looking shy and lost, as he always did.

Captain Shumkov cleared his throat and began. "Carry on, be seated." They all sat or squatted down; there weren't enough places for all to sit. They looked very much alive, and their eyes shone. He could tell that this was an important moment for them. His mind raced. How was he to impart what he had just learned from the admiral, that they were basically under house arrest? And to do so without dashing that spirit that was visible in their faces—that look of curiosity to know what the admiral had said and what was to happen next to them after the harrowing months of uncertainty.

"Men," Shumkov began, "first let me say that I am proud of each of you. As you may have heard, we will be confined to the boat until the others in the brigade return and until we give our full patrol report." He avoided using the word "investigation." "The admiral asked that I compliment each and every one of you for a job well done under the very trying and uncertain circumstances. I will do everything in my power to obtain leave and recreation authorization for all of you as soon as possible. In the meantime, make the best of the situation; get some rest, you all need it. There are no watches to stand other than the engineering sound and security watch; base personnel will be standing our topside watches. So make the best of the time. We will have a freshwater barge alongside soon, so there will be showers for all."

Shumkov turned to go, but the senior petty officer aboard called out, "Captain, here," and he handed him a small glass of vodka. It was not customary for a commanding officer to drink with the crew, but protocol on this operation had disappeared long ago. He took the glass, his hand shaking.

"Sir"—the petty officer stood rigidly—"we wish to drink with you, to our boat, our families, and . . . well . . ." He hesitated nervously. It was not normal for men to speak in this way before their commander. "We appreciate your, ah, close . . . leadership." Then he looked around, and the entire group broke into a cheer.

"Oorah, Shumkov." They drank; Shumkov drained the glass and then raised his hand.

He glanced around the space, taking in their grinning faces. "We could not have done better. Remember, I am nothing without you."

Shumkov quickly turned and began walking forward toward the officers' mess. He walked slowly because his legs still gave him great pain and, of course, he didn't want the officers to see that his eyes had filled. Shumkov was tired and would be able to sleep through the night without being awakened. And he did—for twelve full hours.

B-130 had returned to Sayda Bay on December 7. On the sixteenth Ketov and the brigade commander arrived in *B-4*. They were all still confined to the boats, waiting for Savitsky and Dubivko. The second day after Ketov moored, the freshwater barge had returned alongside, and a resupply of fresh stores arrived. The crews were anxious to get off the boats, but at least they had real food. The next hurdle was to obtain continuous freshwater from ashore, since they had already depleted the first two barges. That process took the chief mechanics two full days to arrange when finally a third water barge pulled up alongside, and they filled their potable water tanks and had their first full showers in weeks. The two commanding officers would have preferred to have the men billeted ashore in the barracks or in the more comfortable berths they knew were available aboard the submarine tender *Dmitri Galkan*, only fifteen kilometers away in Polyarny. However, for some reason they were ordered to remain isolated and pretty much incognito until all the others returned. Shumkov and Ketov had no idea at the time why this was so, other than what Rybalko had told them. As time went on they realized it was for security purposes, since the authorities wanted no unofficial word of the Soviet Navy's plight in the Caribbean at the hands of the U.S. ASW forces to leak out. So just as it frequently was in the USSR in those years, security became their worst enemy: they stewed and waited in the still-fetid boats. At least the temperature was considerably cooler, but the inherent odor of diesel and chlorine fumes still permeated their clothing and everything in the boats.

The second day in port a team of medical officers arrived to inspect the two crews. They were appalled by the condition of the men, prescribed some medication, and gave salve for the rashes and the sores. The two boats still had not received adequate freshwater; the third barge alongside had run out after the second day, and therefore some crewmen were still unable to scrub in warm freshwater.

Two days later they were overjoyed to see that Savitsky arrived with B-59. It was early in the morning hours and still pitch dark as usual when they heard the sound of a tug tooting in response to a command from Savitsky as they moored next to B-130 in the nest. Despite the early hour, the entire crew of both boats turned out on the weather decks to welcome them home. The next morning, while the men sat around and exchanged stories, the brigade chief of staff, Arkhipov, went ashore to try to obtain permission for the crews of all three submarines and the others when they arrived to be berthed ashore. He, too, ran into the same order from the flotilla. The crews were all to remain aboard ship until the remainder of the brigade arrived. Many of the crew still had only the silly khaki shorts and tropical shirts issued before they left. Their other clothing was sodden and smelled terrible due to the mildew from the warm humidity of the South. Finally, after several days of demands to the shore station, a truck with foul-weather jackets and winter caps arrived on the pier. At least they were warm, although they still stank.

Shortly after Savitsky arrived, they learned that Dubivko in B-36 had signaled that he was at North Cape with only a few liters of fuel remaining. They all settled down to await the last boat. To add insult to injury, the three crews were told that they should not intermingle with the crews of the other boats, since they were to be debriefed soon and they were not to cloud their memories with the words of the other crewmen. That was the most ridiculous order they had ever received. But they obeyed, mostly. What was really insulting was that the flotilla staff sent a detachment of guards from the naval infantry to cordon off the pier and to literally keep them as prisoners in their boats.

At first Shumkov and the other skippers were enraged, but when a heavy snowstorm hit, they realized they were not required to have deck sentries or a pier watch out in the storm, as those posts were being guarded by the naval infantry. So the submariners enjoyed the respite of no watch standing, except for a skeleton engineering watch to guard against sinking next to the pier by accident. They all slept a lot.

Two days later, Dubivko arrived in B-36. What a story he had to tell!

DECEMBER 15, 1962
CAPTAIN ALEKSEI DUBIVKO
B-36
NORTHERN NORWEGIAN SEA

The weather during the entire transit north from the time they left their combat patrol station was terrible. The seas were perpetually mountainous, and the winds strong from the northeast. It was sheer hell to stand watch on the navigation bridge when they were on the surface or near the surface, snorkeling. Dubivko was seriously concerned about their remaining fuel.

Dubivko called the chief mechanic to the central command. "Chief, what's our fuel status now?" The engineer looked crestfallen.

"Comrade Commander, we have made an error somewhere along the line."

"What do you mean, 'an error'?" He was growing more concerned.

"Well, sir, we lost some two tons of fuel somehow."

"How could that happen?" Dubivko was astounded. "Did you miscalculate, or did we lose it during the heavy rolling?" It was possible to lose fuel from the ballast tanks in heavy weather if on the surface when taking heavy rolls. All the fuel was not actually contained by the walls of the tanks, but floated atop the seawater, which forced the diesel fuel on the top to be held securely in the open-bottomed ballast tanks. If the boat took extremely heavy rolls it was not out of the question to lose fuel. That, however, happened only in extreme rolls. Although they had taken some heavy rolls, up to fifty degrees, that was not considered extreme enough to lose fuel.

"Well, sir, we're still taking more soundings and trying to find out what happened. I've already done it three complete times and we still come up two tons short."

"How far will that take us?"

"Well, sir, depending on how long it takes us to recharge each day, we're not going to make it much beyond North Cape!"

Dubivko was stunned when he heard the engineer's words. The going had been tough all along, but they had managed, even after suffering the leaks from the sprung hatch and loss of electrical power several times when water had cascaded in through the leaking hatch, shorting out the after switchboard. To run short of fuel was not something the captain particularly wished to do. In fact, it would be not only dangerous but also professionally the end for him.

Dubivko looked at the chief, and he looked so poorly that the captain could not feel any anger toward him; rather he sort of felt sorry for him. It seemed he never got rest, but neither had most of the crew.

"Sir, we'll recalculate, resound all tanks, and then come up with a solution. There are ways."

Dubivko looked at him, puzzled. "What do you mean? If we're out of fuel, we're out! That's it! We can make an emergency call in to request a tug to fuel from, but by the time they make it out here we'll be dead in the water. We also can put out an emergency call for a passing merchant from Morflot [the Ministry of Merchant Shipping], but that would be a violation of regulations. What else can you recommend, Chief?"

The engineer looked at Dubivko with his filthy face and deep, penetrating eyes, which were ringed in red, and smiled. "We have twenty tons of lubricating oil in the after port tank outboard of compartment four. I know we haven't lost any of it because we keep resounding and finding the same amount. We don't need it for any other purpose."

Dubivko looked at him, still puzzled. "We can't burn lube oil in the diesels for propulsion. Or can we?"

"Not for propulsion, but we could mix it with the diesel we have left and water to feed one diesel to charge batteries and run on the electric drive. The lube oil can fire in the cylinders, but will give us only a fraction of normal power—enough to keep a small charge on the batteries, which can drive us home. It all depends on the weather, since we'll have to run at snorkel depth or on the surface. If the seas continue this high we won't be able to do it."

Well, they did it. B-36 steamed home on twenty tons of lube oil mixed three parts to one part with seawater and the remaining diesel fuel. The designers of those diesel engines were masters. Dubivko knew it was taking quite a gamble, but at this point, after all they had been through, he didn't think it was so bad. He trusted his engineers. They pumped the mixture and shifted suction and, to Dubivko's amazement, the last diesel merely coughed and continued running, although at a much lower power ratio.

B-36 steamed through the Barents with the sail awash so as to vent the diesels but without having to extend the snorkel. In this fashion

Zhukov with crewman of *B-36* heading home in November 1962
(courtesy Yuri Zhukov)

they had better air inside the hull, although now temperature was not the problem. In December there was little ice out in the deep water. Only once did they have some doubts and a little panic. The navigator, Zhukov, did a superb job bringing them to the landfall.

After steaming for the better part of the first day on the curious but necessary fuel mixture, the diesel suddenly began to slow and shutter alarmingly. Dubivko immediately stopped the electric drive. For a while nothing happened. Then they lost all power and the lights went out. There was much scampering about back in the engineering compartments, and as Dubivko listened on the phone circuit he decided to let the engineers have a free hand. After a period of about ten frightening minutes, as they wallowed in the gentle swell, the single diesel rumbled back to life and the lights came on again. Later Dubivko asked the chief how he had managed to start the diesel using that dreadful mix of lube oil and seawater. The chief stood before the captain in the evening glow as the snowflakes blew against the open cockpit windshield, wiping his hands on an oily rag.

"Comrade Commander, on the recommendation of several days ago by one of my enginemen, we saved about ten liters of pure diesel fuel. Once we lost power it was impossible to restart on that horrible mixture, so we hand-pumped in the good fuel and she started right up.

Once she was purring away, we shifted back to that mix. It was, in a way, cheating on the engine, but she took it well. We won't have that problem again. We lost the power because, with that lube oil mix, we have to shift and clean fuel strainers about four times an hour to remove the sediment and thick gum, which piled up in the strainers."

The chief was a genius, Dubivko thought. Once they got used to that operation, it was smooth sailing. And it worked all the way back into Sayda Bay. As B-36 rounded the last turn in the channel, with all systems working except for the two damaged diesels, they came in smartly and to their great relief saw that all three of the other boats of the brigade were moored in a nest to the pier. They saw that the weather decks and navigation bridges of all three boats were crowded with their comrades, who cheered as they tied up.

December 25, 1962
Sayda Bay

The day Dubivko arrived in B-36, Admiral Rybalko, the squadron commander, came down the pier again. The crews of all four submarines formed on the pier in the gentle snow. Captains Dubivko, Savitsky, Ketov, and Shumkov stood together on the edge of the pier as their men fell in for the formation. They were highly spirited now after some rest and a cleanup. And were anxious to get home.

"Here he comes," Shumkov said as the four captains took their places at the head of the assembled crews. Admiral Rybalko came down the pier. Shumkov had kept the conversation he had had with the admiral on his arrival to himself.

Admiral Rybalko walked slowly to the front of the formation, stopped, and looked over the men. He seemed moved as he scanned the motley-looking formation. Some of the men wore proper winter uniforms with the *mushanka* winter caps; others wore the blue coveralls with merely a foul-weather jacket and the *pilotka* garrison cap. Despite the cold and their haggard and thin appearance, their eyes seemed to glow; they stood tall. Rybalko stood in front of the formation and began to speak. He spoke slowly and seemed somewhat downcast. As he spoke, Shumkov noticed that the sparkle began to return to his eyes and he, too, stood taller. He gave the assembly a summary, the first they had heard except for bits and pieces they had intercepted over the U.S. radio, of how the whole Cuban fiasco had gone sour. Rybalko said with some pride that the brigade had wandered quite by chance into the greatest antisubmarine armada ever assembled in the Atlantic, and despite what they would hear about compromising the covert transit, they had nevertheless done well. Most important, they had all returned without having triggered a more serious confrontation with the Americans. He said that regardless of how this would all turn out, he was proud of each of them and would recommend each and every one for rest and recuperation leave in the naval rest centers on the Black Sea, to commence as soon as possible.

After the talk to the crews, the men were released to the boats and the four commanders, the squadron commander, and the chief of staff were summoned to the shed, the same small shed on the pier where they had received their send-off that midnight on September 30 before sailing.

The four commanding officers and the brigade commander and staff walked down the snowy pier together and entered the shed. A small security watch had a coal fire going in the stove. The room smelled like coal fumes but was warm. All the officers were relieved to be off the boats and in a room where they could share the tales of their individual adventures. Dubivko produced two bottles of vodka, and they all lit cigarettes. A little later Savitsky's supply officer came through the door covered with snowflakes. He was carrying a large box.

"What's inside, more of your abominable rations?" Ketov was always critical.

"No, sir, we just received these from the squadron headquarters; Galina, Admiral Rybalko's wife, sent them to us." He uncovered a tray of delicious-looking *zakuski*. The officers stared silently at the luscious tray—except for Shumkov after B-130 arrived, they had not seen fresh food like that in months. They all knew that Rybalko had tried hard to help them and probably would soon disappear from the scene. He would no doubt be relieved of his command for his unauthorized transmission by the submarine support broadcast of the U.S. notice to mariners on October 25, against the specific orders of the commander in chief, Fleet Admiral Gorshkov.

"Rybalko didn't look so good when we came in today," Ketov said darkly.

"No, I noticed that, too." Shumkov disclosed, "When we first came in he came down just for a few minutes and told us we were confined aboard until further notice. Although the navy is treating us like quarantined sick people, Rybalko tried to cushion the blow."

"We don't look that good either, after those months of heat." They all found it hard to get accustomed to the cold again.

Suddenly the door of the shed opened and Chief of Staff Arkhipov walked in. They all rose out of respect and shook hands all around, then sat down again. "Nikolai," the chief of staff began, "we heard about your casualty. How did you make it back? Did all your men survive?" The officers began a robust conversation about their experiences. While they spoke, the noise level grew, and they didn't notice the door open and a figure in a navy blue greatcoat come in quietly, covered with snow. The figure shook off the snow and stomped his feet. Ketov suddenly recognized the brigade commander, Vitali Agafonov. The conversation died suddenly, and the officers rose slowly to their feet.

Agafonov motioned for them to carry on. They pulled a bench out and gave him room, and the four submarine commanders, their brigade commander, and the chief of staff sat for hours discussing their adventures and their fate.

Agafonov gave them a summary, the first details they had heard about his efforts to provide them with information, and how he had fought with the Main Navy Staff and lost. He said that they had encountered the greatest ASW armada ever assembled in the Atlantic, just as Rybalko had said. He also said that he had received a message from the commander of the U.S. Atlantic Fleet sarcastically thanking them for the ASW services! He said that regardless of how this would all turn out, he, too, was proud of them, and would recommend them all for rest and recuperation and leave in the naval rest centers on the Black Sea. Then he proposed a toast to the navy and quietly left the shed.

They were later to learn that Agafonov had gone out of his way to ensure that they were treated with respect during the weeks ahead. He had been a good brigade commander, but his hands had been tied by the lack of ability to communicate. He would later be promoted to kontr admiral and go on to command a division of new nuclear-powered submarines in the Northern Fleet.

Later the four captains heard of the strained condition in the Ministry of Defense and that Minister of Defense Malinovsky had been sacked and replaced by Marshal Grechko. Navy commander in chief Gorshkov continued in his post. Admiral Yegorov, the Sayda Bay squadron commander, who was in charge of the tender there and the entire installation, came in later and spoke with the submariners.

When Shumkov informed Yegorov that they needed a place for the crews to be berthed after such a long and arduous patrol, Yegorov looked at him sadly and said, "Nikolai, unfortunately your place along-side the tender is already taken. There is nothing I can do for you."

They were astounded. Admiral Rybalko had always looked after them with such grace that nothing was left wanting. It appeared as if they were under a dark cloud, and it was obvious by looking at the face of the base commander that the four submarines were to be given very little support. All four commanders returned to their boats angry and let down. They continued preparations for standing down in port, and told their executive officers to stand by for instructions. Rybalko had gone to Severomorsk after their session on the pier and was not seen again.

Chief of Staff Arkhipov grew angry and, in his outspoken manner, said jokingly, "Let's draft a message to the Main Navy Staff saying 'If we are not provided berthing for our crews off the boats we will turn around and return to Cuba to the base where we were going to be home ported.'" The four commanders didn't realize it, but Arkhipov had already sent a scathing message directly to the Northern Fleet commander in chief. They never saw the content of the message, but it produced results.

The following day the Northern Fleet commander in chief's barge, *Albatross*, arrived, with the fleet commander, Admiral Kasatanov, and several of his staff aboard. He ordered that the crews of all four submarines be given billets ashore and the commanding officers to grant leave to all hands, and that all four boats would begin a period of maintenance alongside a submarine tender.

Within an hour after he arrived, the fleet commander came aboard Ketov's submarine amid great fanfare, despite insisting on no ceremony. He met Ketov, whom he mistakenly addressed as Savitsky by name, and began asking all kinds of personal questions. Ketov told him that his name was not Savitsky but Ketov, and that of all four submarines, the Americans never forced him to the surface. The admiral responded, "Well, then, where do you want to serve next?"

Ketov responded that he already had requested duty in nuclear submarines. Admiral Kasatanov asked what answer he had received to that request. Ketov responded that he had been offered a command of a unit of submarines. Said the admiral, "Don't you want to become a brigade chief of staff?"

"No, Comrade Admiral," he said, "I wish to command an atomic submarine." Several days after that exchange he was ordered to return to Polyarny and report as the prospective commanding officer of a second-generation nuclear submarine. He returned to his home, the first of the four skippers to arrive back in Polyarny.

At about that time all four were given passes to take leave with their crews at the navy resort of Solnechnogorsk, outside Yalta. That was December 30. They all went and enjoyed the first days immensely.

After several days at the center the director of the resort came to Shumkov and said he was wanted on the telephone. He went to the phone and spoke with a Main Navy Staff officer. All four skippers were directed to report immediately to naval headquarters in Moscow. Shumkov got there just following the New Year's holiday. The other skippers arrived soon after. They spent the next twenty-six days at the Main Navy Staff preparing a report about the patrol to Cuba for the Party Central Committee and Premier Nikita Khrushchev himself. They were treated like pawns; one day they were heroes, the next no one would speak to them. They were very much ill at ease.

While preparing their report in person for the navy commander in chief, they were coached when to speak and when not to speak and what to say. After days of practice, the meeting with Khrushchev was canceled. He was busy, and they met instead with the new minister of defense, Marshal Grechko. They spent a whole day with him, briefing him and the Military Council of the USSR on what had happened. While they were there they learned that their squadron commander, Kontr Admiral Leonid Rybalko, had been forced to retire. He had left Polyarny quietly for Moscow and was never seen again by his four commanding officers.

The four skippers had been thanked by the U.S. Fleet commander for their services provided to the U.S. ASW forces, while they were treated as pariahs at home. Neither Shumkov nor any of his crewmen or the others received any awards for their efforts, with the exception of the appendicitis patient on Dubivko's boat.

In late January all four skippers received letters inviting them to a meeting and dinner in honor of a Cuban delegation that was visiting the country. They were told that the Cuban leader, Fidel Castro himself, was coming. Agafonov accepted the invitations for all four commanding officers of the submarines that had been in the Caribbean during October and November. They were naturally excited about the occasion. Ketov's B-4 was selected to sail into Severomorsk and moor alongside the floating dress pier in the bay below the headquarters building, along with one of the Project 629 ballistic missile boats, which had

Fidel Castro visits Soviet submarine in Severomorsk, January 1963
(courtesy Vitali Agafonov)

been earmarked for transfer to Mariel but never sailed. The two diesels
plus a new nuclear-powered submarine were tied up there in anticipation that the Cuban leader might visit aboard. *B-4* was clean and freshly
painted.

When the big day came, they all watched in anticipation as the
group of visiting Cubans walked down the hill from the Northern Fleet
headquarters building, accompanied by a gaggle of Soviet staff officers.
Admiral Kasatanov and the new minister of defense, Grechko, whom
they had spent a full day briefing in Moscow, were in the group. They
were all certain this was going to be the marshal's first visit aboard a
real submarine. To their chagrin, however, when the delegation moved
down the pier, they walked straight past the two diesel boats and out to
a newly commissioned Project 658 nuclear-powered ballistic missile
boat. They watched crestfallen as the bearded Cuban leader, followed
by Marshal Grechko, climbed aboard the nuclear boat and disappeared
below, inside the sail.

Shumkov looked at Dubivko and said with a shrug, "I guess what we
did was of little note." Dubivko did not respond, but he, too, was disappointed. They watched, highly irritated at the shunning, only relieved
that their crews had not been there to feel the affront. They later attended the banquet but had little to say and merely watched as the seniors toasted to the International Socialist Brotherhood.

Newport Farewell

After returning to Newport in December, Captain Kelley had been told that *Blandy* was to receive the Marjorie Sterett Navy League Trophy for excellence in ASW. Kelley was happy but not surprised. The ship had won the same award in 1960 for its superb work in holding on to a U.S. nuclear submarine.

The week after receiving the ASW trophy in Providence on a cold and foggy January day, *Blandy* began preparing for Captain Kelley's change-of-command ceremony. He had orders to the missile cruiser USS *Albany* as executive officer, and was due to receive his captain's fourth stripe the day he left the ship. Although referred to aboard *Blandy* as "captain," he wore the three stripes of a navy commander.

The event called for a double-barreled ceremony. The new commanding officer was Commander George Grove, who came from a fleet destroyer in the Pacific. But the protocol carefully dictated that he stay away from the ship until the change-of-command ceremony, so we never laid eyes on the new commander until the day he relieved Kelley.

We had all settled down to life in port. *Blandy* was moored inboard in a nest on Pier One, just ahead of the destroyer tender *Yellowstone*. The exec had planned a farewell party at the Newport Main Officers' Club the night before. It turned out initially to be a stuffy affair, with the wardroom mostly subdued in the presence of the new captain, who had been invited. After a polite period, the relieving captain, Commander Grove, departed with his wife, feeling that we were just waiting until he left before we could show our real appreciation to the Kelleys. The usual group of bachelors stayed way too late, and after the Kelleys left, we made our way to the Sportsman Bar in Island Park to drown our sorrow.

"Seems to me Kelley ought to have gotten command of a squadron of tin cans," Flanagan moaned. "The cruiser navy's much too formal for him."

"But it's a missile ship," Morgan replied. "That's where it is today. *Blandy*'s one step from an old World War II tub; we'll all be on the new types someday."

"No, I can't see Kelley on a cruiser, Frank; he belongs to the old school. He'll step on some staff officer's crank and be up the creek, doesn't know how to be diplomatic." Westerman, too, was becoming morose.

"Well, he sure knows how to sniff out subs, we proved that. Look at our record." Morgan as usual was agitating. Westerman was silent, and Brad Sherman was beginning to talk to himself, as he often did late in the evening.

"Can't you just see Kelley on the bridge of cruiser *Albany*, kicking ass and teaching the bridge watch how to hunt subs?"

"Or standing on the quarterdeck while they pipe some staff officers aboard. I understand they even have an old-fashioned 'headboard.'"

"The hell's a 'headboard'?" Westerman asked.

"That's a highly polished oak decoration board hanging over the main deck on the side of the ship; old battleships used to have them. The rule was, when the head of the officer being piped aboard reached the top of the board, the bosun began piping, and finished when the senior's feet reached the main deck." Morgan knew all the old traditions. "What's a' matter, Duck, didn't they teach you that at the boat school?"

"Not that old battleship navy stuff. Never heard of a headboard before."

"Ask Bosun Petit, he'll know." Flanagan always had the last word.

"Anyway, did you ever see the XO as hyped up for an event? Acts like the queen's coming aboard tomorrow instead of a bunch of old fat-assed admirals and commodores. Speaking of which, don't you have the honor guard tomorrow, Duck?"

"Yes, and I'm ready, sword's polished and my blues are clean, all I have to do is get someone to prop me up and look pretty. I'm gonna miss the Old Man."

Frank looked at me and shook his head. "Don't go getting senti-mental on us, Duck." But it turned out to be quite different the next day—that is, concerning what we all thought about Frank Flanagan's hard soul. He had been aboard longer than all of us and had conse-quently known Kelley the longest. We finished our beers and headed out the door. We were all feeling a little blue and a little dejected, and returned to the ship to get ready for the change-of-command ceremony the next morning.

What followed the next day was the usual shipboard change-of-command ceremony, except that being *Blandy*, it was always a little more than normal. The crew stood in ranks on the 01 level in dress blues. The division leading chiefs and division officers stood together before each division, department heads in line ahead of the ranks. The staff were all seated in the folding chairs with the wives and the guests. Bill Morgan's signalmen had draped bunting and dress ship flags around the lifelines. The exec, to go the second mile, had booked the Cruiser Destroyer Force Command band, which was paraded aft, with barely space left on the deck for another soul. The Destroyer Division commander, Captain Ed Carter, stood with his chief staff officer next to Commodore Morrison. Rear Admiral Robert Speck, from the Atlantic Fleet Cruiser-Destroyer Force, was expected, with some of his staff. This, plus the commodores from two other Newport destroyer squadrons, 10 and 12, made the ship virtually alive with gold braid and dress blues.

The exec was in an advanced state of nervous agitation. I was officer of the deck, in dress blues and sword, and had the ship's honor guard mustered on the fantail. Next to the guard were six sideboys in ranks, wearing dress blues. As each senior officer—ships' commanding officers, squadron commanders, and staff—came aboard, Bosun Petit would set the number of sideboys from two to six, depending on grade arriving, then pipe "Attention to Port." All hands topside came to attention, while the senior officer with his lady would cross the brow to the long pipe and be ushered to the 01 level. That day we saw more senior officers than I had ever laid eyes on in Newport.

Stonewall Jackson's Ship's Service Division had laid out a table with sweet rolls, a cake, his usual colored drink (called bug juice), cookies, and coffee under the spotless white awning on the fo'c'sle for after the ceremony. The deck force, under Les Westerman's quiet urging, had washed the decks down and worked on the brightwork until it shone. The ship looked good, its very best. Bill Bangert had reluctantly agreed not to blow tubes that night and would wait until the midwatch, after the ceremony, to blast his soot from the stacks and wipe out the dress white canvas awnings now tightly cinched over the quarterdeck and fo'c'sle.

The usual scramble was under way ten minutes before the senior guests were due when, for some reason, the shore power failed. With the exec in a panic, Bill Bangert had his engineers shift to the auxiliary plant to regain power. The lights went back on just in time, as Commodore Morrison and Admiral Speck came walking down the pier.

"Can't trust the goddamn shore power on Pier One. That's why I always keep one plant under a steam blanket so we can shift," Bangert injected. "Don't ever trust the bastards to provide shore power or steam—they'll lose it every time."

The exec scrambled to the quarterdeck to ensure that the sideboys were ready. That day the ceremony went pretty much as planned, except when Chaplain Ahrensbach began the invocation and suddenly something happened to the sound; a loud squeal screeched from the speakers. The exec scowled at me, which happened any time electronic equipment failed on board. Leading Electronic Technician Chief Tyler sprang forward and fiddled with the amplifier just as one of the troops in the deck force keeled over from the ranks and bounced off the lifeline. One of his mates caught him, preventing a potentially larger disaster, and carried him below.

In a surprise move, Admiral Speck, commanding the Atlantic Fleet Cruiser-Destroyer Force, awarded Kelley the Legion of Merit, for superlative leadership and ASW excellence during the October Cuban blockade. The words of the citation danced carefully around the fact that a Soviet submarine had been forced to the surface after seventeen hours of grueling contact—that was still an official secret, although the Soviets knew about it and we all had our own personal photos of the submarine on the surface.

We all understood, and Kelley's face grew crimson. He read his orders to *Albany*, then stepped to one side and the new skipper, Commander George Grove, read his orders. Then he turned and, as was traditional, saluted Kelley and said loudly, "I relieve you, sir."

We all went to the fo'c'sle for coffee and Stonewall's cake and cookies. There was just something strange about the fact that Captain Ed Kelley was now there with us wearing his new four stripes, and he wasn't our captain anymore.

The junior officers didn't say much. I had to get to the quarterdeck early as the senior guests were piped ashore. Then the exec looked at his watch, which was the signal for all officers to hightail it to the quarterdeck for Kelley's departure. He and Grace had gone up to the in-port cabin with the Groves, and we knew that within five or six minutes they would emerge and begin the slow walk, his last down the 01 deck, down the portside ladder, and toward the quarterdeck.

As was the custom, all the ship's officers lined the side in two ranks, facing one another. I had dismissed the honor guard, but all the crew aboard were manning the rail on all other decks. As we shuffled into place, I took my spot at the top of the brow next to the exec as the officer of the deck.

I looked down the double rank of blue-clad officers, department heads closest the brow, Bill Bangert, Bob Briner, Jim Bassett, Jim Eilberg, then the more senior lieutenants junior grade, Frank Flanagan closest to Briner, then down the rank to the last ensign, Dan Davidson. I felt something strange, but wasn't sure what it was; I just wanted time to freeze. My thoughts raced back to the many days and nights on the bridge, the long, boring watches interrupted by moments of sheer havoc and terror while running to station, sonar contact, the awful sight of the live Hedgehogs on the launchers and the storms, and always Captain Ed Kelley with us, stern, smiling, or scolding. I was glad I didn't have to say anything; I wasn't sure my voice would work right.

At that moment my mind raced back to my first week at Annapolis, when with a group of eleven other first-year men I had sat with both hands resting on a large wooden oar in the twelve-man pulling whaleboat in the center of the Severn River. A gnarled, old, retired chief petty officer with more than thirty-five years of navy service sat in the coxswain's position and spun yarns of the old fleet. He had spoken of how all ships, like humans, had souls, and how we would always look back at our first ship with special thoughts. At the time his meaning had gone right over our heads.

The exec stiffened. "Okay. Stand tall, here they come! Morgan, stop fidgeting."

I could see the captain with Grace on his arm walking slowly down the ladder, then toward the rank of pressed blue uniforms. He stopped and hesitated slightly, then proceeded to the end of the line and began. He didn't stop to shake hands with each officer, as some departing captains did; he considered that too corny. Kelley took the straight, old-fashioned way. I noticed as he slowly passed each officer that he looked into his eyes, each one on both sides one at a time. I was transfixed as I watched, and the events of the past year slowly drifted through my mind.

Suddenly I felt a sharp kick on my right foot. It was the exec next to me. "Damn it, get Petit to pipe. He's late! Pipe now!" The bosun mate should have begun piping as Captain Kelley entered the double rank of officers, but he had already passed three or four, and Petit stood frozen at the top of the brow, next to me.

"Petit, pipe!" I whispered as the captain grew slowly closer. Then I looked at Petit's eyes, wondering what was wrong. His face was red, the pipe inserted in his mouth, his left hand held in the hand salute position, the only left-handed salute allowed in the navy. But his pipe was silent, and I noticed it was trembling.

USS *Blandy* officers, from left:
Flanagan, Morgan, Briner,
author (courtesy Robert Briner)

The exec was losing patience; he poked me again. "Get him to start piping now!" I looked at Petit again, then whispered, "What's the matter, Petit?"

He blinked and took the pipe a fraction of an inch from his mouth and muttered a little too loudly, "Me fookin' mouth don't work, sir." I saw his lips tremble, his eyes glazed over. Suddenly his bosun pipe burst into a loud shrill and he began a long pipe, and held it as Captain Kelley approached the head of the brow, with Grace following silently. He paused, looked straight at Flanagan, and it seemed like the air was filled with a warm breeze. Kelley then faced the flagstaff and to no one in particular said loudly, "Permission to leave your ship."

"Permission granted, sir. Godspeed, sir," the exec answered, because as OOD I should have, but I couldn't seem to find any words.

Then Petit piped "Attention to Port."

Captain and Mrs. Kelley walked across the brow, then began down the pier. We all stood stock still and watched. The eyes of more than two hundred *Blandy* crewmen followed Kelley down the pier. I noticed he began walking slightly closer to the side of the ship, stepping nimbly over the shore steam and power cables. As Grace walked more in the center of the pier, Kelley came close to the ship, and when reaching the break on the main deck, about halfway down the ship, he paused and suddenly leaned over and touched the side of the ship, as a man would gently touch the nose of a horse.

Ed Kelley stopped, then looked up toward the signal bridge scanning the men standing at attention all along the topside spaces, main deck, 01, 02, and the bridge levels. He turned back toward the quarterdeck and, in a voice that wasn't a shout but that most of us could hear, said, "A little running rust there, 01 level, frame 125, better get the first lieutenant to see to that," then paused and said, "tomorrow will do." And he continued walking down the pier.

We all watched until we saw him climb into his orange-and-white Edsel, on the passenger side. Grace always drove onto the pier for some reason. Then he was gone.

I looked at Petit and then Flanagan. Frank's eyes had welled up, and he saw me looking, so I glanced away. Then I looked at Petit, who caught my gaze.

"Sir, got sumpin' in my throat, musta bin some soot. Damn Snipes, knew they went and blew tubes, weren't supposed to."

Then Frank said, "Yeah, just got some in my eye, too, Boats."

Then as we stood looking down the empty pier, Bill Morgan broke the silence: "You know, I swear Kelley was talking to the ship while he was walking down the pier."

Bill Bangert, who had been exceptionally quiet, spoke up: "Ain't you never heard Kelley talk to the ship? I used to see him do it a lot when he thought no one was around."

"No one talks to a ship," the XO injected. "Anyway, he was quite a captain, but he wasn't nuts."

"Sir, talkin' to a ship don't mean a man's nuts, sir." Petit was wiping his eyes. We all looked at him and understood.

NOTES

PROLOGUE

1. "Anadyr," Soviet General Staff Archives, file 6, vol. 2, p. 144.

PART I *Cuba Libre*

1. General Staff archives of the armed forces of the Russian Federation.

2. Joint General Zakharov and Admiral Fokin memorandum to the Soviet Presidium, September 25, 1962, archive of the president of the Russian Federation.

3. General Staff archives of the armed forces of the Russian Federation.

4. General Staff archives of the armed forces of the Russian Federation.

5. Excerpt from the address by President Kennedy from Robert F. Kennedy, *Thirteen Days: A Memoir of the Cuban Missile Crisis* (New York: W. W. Norton, 1969), p. 167.

PART III *Russian Roulette*

1. From an account of that event in Deborah Shapley, *Promise and Power: The Life and Times of Robert McNamara* (Boston: Little, Brown, 1993), pp. 176–177.

2. A description of this conversation appears in James G. Blight and David A. Welsh, *On the Brink: Americans and Soviets Reexamine the Cuban Missile Crisis* (New York: Noonday Press, 1990), pp. 63–64.

3. Shapley, p. 177.

4. Aleksandr Fursenko and Timothy Naftali, *One Hell of a Gamble: The Secret History of the Cuban Missile Crisis, Khrushchev, Castro, and Kennedy, 1958–1964* (New York: W. W. Norton, 1997).

5. A detailed account of that interview is contained in William E. Knox, "Close–up of Khrushchev during a Crisis," *New York Times Magazine* (November 18, 1962), p. 32.

6. Robert F. Kennedy, *Thirteen Days: A Memoir of the Cuban Missile Crisis* (New York: W. W. Norton, 1969), p. 70.

7. Information regarding the operations of U.S. submarines during the Cuban missile crisis is still unavailable and classified secret.

PART IV *Hide-and-Seek*

1. *Washington Star* (November 12, 1962), p. 1.

Bibliography

Primary Sources

Russian

Adzhubei, Alexei. Son-in-law and special press assistant to Premier Nikita Khrushchev. Author's interview, Moscow, September 5, 1991.

Adzhubei, Nikita Alekseevich. Grandson of Premier Nikita Khrushchev. Multiple author's interviews, Moscow, 1991–1992.

Chernavin, Lev Davidovich. Rear admiral, former Foxtrot class submarine commanding officer and division commander in 1962. President, St. Petersburg Club for Mariners and Submariners. Close colleague of Rear Admiral Rybalko. Author's interview, St. Petersburg, September 29, 1996.

Chernavin, Vladimir Nikolayevich. Fleet admiral, former commander in chief, Soviet Navy, 1985–1991. Submarine officer during the 1962 Cuban missile crisis. Author's interviews, Moscow, July 14, 1992, St. Petersburg, July 29, 1996.

Dubivko, Aleksei Fedoseevich. Commanding officer, submarine B-36. Interviews, Moscow, October 2 and 10, 2000.

Kapitanets, Ivan Matveevich. Fleet admiral, former Northern Fleet commander in chief, first deputy commander in chief, Soviet Navy. Submarine officer during the 1962 Cuban missile crisis. Close colleague of Rear Admiral Rybalko. Author's interview, Moscow, June 8, 1992.

Ketov, Ryurik Aleksandrovich. Commanding officer, submarine B-4. Interview, Moscow, October 30, 2000.

Loikanen, Gary Genrikovich. Rear admiral, former Northern Fleet Yankee class SSBN flotilla. Submarine officer during the 1962 Cuban missile crisis. Colleague of Rear Admiral Rybalko. Author's interview, St. Petersburg, September 27, 1995.

Makarov, Konstantin Valentinovich. Admiral, former chief of the Main Navy Staff, 1985–1990. Submarine officer aboard a Foxtrot class submarine in 1962. Colleague of Rear Admiral Rybalko. Author's interview, Moscow, June 8, 1992.

Orlov, Vadim Pavlovich. Head, Radio-Intelligence Division, submarine B-59. Interview, Moscow, October 5, 2000.

Shumkov, Nikolai Aleksandrovich. Commanding officer, submarine B-130, Interview, Moscow, October 2, 2000.

Vtorygin, Lev Alekseevich. Captain first rank, Soviet Navy, Retired. Former assistant naval attaché, embassy of the USSR, Washington, D.C., 1960–1965. Author's interviews, Hiram, Maine, September 12–17, 2000; Frye Island, September 27–30, 1999.

Zhukov, Yuri Aleksandrovich. Radio-electronics officer, submarine B-36. Interview, Moscow, October 1, 2000.

American

- *USS* Blandy (DD-943). *Interviews and Accounts*

Adcock, Jerry. Sonarman first class. E-mail account, August 6, 2001.

Bangert, Dorothy. Wife of chief engineer. Pensacola, Florida, November 9–12, 2000.

Bangert, William. Chief engineer. Pensacola, November 9–12, 2000.

Barnard, Ray. Electronics technician. E-mail account, November 27, 2000.

Bassett, James. Weapons officer. Newport, Rhode Island, October 15–17, 1998.

Briner, Esther. Wife of operations officer. Pensacola, November 9–12, 2000.

Briner, Robert R. Operations officer. Pensacola, November 9–12, 2000.

Brown, Charles. Electronics technician. Pensacola, November 9–12, 2000.

Bump, Rudi. Radarman. Pensacola, November 9–12, 2000.

Cogswell, Bruce. Radarman. Newport, October 15–17, 1998; Pensacola, November 9–12, 2000.

Davidson, Dan. Assistant combat information center officer. Pensacola, November 9–12, 2000; Hiram, Maine, September 20, 1999.

Davidson, Edie. Wife of assistant combat information center officer. Hiram, September 20, 1999.

Flanagan, Frank. Combat information center officer. Hiram, September 20, 1999.

Kelley, Grace. Wife of Edward G. Kelley, late commanding officer. Pensacola, November 9–12, 2000.

Morgan, William O. Communications officer. Newport, October 15–17, 1998; Pensacola, November 9–12, 2000.

Raethka, Gary. Radarman. E-mail account, September 21, 2000.

Westerman, Lester M. First division officer. Pensacola, November 9–12, 2000.

- *USS* Charles P. Cecil (DDR-835). *Interviews and Accounts*

Alford, Clarence. Operations radarman. E-mail account, August 21, 2000.

Hunter, John G. Combat information center officer. E-mail account, October 18, 2000.

Jordan, Jim. Junior officer of the deck. E-mail summary, August 23, 2000.

Rozier, Charles P. Commanding officer. Letter summary, March 17, 1992; e-mail accounts, August 2000.

- *USS* Cony (DDE-508)

Slaughter, Gary. Communications officer and 1JS bridge talker. E-mail interview/account, August 31, 2000.

Memoirs and Major Studies

Agafonov, Vitali Naumovich. "Submarine Participation in Operation *Anadyr*." *Rodina* (March 2000).

Allyn, Bruce, J., James G. Blight, and David A. Welsh. *Back to the Brink: Proceedings of the Moscow Conference on the Cuban Missile Crisis, January 27–28, 1989.* Lanham, Md.: University Press of America, 1992.

Gribkov, General Anatoli I. *U Kraya Yadernoi Bezdni (On the Edge of the Nuclear Chasm: From the History of the Caribbean Crisis, 1962: Facts, Witnesses, Analysis.* Moscow: Gregori-Page, 1998.

Jones, Forrest Ronald, "U.S. Naval Quarantine of Cuba, 1962." Master's thesis, University of California–San Diego, 1984.

Utz, Curtis A. *Cordon of Steel: The U.S. Navy and the Cuban Missile Crisis.* The U.S. Navy in the Modern World Series. Washington, D.C.: Naval Historical Center, 1993.

SECONDARY SOURCES

Books and Articles

Abel, Elie. *The Missile Crisis.* Philadelphia: J. B. Lippincott, 1996.

Allbeury, Joseph. *B-437 Foxtrot Class Submarine.* Sydney: Jasper Communications, 1998.

Baer, George W. *The U.S. Navy, 1890–1990: One Hundred Years of Seapower.* Stanford, Calif.: Stanford University Press, 1994.

Beschloss, Michael. *The Crisis Years.* New York: HarperCollins, 1992.

Blight, James G., and David A. Welsh. *On the Brink: Americans and Soviets Reexamine the Cuban Missile Crisis.* New York: Noonday Press, 1990.

Brugioni, Dino. *Eyeball to Eyeball.* New York: Random House, 1991.

Buckley, William F. *See You Later, Alligator.* New York: Arrow Books, 1994.

Chang, Laurensen. *The Cuban Missile Crisis, 1962.* New York: New Press, 1992.

Cherkashin, Nikolai. "Geroi Sargassova Morya" (Heroes of the Sargasso Sea). *Rossiiskaya Gazeta* (March 19, 1999).

———. "Karibiskaya korrida" (Caribbean cordon). *Rodina* (December 2000).

———. "Velikolepnaya chetverka" (Wonderful four); "Kholodnaya Voina" (Cold War). *Rodina* (March 2000).

Fursenko, Aleksandr, and Timothy Naftali. *One Hell of a Gamble: The Secret History of the Cuban Missile Crisis, Khrushchev, Castro, and Kennedy, 1958–1964.* New York: W. W. Norton, 1997.

Graham, Allison T. *Essence of Decision: Explaining the Cuban Missile Crisis.* Boston: Little, Brown, 1971.

Gribkov, General Anatoli, and General William Y. Smith. *Operation* Anadyr: *U.S. and Soviet Generals Recount the Cuban Missile Crisis.* Chicago: edition q, 1994.

Hill, J. R. *Anti-Submarine Warfare.* 2nd ed. Annapolis, Md.: Naval Institute Press, 1989.

Kennedy, Robert F. *Thirteen Days: A Memoir of the Cuban Missle Crisis*, New York: W. W. Norton, 1969.

Knox, William E. "Close-up of Khrushchev during a Crisis." *New York Times Magazine* (November 18, 1962).

Kostev, G. "Karibiskii krizis glazami ochividsev" (Caribbean crisis in the eyes of witnesses). *Morskoi sbornik* 11 (1994).

May, Ernest, and Philip Zelikow. *Kennedy Tapes: Inside the White House during the Cuban Missile Crisis.* Cambridge, Mass.: Harvard University Press, 1997.

McAuliff, Mary S. *CIA Documents on the Cuban Missile Crisis, 1962.* New York: W. W. Norton, 1969.

Polmar, Norman. "Osen' 1962 KUBOT: Amerikanskie protivolodochn'ie operacii vo vrema Kubinskogo krizica" (Autumn 1962 CUBEX: American Antisubmarine Operations during the Cuban Crisis). *Morskoi sbornik* 11 (1994).

Scott, William F. "Attaché Observations: The Face of Moscow in the Missile Crisis." Central Intelligence Agency, *Studies in Intelligence* 37, no. 5 (1994).

Shapley, Deborah. *Promise and Power: The Life and Times of Robert McNamara.* Boston: Little, Brown, 1994.

Shigin, V. V. *Nad bezdnoi (On the chasm).* Documentary account from the series *Secret Diaries of the Past.* St. Petersburg: Andreevski Flag, 1997.

Spagnolo, Ed. "Cat and Mouse." *American Heritage* (November 2000), p. 31.

Thompson, Robert S. *The Missiles of October.* New York: Simon & Schuster, 1992.

White, Mark J. *The Cuban Missile Crisis.* New York: Macmillan, 1996.

INDEX